Creating Labor-Management Partnerships

Creating Labor-Management Partnerships

Warner P. Woodworth
Christopher B. Meek
Brigham Young University

ADDISON-WESLEY PUBLISHING COMPANY
Reading, Massachusetts • Menlo Park, California • New York
Don Mills, Ontario • Wokingham, England • Amsterdam • Bonn
Sydney • Singapore • Tokyo • Madrid • San Juan • Milan • Paris

Library of Congress Cataloging-in-Publication Data

Woodworth, Warner
    Creating labor management partnerships / Warner P. Woodworth &
Christopher B. Meek.
        p.   cm. -- (Addison-Wesley series on organizational
    development)
    Includes index.
    ISBN 0-201-58823-4
    1. Trade-unions—United States. 2. Industrial relations—
United States. 3. Industrial management—Employee participa-
tion—United States. I. Meek, Christopher. II. Title. III.
Series.
HD6508.W635   1994
331'.0973--dc20   94-12851
                                                CIP

This book is in the Addison-Wesley Series on Organization Development.
Editors: Edgar H. Schein, Richard Beckhard

ISBN 0-201-58823-4
1 2 3 4 5 6 7 8 9 10-BAM-97969594

Other Titles in the Organization Development Series

Team Building: Current Issues and New Alternatives, Third Edition

William G. Dyer

1995 (62882)

One of the major developments in the field of organization redesign has been the emergence of self-directed work teams. This book explains how teams are most successful when the team becomes part of the culture and structure or systems of the organization. It discusses the major new trends and emphasizes the degree of commitment that managers and members must bring to the team-building process. It is written for managers and human resource professionals who want to develop a more systematic program of team building in their organization or work unit.

Competing with Flexible Lateral Organizations, Second Edition

Jay R. Galbraith

1994 (50836)

This book focuses on creating competitive advantage by building a lateral capability, enabling a firm to respond flexibly in an uncertain world. The book addresses international coordination and cross business coordination as well as the usual cross functional efforts. It is unique in covering both cross functional (lateral or horizontal) coordination, as well as international and corporate issues.

Organization Development: A Process of Learning and Changing, Second Edition

W. Warner Burke

1994 (50835)

This text presents an overview of OD and looks at OD in part as a change of an organization's culture. It looks at the organization and factors that will influence structure and development in the future. The author also introduces new topics such as information management and strategy implementation.

The Dynamics of Organizational Levels: A Change Framework for Managers and Consultants

Nicholas S. Rashford and David Coghlan
1994 (54323)

This book introduces the idea that, for successful change to occur, organizational interventions have to be coordinated across the major levels of issues that all organizations face. Individual level, team level, interunit level, and organizational level issues are identified and analyzed, and the kinds of intervention appropriate to each level are spelled out.

Total Quality: A User's Guide for Implementation
Dan Ciampa

1992 (54992)

This is a book that directly addresses the challenge of how to make Total Quality work in a practical, no-nonsense way. The companies that will dominate markets in the future will be those that deliver high quality, competitively priced products and service just when the customer wants them and in a way that exceeds the customer's expectations. The vehicle by which these companies move to that stage is Total Quality.

Parallel Learning Structures: Increasing Innovation in Bureaucracies
Gervase R. Bushe and A.B. Shani

1991 (52427)

Parallel learning structures are technostructural interventions that promote system-wide change in bureaucracies while retaining the advantages of bureaucratic design. This text serves as a resource of models and theories built around five cases of parallel learning structures that can help those who create and maintain them be more effective and successful. For those new to parallel learning structures, the text provides practical advice as to when and how to use them.

Managing in the New Team Environment: Skills, Tools, and Methods
Larry Hirschhorn

1991 (52503)

This text is designed to help manage the tensions and complexities that arise for managers seeking to guide employees in a team environment. Based on an interactive video course developed at IBM, the text takes managers step by step through the process of building a team and authorizing it to act while they learn to step back and delegate. Specific issues addressed are how to give a team structure, how to facilitate its basic processes, and how to acknowledge differences in relationships among team members and between the manager and individual team members.

Leading Business Teams: How Teams Can Use Technology and Group Process Tools to Enhance Performance

Robert Johansen, David Sibbett, Suzyn Benson, Alexia Martin, Robert Mittman, and Paul Saffo

1991 (52829)

What technology or tools should organization development people or team leaders have at their command, now and in the future? This text explores the intersection of technology and business teams, a new and largely uncharted area that goes by several labels, including "groupware," a term that encompasses both electronic and nonelectronic tools for teams. This is the first book of its kind from the field describing what works for business teams and what does not.

Becoming a Learning Organization: Beyond the Learning Curve

Joop Sweiringa and André Wierdsma

1991 (62753)

As organizations evolve with time, the ability to learn and change is becoming increasingly more important. The future poses numerous obstacles and challenges for all organizations, and having the proper learning tools will provide a necessary competitive advantage. This text not only analyzes what a learning organization is, it also explores practical approaches and tools that teach a company to "learn to learn." The aim of this book is to identify and define the learning process, but also to begin the implementation of it in order to gain an advantage in a highly competitive environment.

The Conflict-Positive Organization: Stimulate Diversity and Create Unity

Dean Tjosvold

1991 (51485)

This book describes how managers and employees can use conflict to find common ground, solve problems, and strengthen morale and relationships. By showing how well-managed conflict invigorates and empowers teams and organizations, the text demonstrates how conflict is vital for a company's continuous improvement and increased competitive advantage.

Change by Design

Robert R. Blake, Jane Srygley Mouton, and Anne Adams McCanse

1989 (50748)

This book develops a systematic approach to organization development and provides readers with rich illustrations of coherent planned change.

The book involves testing, examining, revising, and strengthening conceptual foundations in order to create sharper corporate focus and increased predictability of successful organization development.

Organization Development in Health Care

R. Wayne Boss

1989 (18364)

This is the first book to discuss the intricacies of the health care industry. The book explains the impact of OD in creating healthy and viable organizations in the health care sector. Through unique and innovative techniques, hospitals are able to reduce nursing turnover, thereby resolving the nursing shortage problem. The text also addresses how OD can improve such bottom-line variables as cash flow and net profits.

Self-Designing Organizations: Learning How to Create High Performance

Susan Albers Mohrman and Thomas G. Cummings

1989 (14603)

This book looks beyond traditional approaches to organizational transition, offering a strategy for developing organizations that enables them to learn not only how to adjust to the dynamic environment in which they exist, but also how to achieve a higher level of performance. This strategy assumes that change is a learning process: the goal is continually refined as organizational members learn how to function more effectively and respond to dynamic conditions in their environment.

Power and Organization Development: Mobilizing Power to Implement Change

Larry E. Greiner and Virginia E. Schein

1988 (12185)

This book forges an important collaborative approach between two opposing and often contradictory approaches to management: OD practitioners who espouse a "more humane" workplace without understanding the political realities of getting things done, and practicing managers who feel comfortable with power but overlook the role of human potential in contributing to positive results.

Designing Organizations for High Performance

David P. Hanna

1988 (12693)

This book is the first to give insight into the actual processes you can use to translate organizational concepts into bottom-line improvements. Hanna's "how-to" approach shows not only the successful methods of intervention, but also the plans behind them and the corresponding results.

Process Consultation, Volume 1: Its Role in Organization Development, Second Edition

Edgar H. Schein

1988 (06736)

How can a situation be influenced in the workplace without the direct use of power or formal authority? This book presents the core theoretical foundations and basic prescriptions for effective management.

Organizational Transitions: Managing Complex Change, Second Edition

Richard Beckhard and Reuben T. Harris

1987 (10887)

This book discusses the choices involved in developing a management system appropriate to the "transition state." It also discusses commitment to change, organizational culture, and increasing and maintaining productivity, creativity, and innovation

Organization Development: A Normative View

W. Warner Burke

1987 (10697)

This book concisely describes and defines the theories and practices of organization development and also looks at organization development as change in an organization's culture. It is a useful guide to the field of organization development and is invaluable to managers, executives, practitioners, and anyone desiring an excellent overview of this multi-faceted field.

The Technology Connection: Strategy and Change in the Information Age

Marc S. Gerstein

1987 (12188)

This is a book that guides managers and consultants through crucial decisions about the use of technology for increasing effectiveness and competitive advantage. It provides a useful way to think about the relationship between information technology, business strategy, and the process of change in organizations.

Stream Analysis: A Powerful Way to Diagnose and Manage Organizational Change

Jerry I. Porras

1987 (05693)

Drawing on a conceptual framework that helps the reader to better understand organizations, this book shows how to diagnose failings in organizational functioning and how to plan a comprehensive set of actions needed to change the organization into a more effective system.

Process Consultation, Volume II: Lessons for Managers and Consultants
Edgar H. Schein

1987 (06744)

This book shows the viability of the process consultation model for working with human systems. Like Schein's first volume on process consultation, the second volume focuses on the moment-to-moment behavior of the manager or consultant rather than on the design of the OD program.

Managing Conflict: Interpersonal Dialogue and Third-Party Roles, Second Edition
Richard E. Walton

1987 (08859)

This book shows how to implement a dialogue approach to conflict management. It presents a framework for diagnosing recurring conflicts and suggests several basic options for controlling or resolving them.

Pay and Organization Development
Edward E. Lawler

1981 (03990)

This book examines the important role that reward systems play in organization development efforts. By combining examples and specific recommendations with conceptual material, it organizes the various topics and puts them into a total systems perspective. Specific pay approaches such as gainsharing, skill-based pay, and flexible benefits are discussed and their impact on productivity and the quality of work life is analyzed.

Work Redesign
J. Richard Hackman and Greg R. Oldham

1980 (02779)

This book is a comprehensive, clearly written study of work design as a strategy for personal and organizational change. Linking theory and practical technologies, it develops traditional and alternative approaches to work design that can benefit both individuals and organizations.

Organizational Dynamics: Diagnosis and Intervention
John P. Kotter

1978 (03890)

This book offers managers and OD specialists a powerful method of diagnosing organizational problems and of deciding when, where, and how to use (or not use) the diverse and growing number of organizational improvement tools that are available today. Comprehensive and fully integrated, the book includes many different concepts, research findings, and competing philosophies and provides specific examples of how to use the information to improve organizational functioning.

Career Dynamics: Matching Individual and Organizational Needs
Edgar H. Schein

1978 (06834)

This book studies the complexities of career development from both an individual and an organizational perspective. Changing needs throughout the adult life cycle, interaction of work and family, and integration of individual and organizational goals through human resource planning and development are all thoroughly explored.

Matrix
Stanley M. Davis and Paul Lawrence

1977 (01115)

This book defines and describes the matrix organization, a significant departure from the traditional "one man-one boss" management system. The author notes that the tension between the need for independence (fostering innovation) and order (fostering efficiency) drives organizations to consider a matrix system. Among the issues addressed are reasons for using a matrix, methods for establishing one, the impact of the system on individuals, its hazards, and what types of organizations can use a matrix system.

Feedback and Organization Development: Using Data-Based Methods
David A. Nadler

1977 (05006)

This book addresses the use of data as a tool for organizational change. It attempts to bring together some of what is known from experience and research and to translate that knowledge into useful insights for those who are thinking about using data-based methods in organizations. The broad approach of the text is to treat a whole range of questions and issues considering the various uses of data as an organizational change tool.

Designing Complex Organizations
Jay Galbraith

1973 (02559)

This book attempts to present an analytical framework of the design of organizations, particularly of types of organizations that apply lateral decision processes or matrix forms. These forms have become pervasive in all types of organizations, yet there is little systematic public knowledge about them. This book helps fill this gap.

Organization Development: Strategies and Models

Richard Beckhard

1969 (00448)

This book is written for managers, specialists, and students of management who are concerned with the planning of organization development programs to resolve the dilemmas brought about by a rapidly changing environment. Practiced teams of interdependent people must spend real time improving their methods of working, decision making, and communicating, and a planned, managed change is the first step toward effecting and maintaining these improvements.

Organization Development: Its Nature, Origins, and Prospects

Warren G. Bennis

1969 (00523)

This primer on OD is written with an eye toward the people in organizations who are interested in learning more about this educational strategy as well as for those practitioners and students of OD who may want a basic statement both to learn from and to argue with. The author treats the subject with a minimum of academic jargon and a maximum of concrete examples drawn from his own and others' experience.

Developing Organizations: Diagnosis and Action

Paul R. Lawrence and Jay W. Lorsch

1969 (04204)

This book is a personal statement of the authors' evolving experience, through research and consulting, in the work of developing organizations. The text presents the authors' overview of organization development, then proceeds to examine issues at each of three critical interfaces: the organization-environment interface, the group-group interface, and the individual-organization interface, including brief examples of work on each. The text concludes by pulling the themes together in a set of conclusions about organizational development issues as they present themselves to practicing managers.

About the Authors

Warner P. Woodworth received his Ph.D. from the University of Michigan in 1974. He has been a consultant with Arthur D. Little, Inc., and Rensis Likert Associates. He has been an adviser to major corporate clients including Clark Equipment, General Motors, Chrysler, PPG, Exxon, Signetics, and Westinghouse. He has also worked with a number of unions such as the UAW, steelworkers, rubberworkers, and UFCW. He was elected in 1984 to the board of the National Center for Employee Ownership and served as director of the SBA's Small Business Development Center. He also serves on the OD Advisory Board in Warsaw, Poland.

Dr. Woodworth is on the faculty of the Department of Organizational Behavior, Marriott School of Management, Brigham Young University. He has written over a hundred articles and has made presentations at a number of universities including Harvard, Yale, and Berkeley as well as in some two dozen nations. He has been a researcher at the Institute for Labor Studies in Geneva, Switzerland, and the University of Rio de Janeiro, Brazil. He has coauthored three books: *Managing by the Numbers* (Addison-Wesley, 1988), *Industrial Democracy* (Sage, 1985), and *Desteeling: Structural Disinvestment of U.S. Steel and Its Implications for Regional Economics* (Alexander, 1984).

Christopher B. Meek received his Ph.D. in Industrial & Labor Relations from Cornell University in 1983. He received the Kellogg National Fellowship (1988–1991), was appointed director of International Development, Kennedy International

Center at Brigham Young University (1990–1993), and was Fulbright Lecturer at the University of Ryukus, Okinawa, Japan (1993–1994).

Dr. Meek was assistant professor of Human Resource Management at Boston College and is now associate professor of Organizational Behavior at Brigham Young University. He was a staff consultant for the ground-breaking Jamestown Labor-Management Committee (1976–1981) and is coauthor of *Labor-Management Cooperation at Eastern Airlines* (U.S. Department of Labor, 1987). Dr. Meek was also coauthor of *Managing by the Numbers* (Addison-Wesley, 1988) and *Worker Participation and Ownership* (ILR Press, 1983). Since 1987 Dr. Meek has been learning to read and speak Korean and Japanese in order to do in-depth research in Asian organizations. He has been heavily involved in creating exchanges between U.S. and Asian executives, assisting both groups in understanding the other's culture. His on-site research with companies in Seoul and Tokyo, especially concerning their system of labor relations, has resulted in numerous book chapters and articles.

Foreword

The Addison-Wesley Series on Organization Development origi-
nated in the late 1960s when a number of us recognized that the
rapidly growing field of "OD" was not well understood or well
defined. We also recognized that there was no one OD philosophy, and hence one could not at that time write a textbook on
the theory and practice of OD, but one could make clear what
various practitioners were doing under that label. So the original six books launched what has since become a continuing
enterprise, the essence of which was to allow different authors to
speak for themselves instead of trying to summarize under one
umbrella what was obviously a rapidly growing and highly
diverse field.

By the early 1980s the series included nineteen titles. OD
was growing by leaps and bounds, and it was expanding into all
kinds of organizational areas and technologies of intervention.
By this time, many textbooks existed as well that tried to capture core concepts of the field, but we felt that diversity and
innovation were still the more salient aspects of OD.

Now as we move into the 1990s our series includes over
thirty titles, and we are beginning to see some real convergence
in the underlying assumptions of OD. As we observe how different professionals working in different kinds of organizations and
occupational communities make their case, we see we are still
far from having a single "theory" of organization development.
Yet, a set of common assumptions is surfacing. We are beginning to see patterns in what works and what does not work, and

we are becoming more articulate about these patterns. We are also seeing the field increasingly connected to other organizational sciences and disciplines such as information technology, coordination theory, and organization theory. In the early 1990s we saw several important themes described with Ciampa's *Total Quality* showing the important link to employee involvement in continuous improvement, Johansen et al.'s *Leading Business Teams* exploring the important arena of electronic information tools for teamwork, Tjosvold's *The Conflict-Positive Organization* showing how conflict management can turn conflict into constructive action, Hirschhorn's *Managing in the New Team Environment* building bridges to group psychodynamic theory, and Bushe and Shani's *Parallel Learning Structures* providing an integrative theory for large-scale organization change.

We continue this trend with three revisions and two new books. Burke has taken his highly successful *Organization Development* into new realms with an updating and expansion. Galbraith has updated and enlarged his classic theory of how information management is at the heart of organization design with his new edition entitled *Competing with Flexible Lateral Organizations,* and Dyer has written an important third edition of his classic book on *Team Building.* In addition, Rashford and Coghlan have introduced the important concept of levels of organizational complexity as a basis for intervention theory in their book entitled *The Dynamics of Organizational Levels.* Finally, Woodworth and Meek in *Creating Labor-Management Partnerships* take us into the critical realm of how OD can help in labor relations, an area that's of increasing importance as productivity issues become critical for global competitiveness.

We welcome these revisions and new titles and will continue to explore the various frontiers of organization development with additional titles as we identify themes that are relevant to the ever more difficult problem of helping organizations to remain effective in an increasingly turbulent environment.

New York, New York   Richard H. Beckhard
Cambridge, Massachusetts   Edgar H. Schein

Preface

Creating Labor-Management Partnerships is written to assist organizations as they attempt to shift from confrontational union-management relationships toward more effective systems of collaboration. This book is itself a direct result of such a collaborative system. The authors have cultivated a partnership over many years and have once again come together to produce a serious and relevant body of work based on two equal efforts. Warner Woodworth has approached the first two and final two chapters from the macro point of view, showing the effects and consequences of labor-management partnerships. In Chapters 3 through 7, Christopher Meek has focused on the nuts and bolts of the micro view with principles and components of the labor-management partnership. Together they have integrated the ideas and principles involved in establishing a successful labor-management relationship into a text much needed in today's business environment. The coauthors hope that their efforts will be used as a valuable tool in sustaining cooperative partnerships and that their example will be proof of its success.

This book is part of the Addison-Wesley Series on Organization Development. It addresses the strategies, techniques, and processes that are involved in developing a cooperative and dynamic partnership between managers and their unionized workforce. Although the general field of organization development (OD) has existed for many years, little has been written on how to actually succeed with OD in unionized settings. This is a fundamental weakness in mainstream literature on change because unionized work settings contain numerous social and political barriers that do not exist in non-union organizations.

The audience for which the book is intended includes human resource management and industrial relations managers and staff, union officials, professional arbitrators and mediators, and government officials. It also includes professors and students involved in the study of organization development, human resource management, and industrial relations and/or master of business administration programs. Others, such as consultants and facilitators, will also benefit as they work to redesign client systems with which they are involved.

This book begins with a call for change, specifying the critical need for union-management cooperation in the present context of international competition. We briefly illustrate how uncooperative and rigid relations between trade unions and companies have contributed to the deterioration of U.S. industry in such fields as automobiles, heavy equipment, steel, and air transportation. These practices are contrasted with the more cooperative systems that have evolved in Western Europe and East Asia.

We next describe the potential that labor-management partnerships offer for building more flexible, productive, and dynamic organizations in either brownfield and/or greenfield settings. Magma Copper Company is a brownfield effort to change the structure of conflicting labor-management relationships in a work setting that has built up years of financial losses and an ineffective organizational culture. The greenfield case involves the creation of a new firm, Saturn Corporation, and its partnership with the United Auto Workers Union.

In order to help the reader understand the logic behind the structures, processes, rules, and leadership roles we advocate in the chapters that follow, we need to explain how the approach to implementing labor-management cooperation has evolved over many years. We begin with the first U.S. labor-management cooperative systems developed, which focused upon resolving traditional labor-management conflicts within the bargaining process. These early joint committees began at the community level and came into play in an effort to prevent negotiation impasses from resulting in strikes and lockouts. The first attempts to create internal cooperative relations began during the late 1960s and early 1970s, during the peak years of traditional human relations–oriented OD. We illustrate how these efforts ultimately failed because of an overemphasis on communications problems, the reactive nature of the OD process, and the inability to achieve a true partnership. We next describe how the general focus of labor-management cooperation shifted away from improving human relations to undertaking specific operational improvements or implementing massive training programs and employee committees focused on improving the quality of working life. Last, we describe the current and more comprehensive approach, which utilizes the strength of past strategies, but also seeks to create new institutions and systems that complement the traditional collective-bargaining relationship.

We then address the practical process for establishing a genuine cooperative partnership. The first step is to lay down the basic philosophy, values, goals, objectives, and guidelines for the new system. We explain why beginning with this step is so important, using case examples as illustrations, and we then describe alternative processes that can be undertaken to establish the parameters for a labor-management partnership. Sample mission and charter statements currently used by progressive companies and unions in the United States are not included, but may be obtained by contacting the authors at Brigham Young University.

Next, a method for designing the roles, rules, and procedures is spelled out, based on more than a decade of our personal experience. Our goal in this is not just to perform an academic exercise nor to review recent research, but to demonstrate a hands-on application of the nitty-gritty realities of change. Many OD efforts in unionized settings commonly attempt to entirely debureaucratize the conduct of cooperative relations, but such actions come into conflict with the typical union-management culture. The disdain of many OD consultants toward anything that looks bureaucratic or rule-bound has further exacerbated this situation. Unfortunately, the open, or laissez-faire, approach to developing cooperative relations has proven to be a dismal failure because of serious conflicts with the traditional bargaining structure, as well as conflicting expectations about objectives and responsibility, that so frequently occur in these situations.

We demonstrate how to create a parallel union-management organization that will ensure that a successful partnership is created, nurtured, and sustained. The appropriate process for creating a parallel structure is described in detail, including key functions such as coleadership roles, goal setting, and supervision through a joint steering committee, creating problem-solving capacity through worker-supervisor teams, and the necessary support system of documentation roles, as well as rules and procedures that govern the overall system.

Labor-management partnerships often live or die because of the implementation strategy undertaken. Frequently, failure is the result of insufficient front-end analysis and consideration of political issues. We illustrate a variety of implementation strategies and help the reader to work through the political risks involved during the early stages of developing a reciprocal relationship. The strategies discussed include top-down as opposed to bottom-up, systemwide, subunit based, ad hoc, multiunit, and single subunit approaches. Also examined are the pros and cons of undertaking deep as opposed to shallow interventions—e.g., projects that are difficult but promise high returns as opposed to efforts that are easier and therefore more likely to be initially successful. The importance of maintaining balance between achieving worker interests as opposed to company interests and the risks posed by imbalance are also examined, and the nuts and bolts of implementation are specified.

With the framework and strategies for cooperation articulated, we then review two organizations that attempted to develop a labor-management partnership, one successful and the other a failure. We provide a description of the flow of events in each case—New United Motor Manufacturing, Inc., and Eastern Airlines—and then analyze why one organization succeeded while the other did not. The objective is to help the reader see and understand how the many recommendations made throughout the book fit together. The reader may observe how the absence of even a few considerations can prove fatal. The basic thrust throughout the book is to demonstrate the integration of the various tactics and tools.

The book concludes with a summary of the key points that have been made and our view of what we believe will be the future for labor-management cooperative partnerships in the United States.

We would like to express our deep appreciation to all those who have helped us in creating this book. First, we want to acknowledge the rich experiences that have emerged from our action research efforts at many firms and unions and the key participants in those settings from whom we gained great insights.

The encouragement from professional colleagues around the country, in government, research institutes, universities, and consulting firms has been warmly received. In particular, our associates in the Department of Organizational Behavior at The Marriott School of Management, Brigham Young University, provided us with positive and critical feedback regarding our intervention work in OD over the years. We also want to thank Pete Sorenson of Boeing, Chuck Mueller of UFCW, Dave Jacobs of James River Corporation, Michael Damer of NUMMI, Gene Caresia of Amoco, Kees Van Langen of Rockwell, Douglas Fraser, former international president of the UAW, O.C. Miller, Chairman of the Airline Pilots Association at Northwest Airlines, and Lynn Williams, president of the steelworkers union.

We must acknowledge the support of the OD Series editors, Edgar Schein and Richard Beckhard, and Beth Toland and her associates at Addison-Wesley. The technical staff at Brigham Young University, Laura Collins, Cathleen Cornaby, Nancy Elkington, and especially Linda Veteto, offered competence and unending patience through the multiple iterations of the manuscript.

Finally, we express our love and appreciation to our wives, Kaye Woodworth and Noriko Meek, along with our many children—seventeen in all. They have taught us much about the deepest meaning of building authentic, cooperative partnerships.

Provo, Utah   W.P.W.
                                                                        C.B.M.

Contents

1

A Call for Change: The Critical Need for Labor-Management Cooperation

The thesis of this book is that building collaborative relationships between workers and managers is critical in today's business environment. Historically, this has not always been so important. In fact, the source of much of today's organizational conflict originates in factors that prevailed in the economic and political context of nearly a century ago. At that time, as the industrial revolution was launched, large factories were built, machine power became harnessed, and mass production was the grand objective.

In the decades that followed, workers were mere pawns in the hands of company leaders, flesh-and-blood extensions of steel, tools, electric furnaces, and rotating gears. Workers encountered unsafe working conditions, low wages, labor exploitation, and "de-skilling"—a monumental shift away from the craft system and toward the creation of a new bureaucracy, the modern corporation. The dehumanization that characterized this era gave rise to the trade union movement, a powerful network intended to combat workplace abuses. This led to an extensive system of industrial relations in which several assumptions were established: that workers would use their muscles while management did the thinking; that workers' primary motivation is wages; that the best way to handle differences is through collective-bargaining mechanisms under federal government control; and that conflict is natural and is to be managed through a divisive, adversarial system.

Such assumptions produced a history of American labor relations replete with violence, strikes, power struggles, and an accompanying loss of production. For union officials, "taking on management" was the way to gain credibility, win elections, and rally the troops in a cause. "Beating labor" both fulfilled managerial ego needs and became the major road to executive promotion. Often these attitudes, whether on the part of labor or management, did crystallize the issues and did lead to new bargaining contracts, but they were very costly. They shattered trust and lowered morale, and they engendered rigid rules and led to considerable waste of time, face-saving maneuvers, and organizational inefficiencies. Labor-management battles heavily affected the bottom line of corporate profits, driving away shareholders and customers.

Nevertheless, as long as U.S. industry remained the major force in the world economy, the costs of the adversarial system were perceived as tolerable. We built our own mass market at home, based on such products as autos, electronics, and construction. And U.S. rubber, plastics, and steel were shipped to other nations. If a firm or industry was beset with strikes, shutdowns, or other forms of industrial tension, the costs of a new settlement were simply passed on to the consumer.

Inroads of Cooperation

Of course, not every firm and its workers engaged in bitter disputes. Suffern (1915) documents the joint efforts of early coal companies and unions to collaborate. Clothing manufacturers and workers a century ago established cooperative programs to resolve labor problems. In construction, contractors and the bricklayers' union in cities like Boston, New York, and Chicago developed innovative and conciliatory approaches to enhance productivity and avoid disputes (Lowell, 1893).

During certain historical periods, waves of labor-management cooperation spread across the national economy. Enlightened company founders in some firms sought to create a "more Christian" approach to dealing with employees. During World Wars I and II extensive cooperative programs were developed to heighten the production of tanks and bombs in the battle to preserve democracy. Yet in a classic study a half century ago, Slichter (1941) observed that "In industry as a whole, the number

of unions pursuing the policy of systematic cooperation is small! ...
The traditional view of unions is that getting out production and
keeping down costs is the employer's responsibility. . . . Unions
have been bitterly opposed by most employers and have had to
fight for the right to exist. . . . Employers have not desired their
help" (pp. 561–562).

In 1945, after World War II, President Truman tried to
convene a National Labor-Management Conference to plan for
the shift from wartime economy to peace. But discussions collapsed when corporate executives insisted on a lengthy list of so-
called exclusive managerial rights that would not be subject to
the collective-bargaining process. Nonnegotiable matters consisted of plant sites to be opened or closed; factory layout and
equipment; "the processes, techniques, methods, and means of
manufacture and distribution"; financial matters; hiring, firing,
and promotions; work assignment; quality; discipline; schedules;
shifts; and safety (U.S. Department of Labor, 1946, pp. 56–62).
Obviously, labor leaders could not continue the pretext of participating in a "conference" where in reality business executives
were attempting to strong-arm American unions into complete
submission to the wishes of top management.

Management-Union Wars

This unwillingness to negotiate only heightened hostility between the two parties and perpetuated distrust and adversarial
behaviors. The amount of working time lost to factory strife in
the late 1940s–early 1950s was between 38 and 43 percent. A
steelworkers' strike in 1959 virtually shut the nation down for
116 days. In the early 1960s there were numerous public sector
strikes in New York City, and in the 1970s there were work stoppages in construction, trucking, and other industries.

Meanwhile, international competition was heating up,
even in nations that the United States had long dominated economically. By the 1980s foreign firms in many industrial sectors
were not only winning the battle against U.S. goods in host nations, they had also successfully infiltrated and eventually dominated the U.S. market at home.

The thing that amazed U.S. managerial and labor officials
most, other than the phenomenal success of foreign firms, was
the radically different system of industrial relations that foreign

competitors tended to practice. Instead of distrust and uncertainty, the interaction between unions and companies was predictable—they placed a high value on no surprises. Instead of numerous strikes, lost working time, and bitter accusations from both sides, as Americans were accustomed to, overseas competitors experienced few conflicts and little production downtime. Rather than secrets, game playing, and other forms of manipulation, foreign labor and management tended to value collaboration and joint problem solving.

Meanwhile, as other nations have improved their ability to build quality products at high levels of compensation, the United States has experienced a decline in market share and a diminishing living standard. Workers' real wages in the United States have not increased since the early 1970s. Rather than banding together in the face of a growing crisis, U.S. labor and management have tended to argue and "point the finger"at each other. It is almost as though, when a firm is on the verge of collapse, the two parties revert to a rhetoric of "Let's fight!" as if the goal were to kill each other before suicide snuffs them out.

Pittston—UMWA

A dramatic illustration of this tendency toward conflict occurred in the coal-rich region of southern Virginia where tiny mining towns dot the landscape. National coal-field strikes broke out in 1977 and 1981, and in 1990, when Pittston Company axed health-care benefits to 1500 retirees and widows, currently employed workers openly fought the decision. After a year of fruitless negotiations and no new contract, a strike erupted, fracturing many commitments. When Pittston sent non-union replacement workers in to keep the mines open, 2500 workers, wives, and townspeople laid their bodies in front of the coal trucks to block company operations. The United Mine Workers of America (UMWA) dressed its workers in camouflage clothes and trained them in nonviolence. Hundreds of protesters were arrested, and Pittston eventually obtained court injunctions enforced by dozens of state police troopers, to prevent pickets. The union was fined millions of dollars for violating court rulings. Family members were divided, depending on their sympathies, as were schoolchildren, shoppers, and churchgoers. High school students boycotted classes after the principal told them they

could not show UMWA support. Yard signs sent various mes-
sages: "UMWA all the way"; "Pittston stole my health benefits";
"Our lives, our kids, our families."

The company had broken the traditional moral code mandating care for pensioners and their survivors. To workers it was
an unforgivable sin. Terrible accidents over the years had led to
loss of limbs or death. Many miners suffered the agony of black
lung disease for years before they succumbed completely. Now
the financial support to prop them up was being denied.

Some 47,000 UMWA workers in nine states walked off the
job in solidarity with the Pittston miners, knocking millions of
dollars out of the U.S. economy. Throughout the 1980s, Pittston
had laid off some 4000 miners, later reopening some of its closed
mines as non-union facilities. Out of fear that the Pittston struggle would become a precedent for all companies in the
Bituminous Coal Operators Association to break their unions,
and that if the UMWA lost, the whole U.S. labor movement
would disappear, the Virginia battle grew into a war. The company hired hundreds of Vance Security guards, riding shotgun in
Pittston trucks to protect replacement workers. Recruited
through ads in magazines like *Soldier of Fortune,* these adven-
ture-seeking security troops had once been in the U.S. Army in
Vietnam. Now, instead of fighting the Viet Cong, they battled fellow Americans with walkie-talkies, steel pipes, and rifles.

In spite of huge increases in firepower and manpower,
Pittston achieved only one-third of the mine production of past
years. Lost profits, union fines, and taxpayer-financed police
troops culminated in over 200 million lost dollars during the ten-
month strike. In the end, workers won a raise of $1.20 per hour
and 100-percent coverage of health benefits for workers, pensioners, and their families. Thus the unpardonable sin was reversed.
The company would enjoy more flexible work schedules, allowing
for round-the-clock operations, and the union received greater
job security and access to new positions in the firm's non-union
mines.

Eastern Airlines

Another case, that of Eastern Airlines (EAL) and its chairman,
Frank Lorenzo, is perhaps most symbolic of the excessive costs of
labor-management conflict. Lorenzo acquired troubled Eastern

in 1986, vowing publicly to slash labor costs by every means at his disposal. Our research and involvement suggest that by declaring war on labor, he precipitated a strike and lost various battles in U.S. courtrooms as he maneuvered in ways that were at odds with labor law. He attempted to cut pilot and machinist wages, but failed because of earlier concessions. As business deteriorated he sold off planes and cannibalized equipment from some planes to keep other aircraft flying. The Federal Aviation Administration investigated employee complaints of unsafe management practices, and subsequent public fear cut passenger traffic by 26 percent (Bernstein, 1988). Lorenzo refused even to meet with the president of the International Association of Machinists, a 10,000-member union local, and the personality clashes between the two men soon resembled a Cain and Abel relationship.

Management sought $250 million in labor cost reductions, including a 12-percent cut in pilot salaries and 50-percent pay reductions for baggage handlers. Top mechanics' wages were cut from nearly $19 per hour to $14. New employees would start at $5 per hour instead of $9.32 per hour. The unions responded with slowdowns and pickets at airport terminals (Orkin and Ames, 1991). Increasingly, the American public began to boycott EAL, once the crown jewel of the airlines industry. Unfunded pension liabilities of $680 million and other failed management devices eventually sent the firm into bankruptcy and liquidation. The feud ultimately forced a sister company, Continental Airlines, into bankruptcy also. Although Continental is still flying today, Lorenzo was ousted by the board of directors. Crisis management, unethical negotiation tactics, and civil war between executives and the unions shredded Eastern's ability to compete. In the end, workers openly exulted in Lorenzo's firing, declaring that although they lost their jobs too, they at least had brought down the labor movement's worst "enemy." The ultimate cost of all this was over 10,000 jobs and $2 billion.

The New York Daily News

Another example of the pain and exorbitant costs of organizational conflict is the *New York Daily News* incident of 1990–1991. The incident began when the management of the Tribune Company, which owned the newspaper, attempted to wrest control of production from the 2500 employees represented by ten different unions. After two decades of bitter strikes throughout the metropolitan area, printers, paperworkers, and other tradespeople had won significant power in the numerous media of New York. The *Daily News* enjoyed the largest circulation of any city paper in the United States. Nevertheless, costs continued to rise as years passed and the equipment and the facility became antiquated.

In April 1990, the firm's owners and executives demanded unilateral changes in the way the business was run and demanded that labor forgo its traditional rights and responsibilities. By that fall, the company also sought numerous business cuts, which the workers agreed to explore in order to reduce operating costs. At no time, however, did management develop a clear proposal with specific dollar amounts. Finally, employees reporting to the night shift on October 24 found themselves locked out, and replacement workers soon began arriving in heavily guarded buses. The confrontation became extremely bitter in the months that followed. Management and the new workers succeeded in operating enough of the business to produce a daily edition, although in reduced format. But widespread support of the unions by advertisers and consumers ate away at Tribune profits.

After five months of aggressive and bitter disputes, and despite efforts of federal mediators, the parent firm threatened to close the press down. Just days before the shutdown, the *News* was rescued by British industrialist Robert Maxwell. He succeeded in negotiating wages, staff cuts, and other cost savings with all ten unions. In the end, the Tribune paid Maxwell $60 million to take over the *News,* rewarding him for the innovative solutions he had developed with labor, a strategy top management had been unable to pursue successfully in the past. The company also lost more money, including $24 million in prelockout preparations, and reduced revenues of $90 million over the five-month period. Tribune owners reported three additional costs: $92 million in noncash changes to write down the value of *News* assets; $86 million for accrued employee compensation, and another $57 million in operating losses before Maxwell took over (Sleigh and Kapsa, 1991). Of course, shareholders also lost significantly because of this war as their equity was reduced by 20 percent, which averaged some $261,000 per striker. Ultimately, the animosity of this tragic situation cost the firm at least $400 million, enough to have built a new state-of-the-art printing plant.

Other Cases of Conflict

Numerous other examples of the economic and social costs of American labor-management conflicts throughout the past decade exist, including President Ronald Reagan's crushing of the air traffic controller's union (Labich and Farnham, 1986), the meat packer's strike against Hormel in 1986 (Hage and Klauda, 1989), and USX vs. its steelworkers (Woodworth, 1984). In 1983, Phelps-Dodge, a copper company in Arizona, was struck by 2400 steelworkers and other union groups, costing over $200 million (English, 1984). Greyhound, once the pride of American bus transportation, engaged in a protracted labor conflict with the Amalgamated Transit Union (Zellner, 1990). Passengers across the nation boycotted the company, costing the firm some $20 million in its defense of unfair labor practice charges. Many workers were replaced by new, non-union employees and the ex-workers are presently engaged in a suit for back pay totaling $125 million more. Ravenswood Aluminum locked out its 1700 employees in the mid-1980s, leading to years of conflict and nearly ruining the business (Mallory and Schroeder, 1992). Ravenswood's board eventually fired the company's chairman and settled with the steelworkers union, but stock values had dropped as sales plummeted from $701 million to $490 million.

Caterpillar suffered the longest strike by the UAW in U.S. history in 1982–83 during a bitter, costly war. More recently, in 1991 Caterpillar locked out its 14,500 UAW workers and threatened to hire permanent replacements. The financial community, worried about the conflict and how a major equipment manufacturer could build products of the same quality with unskilled workers to compete successfully against aggressive foreign firms, lost confidence in Caterpillar. The strike lasted 163 days from November 1991 to April 1992. The company lost $404 million in 1991 and $162 million in the first six months of 1992. The firm's chairman, Donald Fites, has been heavily criticized for his big ego and stubborn attitudes and has been vilified in massive public campaigns in Peoria, Illinois, where the company is based (Vogrin, 1992).

Thus, the historical U.S. adversarial approach continues to be manifest in today's contemporary corporate-union conflicts.

When crisis occurs, when costs increase, when foreign competition begins knocking at the door, labor and management turn to a great American tradition: they start to fight.

International Contrasts

Although U.S. executives and trade unions have clearly shown a propensity for conflict, we see that in many nations the opposite is true. In both Asia and Western Europe a different set of values seems to dominate: maximization of productivity, full employment, and use of new technologies and training to enhance human fulfillment.

Britain

In the 1950s, Glacier Metal, Ltd., an engineering firm, launched an innovative organizational experiment in which management and the union set up a representative system that inverted traditional roles and authority. Rules were decided in tandem rather than dictated by the company or negotiated through collective-bargaining procedures. The goal was to achieve industrial efficiency and employment security. A works council was created through direct election and all decisions had to be unanimous before action could be taken. Social scientists and consultants from the Tavistock Institute and a government ministry all offered support and expertise. The outcome was not only increased productivity and quality, but greater satisfaction and ownership of decisions, with accompanying ease of implementation (Jacques, 1951). The experiment became almost scripture for many other labor-management cases of collaboration in the U.K.

The British model is tied to the considerable political power held by trade unions through their Labor Party. In the 1980s, however, the conservative dominance of the Thatcher government reduced the power of the working class. A peculiar feature of the U.K. system has been that regulation tends to occur at the factory level rather than through industrywide bargaining agreements. The result is powerful shop stewards' organizations which play a significant role in joint consultations regarding production. Since the mid-1970s, management seems to have increasingly sought ways to involve unions in running the enterprise. Over a decade, these efforts grew from some 60 percent of all firms to nearly 80 percent (Batstone, 1984). The

Conservative government also passed legislation in the late 1980s requiring companies to include a section in corporate annual reports on what is being done to enhance worker participation and encourage management-labor cooperation. Union membership has ranged between 40 and 50 percent of the labor force since the 1960s.

While British mining and manufacturing have declined in importance, North Sea oil drilling has become a major industry which has made the island nation the fifth-largest producer of oil in the world. Some 30 percent of the country's gross domestic product is due to exports, and there has been a great surge of foreign investment and new plant start-ups in recent years. Generally, British management seems to pursue economic objectives through union channels, rather than by fighting or attempting to obliterate labor. In 1992 a giant step toward more cooperative relations began when senior executives of companies and unions published *Towards Industrial Partnership*. In this volume a framework for change is outlined in response to the impact of Japanese plants in Britain and new European Community thrusts. The Involvement and Participation Association (1992) is now working to implement the book's recommendations for enhancing U.K. competitiveness.

France

Over the past twenty years, the Paris government has generated a consensus labor-management policy which includes national agreements on unemployment compensation, re-employment training, parity between white- and blue-collar workers' rights, and improvement of working conditions. Today, not only shop-floor workers, but engineers, first-line supervisors, and middle management belong to trade unions. A number of laws have been passed to create agencies that would enhance the quality of working life and encourage joint union-management decisions. While some 45 percent of all French firms with over fifty employees had a union local in the 1970s, by the mid-1980s that figure had grown to 60 percent (Sellier, 1985). And, unlike U.S. policy, which has been to cut back on labor-regulation staffs in the federal government, the number of labor department inspectors in France has doubled since the 1970s. The consequence of the U.S. policy is long delays for investigators researching

NLRB violations, holding hearings on complaints, and conducting union elections.

In contrast to the individualism of Americans, the French seek communitarianism. From the French Revolution onward, key cultural values are *liberté, egalité,* and *fraternité,* and those are strongly manifest in company organizations. Interviews with French executives reveal the considerable extent to which they feel a commitment to their workers, enhancing peaceful labor relations. "I felt responsible for them to be happy. I needed good administration and measurable profits, but just as a means. I knew everyone and used to spend time in the workers' houses to share contact" (Hall, 1989, p. 148). Such concern in caring for one's workers as a means to improving the quality of life for all is heavily emphasized by France's foremost management researcher in his *General Industrial Management,* who stressed the "subordination of individual interests to the general interest," suggesting the importance of *esprit de corps,* for "union is strength . . . harmony is vital" (Fayol, 1949, p. 20).

Sweden

Since the 1930s, Swedish employers and trade unions have been committed to a Basic Agreement which emphasizes the achievement of labor peace through compromise, with minimal government intervention. Having developed a sophisticated, well-functioning system of joint consultation and worker participation in a climate of friendly cooperation, the Swedish model is widely recognized around the world. It has led to impressive, pragmatic results. Wage policy is compatible with national economic goals such as egalitarian income distribution, full employment, stable prices, and growth of the country's economy through free-market practices. The overriding assumption is that the path to economic success and achievement of one of the highest living standards in the world can best occur through the development of two strong economic partners, labor and management. This is in sharp contrast to the assumption of some U.S. business executives and government officials that a diminished labor movement will enhance the well-being of society. The outcome of the Swedish strategy has been that for most of the last twenty years, the Nordic nation has had the best paid workforce on earth. Economic growth over the past decade has been 2.2 percent, not outstanding but on a par with many Western nations. Sweden has also been virtually strike free, unlike the United States.

Of course, Sweden is no utopia. The worldwide oil recessions in 1973 and the early 1980s hit Stockholm very hard because Sweden it has no natural oil reserves of its own. The reputation of Swedish goods for high quality continues to grow, but the high cost of national products has caused demand to decline on the global market. The public sector share of GNP in Sweden was 25 percent in 1950, but has mushroomed to around 70 percent or so over the past decade. So while unemployed workers have a right to government maintenance at about 90 percent of their earlier pay, and paid parental maternity and paternity leaves are offered for up to a year after a baby's birth, such benefits are becoming an increasingly heavy burden to the average Swede. As a consequence, there have been changes in government since 1991, including the election of more moderate politicians, slightly lowered taxes, and the beginnings of deregulation of some industries.

Still, the impact of the Swedish model of joint labor-management problem solving is impressive. Unemployment, for example, has ranged from 1.6 percent to a high of only 5 percent during the past forty years. During most of the 1980s it hovered around 1.5 percent. Beginning in 1978, legislation was enacted mandating at least five weeks' paid vacation for all workers. Total working hours have steadily declined since 1965. The 1978 Working Environment Act was designed not only to improve shop-floor safety, but also to enhance psychological well-being.

Trade unions in Sweden have enjoyed formal participation in plant-level works councils since the 1920s, although early managerial prerogatives gave executives the upper hand. But by the mid-1970s, a new Act on Codetermination at Work was passed, giving labor a voice in all major business decisions, including production, personnel policy, investment, subcontracting, and plant closings. In the 1980s additional rights were agreed to, such as union access to company financial information, budgeting, and company payment for outside union-appointed consultants and advisers. More dramatically, in 1983 the Swedish parliament passed the Workers' Wage Earner Fund Act, which requires companies to place 20 percent of net profits into a central account for purchase of corporate stock by the unions.

Ultimately, the plan calls for labor ownership of a significant portion, if not the majority, of shares in major Swedish businesses, leading to the possibility of a genuine economic democracy (Swedish Institute, 1984). Thus, unions and managers in Sweden have gone beyond simply changing organizational roles and creating mutual problem solving to becoming financial partners in achieving economic and societal well-being.

Germany

In Germany, as in most other nations of Western Europe, the relationship between management and labor is based on a commitment to cooperation among the parties, resulting in low levels of conflict. Whether beset by new, labor-saving technologies, a shift to conservative politics, or the merger of East Germany into the West, which resulted in rising unemployment and huge socioeconomic changes, the traditional system of consensus has succeeded and is likely to continue to succeed. German international competitiveness since World War II has been a resounding success because of social structures that brought employers and trade unions together, forging a partnership to advance technological superiority and integrate worker creativity into business-growth processes.

Union membership in Germany includes about 50 percent of all blue-collar workers and 25 percent of white-collar workers. A number of scholars explain the postwar boom in terms of a strong manufacturing sector, supported by a "beneficent circle" of cooperative relations among many interest groups (Bergman and Muller-Jentsch, 1975; Gourevitch *et al.*, 1984). Key players in this circle include banks, the state, employers, and German unions, working in concert to produce highly competitive manufacturing prices and quality goods through a strong export orientation. State-of-the-art world-class manufacturing enables Germany to dominate the global markets in selling machinery to other factories—34 percent of total world exports of packaging and bottling machines, 35 percent of harvesters and threshers, 37 percent of rubber and plastics-working equipment, 43 percent of spinning and reeling machines, 51 percent of printing presses, 58 percent of reciprocating pumps (Porter, 1990). These strategies have fueled high living standards, low unemployment, and superb working conditions and have reduced working time to a 35-hour week since the mid-1980s.

In spite of three postwar recessions, one homegrown and two the result of oil shocks in the worldwide ruptures of 1974 and 1981–1982, Germany has rebounded from each crisis by means of increasing flexibility and greater innovation. During those recessions, labor, empowered by the leadership of the country's most influential union, I G Metall, has had to make only minimal sacrifices in wages and income distribution. Nominal gross incomes of wage earners have risen each year since World War II. Exports and the nation's trade surplus have grown likewise, comprising roughly one-third of the national product. In the 1980s, Germany enjoyed a 17-percent share of the world's trade in industrial goods, the largest of any nation, while Japan and the United States each had a share of approximately 15 percent. With respect to high technology, it is oft-stated internationally that the Americans are the best innovators, the Japanese are the best imitators, and the Germans are the best perfectionists.

German courts have created a number of legal barriers to block work stoppages. Political strikes are against the law. The workforce of a plant cannot decide to strike. Rather, the national union must make the decision, and even then a strike can occur only after extensive negotiations have failed. Employer lockouts are also rare. Since 1950, the few major strikes that have taken place have been followed by long periods of virtually no strikes at all and minimal working days lost to such conflicts.

Unions obtained one-third of all seats on company boards in the coal and steel industries in the late 1940s as codetermination laws were established, and today the system allows workers half of the board seats in all large companies. In addition, in all firms with more than five employees a works council is elected by employees to deal with personnel matters, obtain company information, consult with executives on business matters, and so forth. Thus, social peace is facilitated from the shop floor to the boardroom as Germany continues to choose cooperation instead of conflict.

Japan

The Asian system of "harmonization of interests" between management and labor resembles that of America's Western competitors. Singapore has a tripartite arrangement in which government serves as a referee to smooth relations. Taiwan has also enjoyed considerable labor peace. But our research suggests that it is perhaps Japan that provides the best Asian example of unions and management working together to forge an impressive system of cooperation and economic strength.

Ever since the labor reforms of the Occupational Era of 1945–1952, Japan has passed through oil crises and other recessions with a highly structured system of labor-management collaboration. Union-management compatibility may be the crux of Japan's remarkable ability to keep unemployment low (1–3 percent), develop a skilled workforce, avoid prolonged periods of inflation, invade and obliterate other national markets, and build world-class industries that produce high-quality goods. Indeed, Japan's model of a labor-management partnership, and its resulting economic transformation, is generally referred to as the "Japanese miracle."

Approximately one-third of Japan's workforce is unionized, and the unionization typically occurs within the enterprise itself, not outside. Company unions are usually assisted and advised by industrywide federations, while companies are similarly supported by national business associations. The Japanese government often brings both groups together to discuss national economic issues in an attempt to do what makes sense for the well-being of society as a whole. Essentially, government works to reduce the growth rate of consumer prices and to maintain employment. In turn, labor agrees to not demand wage hikes that exceed increased national productivity. Employers endeavor to take care of employees through paternalistic practices and to enhance productivity for the good of the nation.

These mutual interests combine to create a Japanese labor-management equilibrium consisting of company investment in worker education, lifetime employment, continuous improvement systems, and quality control circles that utilize worker suggestions. This "social compact" has led not only to superb levels of productivity of upscale, quality goods, but also to a strong social net, social security, high wages, an equitable income distribution, and improved lives for virtually all citizens.

Both in the early 1960s and again in the mid-1970s, government played a major role in fostering increased union-management consultation. The Japan Institute of Labor organized conferences between employers and labor organizations to discuss their perceptions of one another, how differences might be narrowed, and what kinds of long-run policies might be developed that would be mutually beneficial. Over the past two decades, employees and unions created ongoing consultative mechanisms, not to do formal collective bargaining, but to share information and create greater understanding and empathy (Shimada, 1983).

The consequences of these practices have been remarkable: consistent GNP growth rates above 5 percent per annum, the transformation of what was a Third World economy in the 1950s into an advanced economy that was supporting one of the world's highest living standards by the late 1970s, and phenomenal trade surpluses with the West. And all this has been achieved in an economy that is one-third unionized. Firms with 500 or more employees are over 60-percent unionized. The number of actual unions has continued to grow steadily over the past thirty years. Thus, the number of unions with collective-bargaining agreements in the 1980s was roughly double that of the 1960s. Apparently, Japanese employers made no serious attempts to block unionization and have chosen to build cooperative partnerships instead. Under Labor Standards law, all firms with ten or more workers must seek the views of the majority in determining company policy, whether a union is formally organized or not. Enforcement of this law is fully and competently carried out by the government. The outcome is that workers engage in at least an informal, quasi-collective-bargaining process, whether a union is officially established or not.

In the United States the OPEC oil shock of 1974 and the recession of 1981–1982 led to company demands for "givebacks"—major wage concessions, mass layoffs, and plant closings. In contrast, the Japanese approach to the same events was to build national unity so the country could extricate itself from economic crisis. This strategy promoted of a high degree of corporate social responsibility and increased worker-management loyalty and cooperation. Meanwhile, the United States experienced increased adversarial relations, increased distrust and antagonism toward managers, declining world competitiveness, and a drive to seek revenge.

When we compare the U.S. model of confrontation to the more collaborative approach of selected nations, the contrast is

stark. The OECD's *Main Economic Indicators* (1991) reveal the
following unemployment percentages:

	1988	1989	1990
Germany	6.2	5.6	5.1
Japan	2.5	2.3	2.1
Sweden	1.6	1.4	1.5
United States	5.4	5.2	5.4

Other data suggest additional differences. For example, *The
Economist's* annual report on international industrial factors
states that labor-management cooperation in issues of workplace
safety yields such results as 3.0 fatal accidents at work for every
100,000 American workers, but only 1.8 for Swedes and 1.0 for
Japanese (Smith-Morris, 1990). Production days lost per hundred thousand workers to strikes and work stoppages were as follows: Germany, 134; Sweden, 374; Japan, 578; and the United
States, 4034. In the interest of workers, labor compensation in
the manufacturing sectors of these nations is higher than the
conflict-ridden U.S. system. Combining hourly wages and benefits yields total hourly rates as follows: Germany $24.39; Sweden
$22.30; Japan $17.85; France $16.10; United States $15.40; and
Britain $13.71 (Shlaes, 1993). Likewise, while the United States
led the world in 1970 Gross Domestic Product per person and
Japan ranked eighteenth, the picture was different some two
decades later. In 1988 Japan was first, at $23,325 per person;
Sweden was next, at $21,155; and the United States followed, at
$19,815, only a few dollars per person ahead of Germany.

Obviously, as this section suggests, there is sufficient research into the experience and success of labor-management
partnerships in other countries to warrant an entire volume on
international arrangements alone. This book however, is targeted to U.S. managers, union officials, government policymak-
ers, and students of business within the United States, drawing
upon the rich success of innovative firms and labor unions in the
United States.

Research on U.S. Partnerships

As U.S. corporations and unions enter the mid-1990s, the realities of global competition abroad and increasing numbers of non-

union companies at home raise serious questions about the viability of adversarial labor relations. Thus, some companies and unions are attempting to forge new partnerships. Some observers, such as Harvard's John Dunlop (1986) argue that these changes are "nothing new under the sun" (p.14), while M.I.T. faculty argue that the declining turbulence of present industrial relations is nothing less than a complete "transformation" (Kochan, Katz, and McKersie, 1986).

The evidence suggests that while labor-management cooperation in America has grown in recent years, attempts to cooperate in the past were unfortunately somewhat temporary and isolated. The consequence of many short-lived efforts was increased antagonism, as seen in the years following World War II. Literature in the 1980s suggests that perhaps half of the country's largest 400 or so unionized corporations have launched some sort of formalized labor-management cooperative program (Cooke, 1989; Delaney, Ichniowski, and Lewin, 1988; Kochan, McKersie, and Chalykoff, 1986).

We question whether such efforts will expand and become institutionalized throughout society or constrict and all but disappear, as has been the pattern in the past. The lack of staying power that plagued previous efforts may be attributed to the methods used, the effectiveness of their structure, and the competence of outside consultants who advised mangers and unions. Our purpose here is to address some of these deficiencies and to offer a set of tactics and methodologies for OD consultants to use today.

Certainly, programs of labor-management cooperation do not tend to be abandoned because they lack desirable results. A summary of the empirical research literature would argue just the opposite. *For workers,* the data suggest that self-worth and pride in one's job increase (McIntosh, 1988; Work in America Institute, 1982). Working conditions tend to improve (U.S. Department of Labor, 1983) and employees experience higher financial rewards (Cummings and Molloy, 1977; Dulworth, 1985; Ross and Ross, 1986; Schuster, 1984). Relationships between workers and supervisors tend to become more positive (Boyle, 1986; Burck, 1981; Fuller, 1981; Meek and Woodworth, 1982) and grievances decline (Smith, 1988). Labor-management collaboration gives the individual more voice in how the job is carried out (Kochan, Katz, and

Mower, 1984; Woodworth, 1986) and higher internal satisfaction (Goodman, 1980; Guest, 1979; Parker 1985).

For unions, there are a number of studies that report positive results. Labor leaders, for example clearly voice enthusiasm about labor-management joint efforts (see Donahue, 1982; Fraser, 1984; Watts, 1982). Research reports highlight benefits such as greater communication (Driscoll, 1980; Smith, 1988) and more influence and involvement in managerial decisions of the firm (Cohen-Rosenthal and Burton, 1987; Simmons and Mares, 1985; Woodworth, 1985; Work in America Institute, 1982). Joint management and labor efforts are also reported to assist labor officials in running the union, as reported in Bieber, 1984; Burck, 1981; Kochan, Katz, and Mower, 1984; and Watts, 1982. Apparently labor officials also enjoy increased recognition and legitimization from the rank and file (Burck, 1981; Cammann *et al.*, 1984; Dyer, Lispky, and Kochan, 1977).

The implications of labor-management partnerships *for corporations and their executives* also include a number of positive outcomes (see Woodworth, Meek, and Whyte, 1985 for various examples). Many firms report that such arrangements lead to better quality products and services to customers (Boyle, 1986; Camens, 1986; Katz, Kochan, and Weber, 1985; McIntosh, 1988). Others experience improved efficiency and higher productivity, as borne out in the studies of Contino, 1986; Douty, 1975; Meek, Woodworth, and Dyer, 1988; Pearlstein, 1988; Schuster, 1984; and Voos, 1987. The goals of a number of managers who participate in joint labor-management consultations are to cut the costs of overhead, materials, and expenses related to rework and waste, all of which are correlated in research (Boylston, 1986; Camens, 1986; Dulworth, 1985; Lazes and Costanza, 1984; Woodworth, 1991). Managers also enjoy enhanced communication with employees (Boyle, 1986; Driscoll, 1980; Smith, 1988; and U.S. Department of Labor, 1982) as well as more satisfying relationships (Burck, 1981; Fuller, 1981; Kochan, Katz, and Mower, 1984). Partnerships give firms greater flexibility and also tend to generate a closer alignment between workers and organizational goals (Cohen-Rosenthal and Burton, 1987; Goodman, 1980; Schuster, 1984; U.S. Department of Labor, 1982; and Walton, 1985). Finally, firms are reported to experience reductions in costly tardiness, turnover, and absenteeism and a drop in employee grievances (Cammann *et al.*, 1984; Goodman, 1980; Guest, 1979; Smith, 1988; and Watts, 1982).

In spite of the numerous, positive studies cited above, where there are pros there are often cons as well. Simmons and Mares (1985) report that such changes may result in workplace stress for employees and layoffs as productivity increases. Companies are at times required to spend huge sums of time and money for training in labor-management cooperation (Lee, 1987; Siegel and Weinberg, 1982). Meanwhile, unions too may experience certain downsides to cooperation, including role conflicts, potential loss of power, and political problems (Cohen-Rosenthal and Burton, 1987; Guest, 1979; Hoyer and Huszczo, 1988; Kochan, Katz, and Mower, 1984; Strauss, 1980; Woodworth, 1986 and 1988).

In spite of the extensive literature and numerous studies showing the advantages of U.S. labor-management cooperation, it is our view that there is still too little application, there are too many short-term efforts that are later abandoned, and there are too many poorly designed projects that begin with a lot of fanfare but soon disappear. One factor contributing to these problems is the historical OD bias against unions. Because of this bias, many joint efforts are implemented by industrial relations experts or labor lawyers who, while they understand the technical aspects of collective bargaining, often lack third-party consultation skills, appreciation for organizational culture, and competence in designing successful employee-participation schemes.

Our opinion is that OD ineffectiveness in unionized firms has its origins in the conceptual roots of organizational research. The Western Electric studies by Elton Mayo and his associates (Roethlisberger and Dickson, 1964) half a century ago emphasized the rationality and logic of managers, in contrast to workers. The T-group movement in the 1960s focused on the importance of interpersonal trust, illustrated in the writings of Argyris (1964) and Rogers (1961). Barnard (1938) used terms like "authority," which tended to give added legitimacy to the interests of managers, and ignored the notion of "power," which suggests engaged struggle, rather than one party's natural dominance over the other.

Elsewhere, Tichy (1974) raises concerns about consultants who basically provide analysis for those at the top of the organization. Ross (1972) asks who really benefits from one-sided OD efforts that prop up managers but either ignore or operate against workers. Likewise, Woodworth (1981) criticizes the status-quo orientation of much OD and raises questions of ethics, cooptation, and bias (see also Woodworth, Meyer, and Smallwood, 1982). Similarly, Nord (1976) articulates the importance of moving beyond the micro-level focus of conventional OD to consider interorganizational systems (such as trade unions) and to move beyond a simplistic, top-down bias regarding corporate life to consider the needs, interests, and potential involvement of other parties beyond management alone.

The reality today is that many consultants lack an appreciation for labor's role in U.S. productivity and competitiveness. An extensive survey of other studies, as well as the research of Freeman and Medoff (1984), clearly suggest the benefits of a unionized factory. What is needed at this point in OD practice is a delineation of how one might consult with both mangers and trade unions, helping them to jointly create a sustainable partnership that will result in mutual benefits for each and a better life for all Americans. This book will show how this can be done.

References

Argyris, Chris. *Integrating the Individual and the Organization.* New York: Wiley, 1964.

Barnard, Chester. *The Functions of the Executive.* Cambridge, MA: Harvard University Press, 1938.

Batstone, E.V. *Working Order.* Oxford: Blackwell, 1984.

Bergman, Joachim, and Muller-Jentsch, Walther. "The Federal Republic of Germany: Cooperative Unionism and Dual Bargaining System Challenged." In Solomon Barkin (ed.) *Worker Militancy and Its Consequences, 1965–1975.* New York: Praeger, 1975.

Bernstein, Aaron. "Lorenzo No Longer Wants a Brawl." *Business Week,* July 11, 1988, pp. 24–25.

Bieber, Owen. "UAW Views Circles: Not Bad at All." *Labor-Management Cooperation: Perspectives for the Labor Movement.* U.S. Department of Labor, Bureau of Labor-Management Relations and Cooperative Programs, 1984, p. 34.

Boyle, Fosten A. "An Evolving Process of Participation: Honeywell and Teamsters Local 1145." In Jerome M. Rosow (ed.) *Teamwork.* New York: Pergamon, 1986, pp. 146–168.

Boylston, Benjamin C. "Employee Involvement and Cultural Change at Bethlehem Steel." In Jerome M. Rosow (ed.) *Teamwork*. New York: Pergamon, 1986, pp. 89–109.

Burck, Charles G. "Working Smarter." *Fortune,* June 1981, pp. 68–73.

Camens, Sam. "Labor-Management Participation Teams in the Basic Steel Industry." In Jerome M. Rosow (ed.) *Teamwork*. New York: Pergamon, 1986, pp. 110–118.

Cammann, Cortlandt, *et al.* "Management-Labor Cooperation in Quality of Worklife Experiments: Comparative Analysis of Eight Cases." Technical Report to the U.S. Department of Labor, University of Michigan, 1984.

Cohen-Rosenthal, Edward, and Burton, Cynthia E. *Mutual Gains*. New York: Praeger, 1987.

Contino, Ronald. "Productivity Gains Through Labor-Management Cooperation at New York City Department of Sanitation Bureau of Motor Equipment." In Jerome M. Rosow (ed.) *Teamwork*. New York: Pergamon, 1986, pp. 169–186.

Cooke, William N. "Improving Productivity and Quality Through Collaboration." *Industrial Relations,* Vol. 28, No. 2, 1989, pp. 299–319.

Cummings, Thomas G., and Molloy, Edmond S. *Improving Productivity and the Quality of Work Life*. New York: Praeger, 1977.

Delaney, John T.; Ichniowski, Casey; and Lewin, David. "Employee Involvement Programs and Firm Performance." Proceedings of the 41st Industrial Relations Research Association, 1988.

Donahue, Thomas R. Speech at the University of Massachusetts, January 7, 1982 (unpublished manuscript).

Douty, Harry. *Labor-Management Productivity Committees in American Industry*. Washington, D.C.: National Commission on Productivity and Work Quality, 1975.

Driscoll, James W. "Labor-Management Panels: Three Case Studies." *Monthly Labor Review,* Vol. 103, No. 6, June 1980, pp. 41–44.

Dulworth, Michael. "Employee Involvement and Gainsharing Produce Results at Eggers Industries." *Labor-Management Cooperation Brief.* U.S. Department of Labor, Bureau of Labor-Management Relations and Cooperative Programs. March 1985.

Dunlop, John T. "A Decade of National Experience." In Jerome M. Rosow, (ed.) *Teamwork*. New York: Pergamon, 1986, pp. 56–72.

Dyer, Lee; Lipsky, David B.; and Kochan, Thomas. "Union Attitudes Toward Management Cooperation." *Industrial Relations,* Vol. 16, No. 2, May 1977, pp. 163–172.

English, Carey W. "When a Strike Rips a Small Town Apart." *U.S. News and World Report,* March 19, 1984, pp. 81–82.

Fayol, Henri. *General Industrial Management.* London: Pitman, 1949.

Fraser, Douglas. "Straight Talk from a Union Leader." Interview in *Reader's Digest,* March 1984, pp. 85–88.

Freeman, Richard B., and Medoff, James L. *What Do Unions Do?* New York: Basic Books, 1984.

Fuller, Steven H. "Employee Participation for Productivity: A Management View." In Jerome M. Rosow (ed.) *Productivity: Prospects for Growth.* New York: Van Nostrand Reinhold, 1981, pp. 296–309.

Goodman, Paul S. "Reality of Improving the Quality of Work Life: Quality-of-Work-Life Projects in the 1980s." In *Proceedings of the 1980 Spring Meeting.* Industrial Relations Research Association. Madison, WI, 1980, pp. 487–494.

Gourevitch, Peter, *et al. Unions and Economic Crisis: Britain, West Germany, and Sweden.* London: George Allen and Unwin, 1984.

Guest, Robert H. "Quality of Working Life: Learning From Tarrytown." *Harvard Business Review,* Vol. 57, No. 4, July–August 1979, pp. 76–87.

Hage, Dave, and Klauda, Paul. *No Retreat, No Surrender: Labor's War at Hormel.* New York: William Morrow, 1989.

Hall, Edward T. *The Cultures of France and Germany.* New York: Intercultural Press, 1989.

Hoyer, Denise T., and Huszczo, Gregory E. *Forging a Partnership Through Employee Involvement.* U.S. Department of Labor, Bureau of Labor-Management Relations, 1988, BLMR 130.

Involvement and Participation Association. *Towards Industrial Partnership.* London: IPA, 1992.

Jacques, Eliot. *The Changing Culture of a Factory.* London: Tavistock, 1951.

Katz, Harry C.; Kochan, Thomas A.; and Weber, Mark. "Assessing the Effects of Industrial Relations and Quality of Working Life Efforts on Organizational Effectiveness." *Academy of Management Journal,* Vol. 28, September 1985, pp. 509–526.

Kochan, Thomas A.; Katz, Harry C.; and McKersie, Robert B. *The Transformation of American Industrial Relations.* New York: Basic Books, 1986.

Kochan, Thomas A.; Katz, Harry C.; and Mower, Nancy R. *Worker Participation in American Unions.* Kalamazoo, MI: Upjohn Institute, 1984.

Kochan, Thomas A.; McKersie, Robert B.; and Chalykoff, John. "The Effects of Corporate Strategy and Workplace Innovations on Union Representation." *Industrial and Labor Relations Review,* Vol. 39, No. 4, 1986, pp. 487–501.

Labich, Kenneth, and Farnham, Alan. "America's Most Arrogant Union." *Fortune,* November 10, 1986, pp. 153–158.

Lazes, Peter, and Costanza, Tony. "Xerox Cuts Costs Without Layoffs Through Union-Management Collaboration." *Labor-Management Cooperation Brief,* U.S. Department of Labor, Bureau of Labor-Management Relations and Cooperative Programs, July 1984.

Lee, Barbara. "The Ethico/ACTWU Work Involvement Process." U.S. Department of Labor, Bureau of Labor-Management Relations III, 1987.

Lowell, Josephine Shaw. *Industrial Arbitration and Conciliation.* New York: G.P. Putnam's and Sons, 1893.

Main Economic Indicators. Paris: Organization for Economic Cooperation and Development, 1991.

Mallory, M., and Schroeder, M. "How the USW Hit Marc Rich Where It Hurts." *Business Week,* May 11, 1992, p. 42.

McIntosh, Phyliss L. "Labor Compact Key to New Employee-Management Partnership at Dayton Power and Light." U.S. Department of Labor, *Brief,* No. 12, January 1988.

Meek, Christopher, and Woodworth, Warner. "Employee Ownership and Industrial Relations: The Rath Case." *National Productivity Review,* Vol. 1, No. 2, Spring 1982, pp. 151–163.

Meek, Christopher; Woodworth, Warner; and Dyer Jr., W. Gibb. *Managing by the Numbers.* Reading, MA: Addison-Wesley, 1988.

Nord, Walter R. "Economic and Socio-Cultural Barriers to Humanizing Organizations." In H. Meltzer and F.R. Wickert (eds.) *Humanizing Organizational Behavior.* New York: Charles C. Thomas, 1976.

Orkin, N; and Ames, M.B. "Secondary Picketing Under the Railway Labor Act." *Labor Law Journal,* Vol. 42, July 1991, pp. 425–432.

Parker, Mike. *Inside the Circle: A Union Guide to QWL.* Boston: South End Press, 1985.

Pearlstein, Gloria. "Preston Trucking Drives for Productivity." U.S. Department of Labor, *Brief,* No. 15, April 1988.

Porter, Michael E. *The Competitive Advantage of Nations.* New York: Free Press, 1990.

Roethlisberger, F.J., and Dickson, W.J. *Management and the Worker.* New York: Wiley, 1964.

Rogers, Carl. *On Becoming a Person.* Boston: Houghton Mifflin, 1961.

Ross, Robert. "OD For Whom?" *The Journal of Applied Behavioral Science,* 1972, Vol. 7, No. 5, pp. 580–585.

Ross, Timothy L., and Ross, Ruth Ann. "Dana's Hyco Plant Successfully Integrates Quality Circles and Gainsharing." U.S. Department of Labor, *Brief,* No. 7, June 1986.

Schuster, Michael H. *Union-Management Cooperation.* Kalamazoo, MI: Upjohn Institute, 1984.

Sellier, Francois. "Economic Change and Industrial Relations in France. In H. Juris, M. Thompson, and W. Daniels (eds.) *Industrial Relations in a Decade of Economic Change.* Madison, WI: Industrial Relations Research Association, 1985, pp. 177–209.

Shimada, Haruo. "Wage Determination and Information Sharing: An Alternative Approach to Incomes Policy?" *Journal of Industrial Relations,* Vol. 25, June 1983, pp. 177–200.

Shlaes, Amity, "Anywhere But Germany." *The Wall Street Journal,* January 22, 1993, p. A-14.

Siegel, Irving H., and Weinberg, Edgar. *Labor-Management Cooperation: The American Experience.* Kalamazoo, MI: Upjohn Institute, 1982.

Simmons, John, and Mares, William. *Working Together.* New York: New York University Press, 1985.

Sleigh, Steve, and Kapsa, Michael. "The Cost of Aggression." *Across the Table.* The Center for Labor-Management Policy Studies, City University of New York, Summer 1991, pp. 1–3.

Slichter, Sumner H. *Union Policies and Industrial Management.* Washington, D.C.: The Brookings Institution, 1941.

Smith, Michal. "Aladdin's Magic." U.S. Department of Labor, *Brief,* No. 12, January 1988.

Smith-Morris, Miles (ed.). *The Economist: Book of Vital World Statistics.* London: Hutchinson Business Books, 1990.

Strauss, George. Quality of Worklife and Participation as Bargaining Issues." In Harvey Juris and Myron Roomkin (eds.) *The Shrinking Perimeter.* Lexington, MA: Lexington Books, 1980.

Suffern, Arthur E. *Conciliation and Arbitration in the Coal Industry of America.* Boston: Houghton Mifflin, 1915.

Swedish Institute. *Fact Sheets on Sweden: Labor Relations in Sweden.* Stockholm, 1984.

Tichy, Noel M. "Agents of Planned Social Change: Congruence of Values, Cognitions, and Actions." *Administrative Science Quarterly,* Vol. 9, 1974, pp. 164–182.

U.S. Department of Labor. Labor-Management Services Administration. "Report of the Secretary of Labor's Southeast Regional Symposium on Cooperative Labor-Management Programs." Washington, D.C., 1983.

U.S. Department of Labor. Labor-Management Services Administration. "Report of the Secretary of Labor's Symposium on Cooperative Labor-Management Programs." Washington, D.C, 1982.

U.S. Department of Labor, Division of Labor Standards. "The President's National Labor-Management Conference." November 5–30, 1945, Bulletin No. 77, Washington, D.C.: U.S. Government Printing Office, 1946.

Vogrin, Bill. "CEO Digs in Against Union and Rivals." *The Sale Lake Tribune,* December 27, 1992, p. D-6.

Voos, Paula B. "The Influence of Cooperative Programs on Union-Management Relation Programs." *Industrial and Labor Relations Review,* Vol. 40, No. 2, January 1987, pp. 195–208.

Walton, Richard E. "From Control to Commitment in the Workplace." *Harvard Business Review,* March–April 1985, pp. 77–84.

Watts, Glen "Quality of Work Life." *Perspective.* Labor Relations Press, October 1982.

Woodworth, Warner. "Weirton Steel: An ESOP Conversion." In Jon D. Wisman (ed.) *Worker Empowerment: The Struggle for Workplace Democracy.* New York: Intermediate Technology Development Group, 1991, pp. 117–130.

———. "Why Success Didn't Take: The Hyatt Clark Experience." *Management Review,* Vol. 77, No. 2, 1988, pp. 50–56.

———. "Blue Collar Boardroom." *New Management: The Magazine of Innovative Management.* Los Angeles, University of Southern California, Vol. 3, No. 3, 1986, pp. 52–57.

———. "Building Worker Democracy." *Dollars and Sense.* No. 108, July-August 1985, pp. 16–18.

———. *De-Steeling: Structural Disinvestment of U.S. Steel and its Implications for Regional Economics.* Provo, UT: Alexander Press, 1984.

———. "Consultants, Conspirators and Colonizers." *Group and Organization Studies,* Vol. 6, No. 1, 1981, pp. 57–64.

Woodworth, Warner; Meek, Christopher; and Whyte, William Foote (eds.). *Industrial Democracy: Strategies for Community Revitalization.* Beverly Hills, CA: Sage, 1985.

Woodworth, Warner; Meyer, Gordon; and Smallwood, Norman. "Organization Development: A Closer Scrutiny." *Human Relations,* Vol. 35, No. 4, 1982, pp. 307–319.

Work in America Institute, Inc. *Productivity Through Work Innovations.* New York: Pergamon, 1982.

Zellner, W. "Labor May Still Have Greyhound Collared." *Business Week,* November 26, 1990, p. 60.

2

Labor-Management Partnerships: Reform Versus New Start-Ups

In the introductory chapter, we argued for the creation of labor-management partnerships as a strategy for achieving national economic success. Having criticized the high costs of adversarial systems and explored the appeal of cooperation, in this chapter we will focus on concrete illustrations of how partnerships may be developed. The basic question is, What do we mean by labor-management partnerships?

To introduce the process of designing structures for labor-management collaboration, we start with a brief overview. The type of partnership defined in this book is that of a *formal, negotiated system of labor and managerial joint consultation and decision making.* Such efforts share broad objectives of improving employees' work lives, as well as improving the productivity and quality of the goods and services of the firm. A common set of procedures governs the cooperative structure and frequency of interaction.

Partnerships are not confined to narrow efforts, such as a safety committee or a quality control circle. Nor do things like a company suggestion program or an "open door" policy fit our criteria for structural change in management-labor relations. OD notions like GRID, team building, and job redesign may be part of a labor-management partnership, but anything done by management alone is too narrow.

It is important to clarify that these new joint partnerships are not a substitute for traditional collective bargaining. Work schedules, compensation, benefits, and basic shop-floor rules should continue to be handled through contractual arrangements between labor and management. True partnerships are created by company management and trade unions, usually with support from international officers on the labor side and corporate officials at company headquarters. Neither side ought to attempt to circumvent collective bargaining, but should build a parallel system of collaboration.

Our underlying assumptions of what constitutes a genuine partnership are that a degree of trust will be established and there will be mutually beneficial outcomes for each group including, perhaps, improved working conditions, increased employee morale, greater job security, enhanced competitive advantage, fewer grievances, and a more positive organizational climate. The expectation is that although conflict will not be eliminated, a more effective relationship between labor and management will develop, reinforced through training and assistance from outside consultants.

Company executives should not create partnerships to undermine the union, nor should labor use them as a vehicle to subvert management. Instead of one-sided dominance, the emphasis should be on reciprocity and other appropriate values that will empower everyone. Communication should be open, problems identified, responsibilities shared, and strategies for improving the situation developed. Rather than devising manipulative games, both parties should attempt to work within a framework of honest dialogue, advice, and joint decision making.

Over time, studies may need to be conducted to collect data on certain problems. Analysis and careful evaluation of the facts and potential solutions should be carried out. Not all difficulties may be resolved and failures will certainly occur. In spite of progress, there may be occasional steps backward due to crises, changing conditions, and even success. Each of these conditions may have unplanned consequences for joint partnerships. But if good faith prevails and the capacity to adjust is built into the process, partnerships can evolve over time to increasingly meet the needs of both management and unions.

The Range of Programs and Partnerships

Our central thesis is that labor-management partnerships hold great promise as American industry attempts to build more productive, flexible, and dynamic organizations. Many innovative efforts to create partnerships have been launched in recent years, but historically there has always been a small, but important cooperative sector of the nation's economy.

In the 1920s and 1930s, the Naumkeag Steam Cotton Company of Salem, Massachusetts, a century-old sheet and pillow producer, created a partnership effort with the United Textile Workers (Nyman and Smith, 1934). A joint committee of representatives from both parties worked to change inefficient production methods and reduce costs. The union obtained management's consent to hire an outside engineer to study more efficient shop-floor methods, leading ultimately to a "joint research" plan which strengthened the firm's competitive position. During the same era, the Baltimore and Ohio Railroad and its rail union reversed its high-cost, low-productivity, and negative industrial relations environment through labor-management committees set up in every roundhouse and maintenance shop. Over 30,000 proposals for improvement were made during a fifteen-year period. The efforts enabled the company to survive the Great Depression, and workers not only retained their jobs but enjoyed improved working conditions, reduced grievances, a strong new apprenticeship program, and somewhat higher wages than their counterparts at other railroads (Wood, 1931).

During World War II, the U.S. Chamber of Commerce and National Association of Manufacturers, together with the original AFL-CIO unions, supported the proposal of Donald Nelson, chairman of the War Production Board, in a 1942 radio broadcast to establish "joint management-labor committees to push production up to and beyond the President's goals" (Schweinitz, 1949). In the end, some 5000 councils were set up in factories employing over 7 million workers. The problems addressed included reducing absenteeism, providing worker transportation to the job, improving plant efficiencies, as well as helping wartime causes such as company blood drives, patriotic rallies, and the buying of government bonds.

In the decades after the war, other partnerships were begun. The Tennessee Valley Authority developed a rather sophisticated system of joint committees (TVA, 1971), and many other federal and local government agencies and unions did similarly. In the mid-1970s the National Commission on Productivity and Work Quality commissioned a report on six in-depth studies of managerial and labor joint programs (U.S. Bureau of Labor

Statistics, 1974). The studies revealed extensive cooperation in such industries as rubber products, baking, and women's fashion accessories.

Throughout the 1970s and into the past decade, other innovative arrangements for joint labor-management consultation were launched, including some that took place on a regional basis. Meek (1985) carefully documented the upstate New York Jamestown Area Labor-Management Committee, which involved thirty companies and their unions in strategies to save troubled businesses, redesign factory floors, train workers in new skills, convert some plants to worker ownership, and so forth. Woodworth (1985) did similar work in Muskegon, Michigan, with another group of unions and firms.

Other applications of partnerships grew out of industry-wide problems in retail food, trucking, basic steel, and railroads (Douty, 1975). Impressive results were achieved by unions and such companies as Rockwell International, Bethlehem Steel, Missouri Pacific Railroad, General Motors, Harmon International, Kaiser Steel, Cummins Engine, and the Rushton Mining Company (see Lawler and Drexler, 1978; Lelyveld, 1977; Zwerdling, 1978). The Federal Mediation and Conciliation Service (FMCS) began to foster labor-management joint projects to encourage "industrial peace." In a national *Report and Recommendations* (1974) the FMCS declared:

> We regard our missionary efforts among labor and management representatives to induce them to accept more rational and peaceful means of settling their differences, as well as the establishing of joint standing committees with a neutral chairman, to be in the nature of preventative mediation. [p. 6]

In the remainder of this chapter, we will focus on two significant cases of labor-management partnerships created in recent years. In order to show how extensive and powerful partnerships can be, both cases are described in considerable detail. The specific context of each case is quite different. One, the Magma Copper Company, is a brownfield site in which the parties attempted to alter their relationship in an old work culture with a long history of conflict and economic problems. The other, the new Saturn-UAW partnership, is a greenfield site, which involved the design of a whole new car, organization, factory, and culture. Juxtaposing these two cases will enable the reader to see clearly the dynamic processes by which effective partnerships can be created.

Magma Copper Company

Headquartered in Tuscon, Arizona, the Magma Copper Company consists of a number of divisions, one in Nevada, the others in central Arizona. They include a large smelter and underground mine at San Manuel and smaller mines at Pinto Valley and Mc-Cabe. These various units together will be referred to as the Magma Company. Total employment is some 4400 workers.

On the labor side, various unions are now affiliated and make up the "Magma Unity Council": United Steel Workers of America, United Transportation Union, International Association of Machinists, as well as locals from the Electrical Workers, Teamsters, Painters, and Boilermakers. While the mix of trade unions represented and the numbers of workers in each group vary, they have begun to collaborate, to reduce turf and jurisdictional disputes, and essentially to bargain jointly as "the union" with Magma and its divisions in an effort to bring coherence to what had historically been a difficult and confusing set of relationships, each with a different collective-bargaining agreement.

Magma has a long history of copper mining, and its smelter makes up roughly one-quarter of all U.S. capacity in the copper industry. Like most of the mining industry, Magma has suffered greatly over the past decade.

Worldwide copper prices dropped dramatically in the early 1980s (Atchison, 1988). Magma faced additional problems of declining copper reserves, aging equipment, and inefficient operations. Economic conditions eventually led to severe financial stress totaling $400 million in debts. To make matters worse, the company and its unions had had an extremely fractious relationship for over three decades—strikes, lockouts, grievances, rigid rules, and "going-by-the-book" practices which led to daily tensions, reduced effectiveness, and hostile attitudes.

By the mid-1980s Magma was in severe pain, and in 1988 a new president, Burgess Winter, was put in charge of the company (Slovak, 1988). One of Winter's first actions was to order that Magma's huge smelter be retrofitted with a new furnace in order to increase production. This modern technology was complemented by the installation of new mining methods and techniques. Magma's problems were far from over, however. "Bugs" in the new approach interfered with the system and production targets were not attained, adding fuel to the fires of management's concern about the long-term viability of the company. The unions also became increasingly concerned, and the buildup of tension seemed more severe each day.

Ultimately, in 1989, management reached a collective-bargaining agreement with labor's Unity Council stipulating that the mines and the smelter would remain in operation rather than suffer another work stoppage. Nevertheless, the various unions were extremely bitter over the state of the company and the labor contract. Efforts were made to increase productivity incrementally, but the need for major change was becoming more critical.

The factor that ultimately served as a catalyst for change was a provision in the new contract for joint union-management participation in issues of concern to either party. Reflecting on this provision, Winter and his team decided to attempt to create greater trust. They began meeting to consider the sources of the problem of distrust that had plagued Magma for so long (*AFL-CIO News*, 1991).

Meanwhile, throughout the 1980s, the steelworkers' union had achieved a number of cooperative successes with managers in steel mills across the nation. In 1989 they began to explore with other unions at Magma how the conflict with management might be better handled so that hostilities could be reduced. The Unity Council soon realized that only by building a better relationship would its workers have a secure future (*Steelabor*, 1990). While copper prices had improved, Magma's profits were in sad shape, which suggested a bleak future for both parties.

Toward a New Partnership

The two groups began to meet, building more open communication and sharing their hopes for the future. Outside experts were brought in to facilitate dialogue and raise the level of trust. Training programs were carried out, and as common concerns began to emerge, the group began to focus on how productivity could be strengthened more quickly. Other issues, like mine safety, also were placed on the agenda for discussion.

At this point, a different view of the new collective-bargaining agreement slowly emerged. It was seen as too traditional, too rigid, and perhaps a major cause of Magma's difficulties. Both groups felt that the contract was more like a straitjacket, locking them into a paradigm that was no longer viable. Although the union-management agreement was typical for the copper industry, both parties determined that a new, more progressive framework was needed.

Contract talks were reopened, but the overarching goal was to proceed in a problem-solving way. Over the next three months, some eighty union and management officials participated in discussions to flesh out a more innovative system. Ultimately, in October 1989, both Winter and the union leaders gave their support to this search for a new beginning, and the revised agreement specified key principles for joint labor-management cooperation. It was a dramatic departure for Magma and a radically different way of thinking for the copper industry as a whole (Charlier, 1991).

The Change Process

The following list captures key aspects we have seen in the Magma change process as it has unfolded over time.

- Beginning in October 1989, 700 managers and union leaders have gone through a two-day educational program for building intergroup trust and creating a climate of collaboration.

- All managers and some union officials went through extensive leadership training beginning in January 1990 to acquire new skills of effectiveness and communication and to learn how to develop problem-solving teams.

- Various projects were launched as both parties began to address crucial business problems through a joint approach.

- In late 1990 a labor-management team began to strategize about how to establish a gainsharing plan through which both parties could enjoy the economic fruits of greater productivity and efficiency.

- By early 1991 Magma decided to begin another problem-solving process, which would lead to a new collective-bargaining contract, one that reflected the changing company/union climate and incorporated the recent innovations.

- In mid-summer 1991 an agreement was reached for doing a massive work-redesign effort, which would overhaul the smelter itself and all the division mines, leading to more efficient operations throughout Magma.

As of early 1993, considerable progress has been made on these various efforts, some of which have been completed while others are ongoing systems of continuous renewal. Together they make up a huge process of organizational transformation at Magma. The essence of all this is summarized in a mission statement adopted by the Unity Council and management on May 30, 1991, declaring that the group has "full credibility and works through collaborative problem-solving techniques . . . which enhance prosperity and security for all employees and shareholders."

Specific objectives include the following:

- To use the talents of all employees
- To improve the quality of work
- To strengthen union involvement
- To increase productivity
- To reduce cost
- To enhance employment security
- To increase pride and satisfaction
- To extend mine life
- To share financial gains

The vehicles to accomplish these ends are numerous. They consist of strategic-planning committees created with participation of union chief stewards and managers to share jointly in developing strategies for change at Magma's various facilities. "Breakthrough projects" have been set up to launch major innovations. Gainshare coordinators were selected and trained to begin educating the workforce about economic results and ways to improve the fruits of one's labor. Magma began a series of regular communication meetings and informational updates so all 4400 workers understand what is going on, how the firm is doing, and what new innovations are being attempted. Ultimately, Magma spent over $3 million and 250,000 hours of management time in seminars and meetings with union leaders (Charlier, 1991). Various employees have become involved in exchange programs with other Magma facilities, learning how different divisions are coping with the complex problems of restructuring.

Finally, Magma has created numerous high-performance teams to begin the process of redesigning their jobs and developing mine plans for the future (Miller, 1992). These teams, made up of union and management representatives, are demonstrating new work relationships and better results, and they are creating new reward systems as well. Essentially, the Magma change process has brought labor and management together in a new partnership for creating what the participants refer to as "a culture of invention"—mobilizing all elements of the system in a search for better ways of running a smelter and its mines. In our view, Magma represents a quantum leap forward from the old, worn-out industrial relations system of the copper industry.

Concrete Outcomes

A number of significant results have occurred since these union-management efforts began in 1988. While it may still be too early to see the long-term impact, trends so far are certainly going in the right direction.

San Manuel Mining Division: According to "Dee" Durazo, General Manager of the mine, people are the source of major changes. San Manuel has not made any major capital expenditures at that site. Yet the parties created a union-management strategic-planning committee, carried out leadership and team-building training programs, and launched a divisionwide redesign of work. Crucial factors for making these initiatives succeed have been the sharing of mutual expectations, trust, openness, patience, tenacity, and the alignment of key goals and operating processes.

The results?

- Pounds of salable copper for each man-hour worked has risen from 48 in 1987 to 84 in 1992, a 75-percent increase.

- Operating unit costs have been reduced from a high of 83 cents per pound of copper in 1987 to only 63 cents per pound currently.

- Mill recovery (percent of TCu) rose steadily from 86 percent five years ago to 90 percent in 1992.

- The annual reportable accident rate went from a high of nearly 8 in 1988 to only 3 in 1992.

- Productivity jumped 42 percent by the end of 1992.

- In 1987 officials were considering closing San Manuel because of depleted ore resources. An untouched body of ore existed but it was so deep that, given current productivity levels, it would not be economically viable to dig for. The problem of how to access this deep source, the Kalamazoo, was addressed by a labor-management team at San Manuel, using new methods to achieve improvements. The objective was successful, giving the mine a new lease on life and salvaging the jobs of 1500 mineworkers.

Magma Copper Company as a Whole: The company and its unions reached agreement on an unprecedented labor contract in November 1991 (Settlement of 1991 Negotiations). It will extend over the next fifteen years and guarantees no strikes or management lockouts for the first eight years. The contract has unusual features, including not only cooperation, but also sections on gainsharing and problem solving. A major new feature added in 1992 is the Memorandum of Understanding on Work Re-Design, which authorizes union and management involvement in planning, shared management control, worker participation in improving "every aspect of the work system: safety, productivity, costs, employment security, the work environment, teamwork, and communication" (Magma Agreement, 1992, p. 42).

The memorandum specifies division-level strategic-planning committees, department steering committees, and design teams, each made up of between six and twelve union and management representatives. A charter clearly specifies how the committee is to perform studies, submit ideas and solutions, and obtain approval. Related issues cover such issues as scope of each project, stakeholder analysis, system demands, needed training, technical and/or customer analysis, and proposals for change.

The sum total of these efforts, which began five years ago, has led to a more formal and institutionalized labor-management partnership called the Joint Union-Management Cooperation Committee (JUMCC). Incremental financial improvements have occurred as well (Campbell, 1992). For instance, the pounds of copper "per manshift" has risen from 350 in 1988 to 550 by 1992, a major rise in overall productivity of approximately 50 percent. Simultaneously, the cash cost per pound before credits has dropped from $0.92 to a record low of $0.75 in late 1992, saving millions of dollars for the business. For Magma workers, this has meant a significant payback through the new gainsharing program, an average amount over the past year of $4500 per worker beyond base wages and benefits.

The integration of greater productivity and lower costs and the sharing of economic results have transformed Magma from an increasingly obsolete company to a new powerhouse in the copper industry. Partnership with the unions has aligned the firm's strategy, structure, and employees to focus on becoming a high-performance organization. Elimination of some supervisors reduced management salary costs as teams became self-directed. Improved financial performance has allowed Magma to acquire 100 percent of a 12,000-acre gold and copper reserve near Ely, Nevada, called the "Robinson District." This new source will provide Magma with cheap copper concentrates far into the future.

In January 1992 a new spinoff venture was started by Magma, Magma Metals Company. It is a completely separate enterprise, which combines smelter, refinery, and marketing into a new, extremely competitive firm.

Other effects of the turnaround at Magma include a dramatic decrease in union grievances, improved safety, and an improved environmental record. The company has been able to recover from years of financial loss, pay down its bank debt, and even create a cash reserve. Essentially, Magma has undergone an organizational rebuilding that has repositioned it for facing the challenges of the copper industry well into the next century.

The joint union-management committee has been championed at the top. It has developed a shared vision and has become proactive in creating its own future, rather than simply attempting to react to turbulence in the copper industry.

Saturn Corporation and the UAW

In contrast to the Magma case in which labor-management cooperation led to the regrouping and revitalization of an old, troubled copper mine, we next turn to the Saturn project, a new, greenfield site. While the project is funded by General Motors, Saturn is not simply another GM plant, or even a division. It is, in essence, the first new American car company in half a century. Its mission: to build an entirely new automobile that will help save the small-car industry of the United States. Among its many unusual features, perhaps the most revolutionary is that for the first time in history, rank-and-file auto workers participated in the creation of a major corporation and a whole new product line.

The Saturn concept is that a radically different approach to auto manufacturing was needed if U.S. products were to compete successfully against the small-car imports from Asia and Europe. New values, new assumptions, and new dreams became the launching pad for a new venture channeling technological and human capabilities. Less restrictive work rules, automation, and an innovative labor-management system were to be the foundation of the huge start-up.

For industry, the strategy was one of countering the flood of foreign competitors that was crashing onto U.S. shores: Mazda, Honda, Renault, Volkswagen, BMW, Audi, Merkur, Toyota, Datsun, Suzuki, and Isuzu. Subsequent competitors could potentially make things worse: Hyundai, Yugo, Mitsubishi, and Nissan. Some of the autos were very expensive and sold to a limited market, but many were small, low-cost vehicles which easily pushed Detroit's big gas-guzzlers off the road. Superb mileage, new comforts, and high-tech features all convinced many Americans that the U.S. auto industry could not cope. Saturn became GM's great hope for a turnaround.

For the UAW, Saturn offered a different set of goals. The opening of the new plant would create a major new source of domestic cars, would offer job security and high pay, and would counter the hemorrhaging of auto workers' jobs. All 400,000 active and laid-off UAW members would be eligible for employment at Saturn. Equally important, the union would move into a position of full parity with management. Instead of playing the typical reactive role of second-guessing or opposing the company, in Saturn the UAW was empowered, and therefore it could be proactive—take initiatives, make proposals, help to create a new corporation from scratch. The result, as *Business Week* said, was that "a new labor era may dawn" (Edid, 1985, p. 65).

Inventing a Brave New Company

Saturn grew out of the vision of some thirty-five GM staff and sixty-four UAW members who spent the years 1984 and 1985 exploring innovative manufacturers around the world. Both Europe and Japan were visited for factory tours and interviews with executives, international unions, academics, and foreign government officials. The "Committee of 99" read cases, studied new management theories, and observed videos in order to understand the best practices. Old models and traditional U.S. assumptions were thrown out in the search for the new, the brave, and the beautiful. The constraints of the past were thrown out as the committee considered not merely how to do things differently, but how to do different things.

In July 1985 the two parties came to full agreement, and negotiations were completed on what is perhaps the most radical union-management paradigm in U.S. history. Shortly thereafter, the UAW's executive board ratified the agreement, and Saturn announced that its new plant would be built in Spring Hill, Tennessee, a town of 1100 near Nashville. A $5 billion investment in the rural area would eventually culminate in construction of a huge new factory complex and generate some 16,000 direct and related jobs. Saturn itself would create employment for between and five and six thousand people.

The research and discussions between the managers and the UAW members culminated in the establishment of the Saturn Study Center. Team members worked to develop a radically new process for product development—design, engineering, manufacturing, assembly, marketing, and human resources. The car was to match the Japanese cost advantage of roughly $2000 per vehicle sold in the United States and, at the same time, possess the same high quality. The manufacturer also would provide outstanding customer service and timely response to changing market conditions—as the Japanese companies did.

Over the period of a year, the study team debated, negotiated, and strategized a common mission and underlying philosophy for the new company. Goals and a structured partnership were designed and appropriate policies were formulated. Rather than leaving engineers in exclusive control of technical areas, cross-functional committees collectively dealt with everything from stamping, painting, and assembly to compensation, safety, and managerial roles. The process maximized a synergistic effect in which the company as a whole grew out of the diversity and rich experience of many participants. It was anything but "business as usual."

As we see it, a major thrust of this effort centered on creating a sense of ownership in all aspects of the business. There were extensive disagreements, as both union and management representatives were often trapped by their past experience in traditional auto plants. The extensive research included surveys of GM dealerships, tours of Volvo in Sweden, interviews with innovative companies outside the auto industry, such as Hewlett-Packard, Fred Meyer, McDonald's, Sanyo, and Lincoln Electric. During one three-month period alone, team members put in 50,000 hours of effort, traveled 20 million miles visiting various sites, and stayed within budget (DeKoker, 1986).

As originally conceived, the Saturn labor-management partnership was a fulfillment of the dream of Walter Reuther, a UAW pioneer who proposed that all hourly workers be put on salary to eliminate distinctions between blue- and white-collar employees. While this suggestion, made in 1961, shook up Detroit executives and the UAW leadership as well, the absence of time clocks is a key feature of Saturn's new agreement. Less-restrictive work rules were established to unleash greater productivity. Instead of management supervisors, teams of between six and fifteen workers would elect a "counselor" to facilitate production and handle such issues as scheduling, budgets, safety, health, and absenteeism. Lifetime employment was guaranteed to 80 percent of the Spring Hill workforce, unless severe economic conditions or "unforeseen or catastrophic" events were to occur (*UAW—GM Report,* 1985, p. 3).

Certain features of the new agreement were of concern to some auto workers. The president of the Warren, Michigan, UAW Local 160 objected to the implications of the agreement for changing UAW seniority rights (Edid, 1985, p. 66). Advisors and consultants to unions were critical, arguing that reduced job classifications, teamwork, and other aspects of the Saturn agreement violated the UAW's principles of shop-floor opposition to management (see Parker and Slaughter, 1988). The National Right-To-Work Committee, an anti-union coalition of businesses, also opposed the agreement and sued in court, arguing that Saturn granted labor too much power. But in spite of challenges and outright resistance, the partnership proceeded.

In spite of the complaints and concerns voiced by a few isolated opponents of the Saturn-UAW pact, the union's leadership was ecstatic. Don Ephlin, the UAW vice president who played a major role in the project, declared: "Consistency of treatment is one principle in the total philosophy of full partnership. UAW members will literally help run the enterprise through joint decision making" (*UAW-GM Report,* 1985, p. 1).

The union envisioned Saturn as showing the way to greater U.S. competitiveness, gaining the country a major advantage in the small-car market of the future. Owen Bieber, UAW International President, promised that the union would "participate fully in the operation of all phases of the business," and others hailed the partnership as a "new milestone in our union's progress—a breakthrough that will rank among our greatest achievements as we look back over the years" (*UAW-GM Report,* 1985, pp. 1–2).

Compensation at Saturn was to start at $13.45 per hour for production workers, all of whom would be in a single job classification. Among skilled trades there would be between three and five categories and base pay would begin at $15.49 per hour. Profit sharing and other benefits would be added on top of regular pay. Instead of the usual term "employee," everyone would be called a "Saturn member." Decisions would be made by consensus from the shop floor to executive levels, and either party could block a potential decision when necessary. This great "leap forward" in union-management relations was touted by Bieber as "a degree of co-determination never before achieved in U.S. collective bargaining" (Cohen, 1985).

The original 1985 Saturn-UAW agreement was to function as a "living document" that either side might choose to alter over time. It was based on the understanding that within six months of actual car production, a new contract would be initiated to reflect more accurately the Saturn experience after several years in the planning process.

Strategy Implementation

With the dream all on paper and the design clearly in place by 1985, Saturn's new strategy moved from formulation to implementation. Over the next three years, more of what the Committee of 99 had planned was put into place. Headquarters was built in Troy, Michigan, and the meetings that we attended there and at UAW offices in Detroit impressed us greatly with the degree of openness, trust, and willingness to experiment that were evidenced. A mile-long factory was constructed in Tennessee. Saturn succeeded in distancing itself from GM so as not to be encumbered by the massive bureaucracy of Detroit, and it succeeded in pitching itself as a new American firm.

The original proposal received some adjustments, however, as the company experienced unanticipated problems. GM's market share in the United States declined by 7 percent, and as profits were squeezed, the original budget for Saturn was cut to $4 billion. The original plan to produce a vehicle that would sell for $6000 was revised to produce a more upscale car priced at $10,000 or more. The car's styling was not dramatically different from other cars in its class, and the goal of producing an engine that gave 50 miles per gallon was dropped in favor of a more realistic target.

The "Japanization" of Saturn's strategy was generally carried out as planned. Drawing upon the NUMMI experience, and employing some of the Fremont facility's managers, Saturn expended considerable effort evaluating potential new hires and then investing heavily in training. *Kanban* assembly processes and the configuration of numerous loading docks at Spring Hill greatly facilitated the flow and exact amount of needed parts. Close linkage between Saturn suppliers and dealers was also developed so that there would be no lack of coordination and harmony. The entire thrust of Saturn's profitability was premised on delivering superb customer service so that word-of-mouth advertising and the personal testimonies of Saturn buyers would convince foreign-car owners to convert to Saturn.

Ford, Chrysler, and foreign auto makers watched the rise of Saturn as intently as did GM, envying the brand-new upstart and hoping for a miscue. Lee Iacocca, chairman of Chrysler, wrote a new book, *Talking Straight,* in 1988. When it hit the bookstores, readers were intrigued to see his prediction that Saturn was going to be just another Chevy for 1990. He assumed the new auto business would dwindle away, becoming merely another headache for GM.

But for the Saturn team, this casual dismissal was a far cry from reality. Declared "Skip" LeFauve, Saturn's president: "We're still exploring, but Saturn is no longer an experiment. We're not a laboratory. We're not a social program. We're a business" (Taylor, 1988, p. 64).

In 1990 packets were released to the media and public showing the first four Saturn models, adding to the over 200 other vehicles Americans could choose from. The company sold 40,000 cars by the end of that year through a limited number of dealerships. By late 1992, Saturn had grown to 250 dealers in forty-two states. The cars—which were built with aerodynamic styling, driver air bags, fuel-injected engines, and high-tech features such as "shift stabilization" and "fuzzy logic"—were an immediate hit with many customers. In 1991 a quarter of the Americans who bought a Saturn traded in their foreign import in making the purchase. This was a key goal of the new company as it sought to reclaim the small-car market from Japan.

Producing four-door sedans, sporty coupes, station wagons, and so on, Saturn was selling seven models by late 1992 and had over 200,000 buyers. This was a record for a new car company, and it suggested that customers did *not* always delay purchasing to see how a new product would hold up over the first few years. Incredibly, Saturn offers a money-back guarantee. Within either the first 1500 miles or first thirty days, purchasers may return their new Saturn if not completely satisfied, for any reason. They can either select another vehicle or get a full refund. The car features a bumper-to-bumper 100-percent warranty on everything for three years or 36,000 miles, and there are no deductibles. In addition, Saturn features free, twenty-four-hour roadside maintenance in case of any problems, allowing owners to call a toll-free hot line and ask for advice or help, or free towing service if necessary. No wonder J.D. Power and Associates ranked Saturn as the best car in America, coming in behind only two luxury cars, Infiniti and Lexus of Japan. Customer-satisfaction index scores rank Saturn above big names like Porsche, Mercedes-Benz, Lincoln, and Jaguar (J.D. Power and Associates, 1992).

Outsiders like ourselves, as well as Saturn participants, tend to agree that it is the partnership between the UAW and management, replicated in alliances with suppliers, customer groups, the Spring Hill community, and other entities that makes the new company so successful. Saturn manager Nancy Brown-Johnston (1992) describes the structure of partnership and company governance as shown in Fig. 2.1.

Essentially, the Saturn Action Council (SAC) consists of Saturn president Skip LeFauve, UAW Local 1853 president Mike Bennett, and their respective associates who share equally in strategy formulation, developing company policies, and making decisions on capital expenditures, pricing, and other major is-

Figure 2.1
Saturn Decisions and Governance

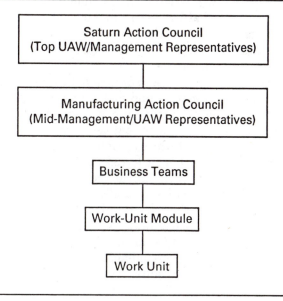

sues. At this level, the UAW even helps determine who Saturn's suppliers will be and what type of advertising campaign will be designed for new models. The second level is a mid-management and labor group, the Manufacturing Action Council (MAC), which resembles the European notion of a workers' council. It collectively runs the factory, plans how to carry out SAC strategies, and begins implementation. The third level is the labor-management Business Team over a given section of the factory, such as the power train or vehicle systems. Union and managerial leaders at this point focus on a more narrow range of administrative issues, providing direction and taking action as appropriate. The next level consists of a work-unit module made up of between three and six work units assigned to a core function, such as engine assembly or working in the paint shop. The most fundamental group at Saturn is the work unit or shop-floor team made up of between six and fifteen workers linked together geographically or by work process. Other resource teams or support organizations provide information, offer engineering and technical advice, and feed back reports from customers.

While most Saturn workers support the partnership between the UAW and management, a recent referendum indicated that some 29 percent prefer the more traditional labor relations model (Woodruff, 1993). Whether this is due to a change in the type of UAW worker that has been hired over the past year, extensive overtime, stressful conditions resulting from growing customer demand for Saturn, or other factors, the meaning of this new opposition is not clear.

At each level, the UAW and Saturn managers work collaboratively to share information and make appropriate decisions. At Saturn, the notion of partnership is defined in various in-house documents as "two or more entities or persons who enter into a basic agreement and who contribute some share of capital and/or labor, as well as share the risk and reward of the venture." Most of the key participants at the various levels of decision making are appointed because of their formal roles in the company or union, but at the work-unit level, an hourly worker is elected as counselor for each crew.

When state-of-the-art technology is fused with these multilayered, self-managed union-management teams, the integration leads to phenomenal results. Key values, commitment to company mission, and the Saturn/UAW Memorandum of Agreement have become the basis for a high-performance operation. But the key to making this work is not simply rhetoric about creating one big, happy family. Rather, it is the shared expectations that management and Local 1853 have agreed upon as practical, working principles and norms of behavior. Signs in the plant and office reflect these shared expectations, noted as follows:

Principles of a Long-term Partnership
Saturn and the UAW

- Begin with Good Clay (Beliefs and Values)
- Be Willing to Work from a Position of Total Commitment
- Always Maintain Respect for Each Other, in Spite of Personal and Emotional Baggage
- Do Not Take Understanding for Granted
- Learn to Accept Each Other's Shortcomings
- Maintain a Balance of Power

The result of adherence to this process has been the creation of over 6000 direct new jobs, as well as indirect employment among suppliers, retailers, and others. Base salaries are currently $32,400 for operators and $37,250 for skilled classifications. It is possible to earn an additional $6000 in bonuses, depending on the success of the company. Each employee was to receive some 92 hours of training in 1993 to enhance on-the-job performance. Since Saturn began producing vehicles, it has become the only American auto maker since the mid-1970s to sell more cars per dealer than Japanese manufacturers. And the Saturn car is 96-percent U.S.-made, unlike many other so-called "made-in-America" vehicles, which contain high percentages of foreign parts.

Our assessment is that the original vision of Saturn has largely been fulfilled. Old assumptions and traditional U.S. organizational practices have been mostly overturned. For instance, Charles Wilson, GM's chairman in the 1940s, often used to declare that as far as he viewed the UAW, there would be "no more of this equal voice back at GM!" Half a century later, labor-management partnership is *the* path to the future of not only GM's spin-off in Tennessee, but perhaps the American auto industry as a whole.

Visitors to Saturn tend to reflect this view, as illustrated in a *Work in America* bulletin (1992): "I see now how maybe union and management can work together better." An electrical union leader from Chicago said of Saturn, "This is an eye-opening experience." And a Raychem manager from California observed, "You have refuted the rumor that U.S. workers are lazy and illiterate and don't have a work ethic," while a well-known consultant suggested that Saturn has "succeeded in slaying many, many dragons" (p. 2).

Saturn had sold 500,000 vehicles by September 1993, including some exports to Canada and Taiwan. It currently employs some 8000 people. It has been so successful that the firm cut back on advertising during the past year and slowed the expansion of new dealerships. However, as sales have declined and new competition, like Chrysler's Neon, enters the automobile market, Saturn executives are increasing ads and dealerships and are launching a three-year lease program. They also are lobbying GM for $1 billion to add a second factory. Saturn also needs huge financing to begin designing new automotive systems for its 1996 models. The company achieved a small net operating profit in 1993, giving workers an attractive bonus, and the firm expects to enjoy a profit in 1994 as well (White, 1994, p. A-6).

As both the new Saturn Corporation and the revitalized Magma Copper Company show, creating labor-management partnerships can produce phenomenal results. Moving next to Chapter 3, we will review and assess the strengths and weaknesses of several models for attempting to build a cooperative partnership.

References

AFL-CIO News, "10 Unions Bargain 'Revolutionary' Pact with Magma Copper." November 11, 1991, p.10.

Atchison, S.D. "As Good As—Well, Copper (copper junk bonds)." *Business Week,* December 19, 1988, p.87.

Brown-Johnson, Nancy. Presentation at National Organizational Behavior Conference, Brigham Young University, Provo, UT, March 5–6, 1992.

Campbell, Marsh. Vice President of Human Resources, Magma Copper Company, Presentation to *The Productivity Forum,* Scottsdale, AZ, October 20–22, 1992.

Charlier, M. "Magma Copper's Workers Approve Pact that Protects Against Strikes for 7 Years." *The Wall Street Journal,* October 23, 1991.

Cohen, Sharon. "UAW Reveals 'Partnership' with GM for Saturn Facility." *The Salt Lake Tribune,* July 27, 1985, p. 1.

DeKoker, Neil. Personal Interview with Warner Woodworth. March 1986.

Douty, H.M. *Labor-Management Productivity Committees in American Industry.* Washington, D.C.: National Commission on Productivity and Work Quality, 1975.

Edid, Maralyn. "A New Labor Era May Dawn at GM's Saturn." *Business Week,* July 22, 1985, pp. 65–66.

Iacocca, Lee. *Talking Straight.* New York: Bantam, 1988.

J.D. Power and Associates. *Special Report,* September 1992.

Lawler, Edward E. III, and Drexler, John A. "Dynamics of Establishing Cooperative Quality-of-Worklife Projects." *Monthly Labor Review,* Vol. 101, March 1978, pp. 23–28.

Lelyveld, Joseph. "The Gone Fishing Syndrome." *New York Times Magazine,* May 29, 1977, p. 62.

Magma—Unity Council Work Redesign Agreement, July, 1992.

Meek, Christopher. "Labor-Management Committee Outcomes: The Jamestown Case." In Warner Woodworth, Christopher Meek, and William Foote Whyte (eds.) *Industrial Democracy.* Beverly Hills, CA: Sage, 1985, pp. 141–159.

Miller, W.H. "Metamorphosis in the Desert." *Industry Week,* March 16, 1992, p. 27.

Nyman, Richmond C., and Smith, Elliott Dunlap. *Union-Management Cooperation in the "Stretch Out."* New Haven, CT: Yale University Press, 1934.

Parker, Mike, and Slaughter, Jane. *Choosing Sides: Unions and the Team Concept.* Boston: South End Press, 1988.

Report and Recommendations, Federal Mediation and Conciliation Service. Washington, D.C.: National Commission on Industrial Peace, 1974.

Schweinitz, Dorothea de. *Labor and Management in a Common Enterprise.* Cambridge, MA: Harvard University Press, 1949.

Settlement of 1991 Negotiations: Magma Copper Company and the Unity Council, November 1991.

Slovak, J. "Magma Copper Company." *Fortune,* December 5, 1988, p. 118.

Steelabor. "USWA Wins Respect at Magma Copper." Vol. 55, No. 6, 1990, pp. 14–15.

Taylor, Alex, III. "Back to the Future at Saturn." *Fortune,* August 1, 1988, pp. 63–72.

TVA. *Guidelines for Union-Management Cooperative Program.* Knoxville, TN: Tennessee Valley Authority, 1971.

UAW-GM Report. Special Saturn Issue. Detroit, MI: Summer 1985.

U.S. Bureau of Labor Statistics. *Report on Joint Productivity Committees to the National Commission on Productivity and Work Quality.* Washington, D.C.: General Report, 1974.

White, Joseph B. "GM Saturn Unit Trumpets Profit Turned in 1993." *The Wall Street Journal,* January 6, 1994, p. A-6.

Wood, Louis A. *Union-Management Cooperation on the Railroads.* New Haven, CT: Yale University Press, 1931.

Woodruff, David. "Saturn: Labor's Love Lost?" *Business Week,* February 8, 1993, pp. 122–124.

Woodworth, Warner. "Achieving Labor-Management Joint Action." In Warner Woodworth, Christopher Meek, and William Foote Whyte (eds.) *Industrial Democracy.* Beverly Hills, CA: Sage, 1985, pp. 121–139.

Work in America. "Productivity Forum." New York: Work in America Institute, Vol. 17, No. 10, October 1992, pp. 1–3.

Zwerdling, Daniel. *Democracy at Work.* Washington, D.C.: Association for Self-Management, 1978.

3

The Evolution of Approaches to Labor-Management Cooperation

The notion of labor-management cooperation has been around for a very long time, perhaps since as early as the turn of the century. Ever since the enactment of the National Labor Relations Act in 1935, many industrial relations theorists and practitioners have proposed a variety of schemes for cooperation in order to promote industrial peace. Since the mid-1970s, however, labor-management cooperation has come to mean many things, ranging from simple two-way communication to the large-scale empowerment of workers and union leaders to participate in decisions ranging from the shop floor to the boardroom. In this chapter we will provide a brief description of the evolution of these approaches before moving on to a step-by-step practical discussion of the techniques involved in implementing cooperation and organizational change in a traditional unionized setting. After reviewing historical developments it should be much easier to understand the logic behind the strategy and tactics we recommend for building labor-management partnerships.

Early Approaches to Labor-Management Cooperation

One of the earliest efforts to create a cooperative relationship between organized labor and management began with Joseph Scanlon. In 1935 Scanlon was a cost accountant at the Empire Steel Company and the president of the United Steel Workers

Union local. The company had just emerged from bankruptcy proceedings and was in a very weak position because of its old and highly inefficient machinery. As president of the local, Scanlon was faced with new collective-bargaining demands from his membership for increased pay and benefits, which he knew could throw the firm back into bankruptcy.

In an effort to find a solution to the problem, Scanlon convinced the president of Empire Steel to meet with USW vice president Clinton Golden. Golden suggested that they return to the mill and hold individual interviews with all employees to seek ideas for increasing efficiency, reducing costs, and improving product quality. At the same time, workers temporarily deferred their contract demands, and eventually Scanlon, working with management, developed a comprehensive employee suggestion and consultation program. Combined, these efforts led to a successful revitalization of Empire Steel, and the firm survived another twenty years until it was acquired by the Studebaker Auto Company (O'Dell, 1981).

Scanlon moved on to other companies, and he continued trying to improve company performance while simultaneously increasing workers' job security through labor-management cooperation. Examples of Scanlon's initiatives include serving as head of the USW's new Production-Engineering Department and the development of his famous Scanlon Gainsharing-Bonus Plan at the Adamson Company in East Palestine, Ohio (O'Dell, 1981). However, these progressive programs in employee involvement and union-management cooperation did not spread very rapidly. A more common focus for labor-management cooperation was upon mediating impasses between unions and companies engaged in contract negotiations. These efforts were commonly undertaken at the community level through joint bodies of union, management, and government officials called *community* or *area labor-management committees* (LMCs).

The first of these community-based labor-management groups was the *Toledo Labor-Management Citizens Committee,* which was initiated by vice-mayor Michael Disalle in Toledo, Ohio, in 1945 (Foltman). Toledo had become notorious as a *strike-prone* city, and the vice-mayor wanted to change that reputation by establishing industrial peace. In 1945 the Federal Mediation and Conciliation Service (FMCS) had not yet been created, nor did a state agency exist in Ohio to help mediate contract disputes. The Toledo LMC was therefore established to provide this service. After hiring a committee director, a forty-eight member board was organized, composed of one-third labor, one-third management, and one-third public-sector leaders. Still in operation today, the Toledo LMC has essentially followed the same process for mediating contract disputes for the past forty-nine years. A report of the National Center for Productivity and Quality of Working Life (1978) describes the process: "Initial mediation efforts are provided by the full-time director. If he is unable to obtain a settlement, or if he deems it necessary, a tripartite panel of one member from the three sectors can be appointed by the chairman to mediate" (p. 142).

Once the FMCS was established by the Taft-Hartley Act in 1947, the need for such community-based mediating bodies was significantly reduced. Nonetheless, area LMCs continued to be established periodically, following the Toledo model, with six more created during the next twenty-odd years. After this point there was a dramatic increase in the number of area LMCs formed, beginning with the creation of the Jamestown Area Labor-Management Committee (JALMC) in 1972. JALMC, which was initiated through the intervention of Mayor Stanley Lundine (currently lieutenant governor of New York State), was established with a somewhat different mandate than prior committees (Meek, 1985).

Like Toledo, Jamestown, New York, had earned a reputation as a *strike-prone* town with what was often referred to as a *bad labor climate*. In 1972 Jamestown was also faced with a 10-percent unemployment rate, due to several plant and company closures and other shutdowns. Jamestown's reputation for antagonistic labor-management relations made it virtually impossible for the city government to recruit new firms into the area. Thus, Mayor Lundine and the JALMC determined that their main order of business was to prevent additional plant closings and to revitalize existing industry through building cooperative relations between labor and management. Eventually JALMC's activities evolved into cooperative problem-solving efforts, assisted by organization development intervention provided by Eric Trist and researchers from the University of Pennsylvania with later assistance from William Foote Whyte and colleagues (1983) at Cornell University's New York State School of Industrial and Labor Relations.

JALMC's activities led to many innovations in labor-management relations which were directed at both operational improvements as well as improving the quality of working life. These activities also served as a model for the efforts of some forty new-area LMCs that followed JALMC over the next twelve years.

Such area LMCs, organized since the 1970s, as well as many plant- and company-level labor-management committees, have sought to reverse the process of industrial decline. Many of these efforts, unfortunately, have been less than aggressive in their efforts to mobilize labor and management. And as we shall see, early efforts tended more toward public relations than toward effecting substantive change at either the shop-floor or upper management and union levels. As time has progressed, though, it has become apparent that the rhetoric of cooperation is meaningless without the creation of new institutions and processes for union-management interaction.

The Labor Relations Strategy

We refer to the early approaches to creating more cooperative labor-management relationships as the *labor relations strategy* because they were generally introduced by federal mediators or other professionals with training and experience in traditional industrial relations. Their sole goal was to reduce friction between union leaders and managers in order to facilitate smoother contract negotiations and reduce grievances. These early practitioners seldom even considered facilitating direct worker and union-official participation in joint problem solving with management and, in fact, this is still the case even today. So even though we characterize the labor relations strategy as an *early approach,* it is important to realize that this strategy continues to be advocated by many consultants and other third-party interventionists even today.

Some of the first efforts to create a less adversarial and more cooperative dialogue between union leaders and managers were undertaken by members of the Federal Mediation and Conciliation Service during the 1960s. These mediators became frustrated with the crisis nature of their involvement in contract negotiations, and they felt that there needed to be some way to get the parties talking about problems before they reached the crisis stage of either arbitration or a negotiation impasse. Federal mediators also lost patience with the intervention of groups like the Toledo Labor-Management Citizens Committee. Mediators came to feel that the activities of these groups were at best unnecessary and at worst a hindrance to reaching contract settlements once the FMCS had become established.

Veteran federal mediator and organizer of numerous labor-management committees Samuel Sackman of the FMCS explains:

> The biggest problem that I had from my experiences in Pennsylvania, going back to 1959 and '64, was where the labor-management committees mediated. It caused an awful lot of problems. . . . When the Mediation Service was moving to create pressure the LMC would intervene and reduce the pressure. The people would sit back and wait and say, "Let's wait and see what the LMC is going to do." The Wilkes-Barre LMC created a situation where a strike continued for an extra five weeks.

Mediators like Sackman concluded that the way to create a more positive role for area LMCs, and also reduce friction between union leaders and managers, was to get involved outside the formal collective-bargaining machinery in facilitating more informal two-way communication. There were two principal assumptions behind these efforts. First, it was believed that if union and management officials could become engaged in informal discussion and socializing outside the traditional adversarial dynamics of collective bargaining, greater trust would develop between the parties, making agreements easier to reach. Second, federal mediators like Sackman felt that if managers and union representatives could become alerted to problem areas early, then confrontations and crises could be minimized.

A typical effort at developing such a process was attempted by Sackman and a labor attorney and former mediator, Raymond Anderson. It occurred informally during the late 1960s in Jamestown, well before the formal creation of the Jamestown Area Labor-Management Committee. Anderson describes their attempt to establish one of these plant-level LMCs at the Watson's Metal Fabrication Company:

> Sam Sackman and I started an in-plant LMC at Watson's. We would have a little smorgasbord, and we would meet with management and the Machinists. Sam Sackman

chaired the thing and . . . the senior business agent took a lead role. The concept here was to have our own in-plant labor-management committee, but then break down into subcommittees so that foremen and stewards would get a coffee break and discuss their problems. We tried to set up a top plant committee and then break it down into subcommittees made up of department stewards and department foremen.

The role of this top steering committee was to see that there was continuity and to develop a philosophy of overall improvement and then to watch it to make sure it flowed down to the departments. Sackman and I would meet with the company and union representatives in the overall plant committee, and they, in turn, with the assistance and advice of Sam Sackman, would break the program down into smaller subcommittees. So, if a foreman and a steward didn't communicate, the idea was to subtly get this communication through coffee breaks, luncheons, bowling, and drinks after work because everything emanates from that level.

Later, as university professors became involved in these kinds of efforts, applied social science techniques such as survey-feedback designs and group-sensing meetings were used to facilitate cooperative communications between labor representatives and management. The objectives behind employing these techniques were to open up the process more rapidly to the entire workforce and to build upon an initial foundation of more objective data. Unfortunately, the mediators' technique and the more sophisticated social science-based method were both seriously flawed and in most instances ultimately doomed to produce failure. In fact, rather than facilitating a more rapid transition to cooperative relations, the introduction of behavioral science technology actually served to speed up the demise of such efforts. Figure 3.1 illustrates the dynamics that developed and ultimately resulted in the collapse of the labor relations strategy.

Essentially, the labor relations strategy fell into the same reactive dynamics that characterize the traditional grievance procedure. In the grievance process *only the union and workers file grievances*. A grievance is filed when it is felt that a violation of the contract has taken place. Of course, a labor-management

Figure 3.1
Dynamics of the Labor Relations Strategy

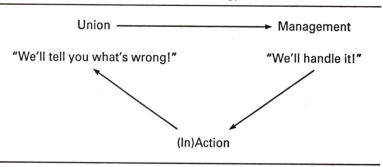

Union ⟶ Management

"We'll tell you what's wrong!"   "We'll handle it!"

(In)Action

contract, like any contract, is a legally enforceable, two-way agreement between the parties. Unlike other contractual arrangements, however, management is free to act if they feel that members of the union have violated the collective-bargaining agreement; that is, management can take disciplinary action against workers if it believes that violations have occurred. Similarly, it is management's role to implement the contract—for example, to assign overtime, pay benefits, assign work, and determine shift differentials. If an individual worker, a group of workers, or the union leadership feels either that disciplinary action has been taken unfairly or that the contract provisions were implemented incorrectly, then their only recourse is to file a grievance. Ultimately, they can take the grievance to binding arbitration if resolution cannot be reached. The fundamental rule is for workers to follow management's orders, unless there is a question of a serious safety hazard, and then file a grievance.

The labor relations strategy pursued a path very similar to this process. As meetings were held, channels were opened which enabled union officials and workers to raise complaints about virtually any issue that concerned them. This means of releasing pent-up frustrations and expressing real problems was, at first, a very positive experience for labor. Since most of the complaints were directed one way, toward management, the experience was naturally less pleasant for managers. Keeping the discussion going, and helping management deal with their defensiveness, became the critical role of the third-party consultant. Once the issues had been raised by labor, management typically agreed to take care of the problems. If the third party was a skilled facilitator, the problems were prioritized once they were listed.

Unfortunately, even with the prioritizing of issues, more items were typically raised in these meetings than management could possibly address in a reasonable period of time. Moreover, putting all of the responsibility on the shoulders of management kept valuable worker input out of the problem-solving and decision-making processes. Consequently, the solutions actually developed were often unsatisfactory to workers or even directed at the wrong problem. Furthermore, since the union assumed no joint responsibility for reaching solutions to the problems they had raised, they were free to step back and join their members in criticizing management for *not doing the right thing* or *acting too slowly* on worker complaints.

Not surprisingly, in such cases management eventually became angry and frustrated by the continued onslaught of complaints. They felt that their efforts were unappreciated by workers or union leaders, and thus they tended more and more to cancel meetings in an effort to avoid more criticism. Conversely, as union officials received complaints from union members for not getting action on *their* issues, they also quietly backed away from the process, trying to pretend it had never happened. Even worse, there were sometimes public protests against management in an effort to absolve labor of any hint of responsibility for the failed program.

When survey-feedback techniques were introduced into the process, or when group-sensing meetings were held in departments to obtain broad input and objective data, problems were actually exacerbated. For example, at a ceramic mould manufacturing plant, third-party consultants, union leaders, and top management decided to hold sensing meetings in every plant department in order to begin work on creating a more favorable labor-management climate. Over a period of approximately six to seven months they met with all employees and asked them what problems and suggestions they wanted the newly formed LMC to address.

As a result of these meetings, some 135 problems and suggestions were compiled. Unfortunately, because of regular work responsibilities and the complexity of many of the problems—to say nothing of the expense involved in addressing them—only a very small number of items were actually resolved. The few issues that were addressed paled in comparison to the more than one hundred remaining on the LMC's agenda. Moreover, not only did the formal labor representatives become frustrated with the process, but, since the entire workforce's expectations had been raised, all employees became angry with the lack of progress. Managers began to feel attacked and unappreciated, and labor leaders concluded that cooperation involved "nothing more than talk." As the former union president explains:

> When we first started holding labor-management meetings, I think we all thought that if we just sat down and talked, everything would work out. It was really frustrating. We talked and we talked and we talked about problems as if we talked about them enough they'd somehow go away, but they didn't.

Not surprisingly, this LMC ceased meeting after less than a year of operation. Virtually everyone in the factory was unhappy with the experience and cynical about the idea of cooperation. Similar results occurred even when management did take action if it was done without worker input.

The case of a metal caseworking company in upstate New York provides an excellent illustration of this situation. A consultant who worked on the effort explains:

> When we went on a plant tour, there were about ten machine operators waiting to have their piece on a production run inspected. And we asked them, "What are you dong?" They said, "Well, we're waiting to have our pieces inspected."
>
> Right after that, we had a kind of general labor-management meeting with just some people from both sides. . . . And we said, "Why don't you have some kind of system of levels of inspection so that people can inspect their own first pieces within a given range?" That was their first project.
>
> Now they blew that as I learned when I went back. And the way they blew it was they took that idea and they just went out on the floor . . . and they never went back to the

people in that department to get some input on how that specific process ought to have been designed—*which is a typical labor relations thing.* A problem gets identified, it's a kind of top-down kind of problem solving. And they went out and they built this big measuring table, and got all these tools. They just laid it on them and people never used it because they didn't understand what they were supposed to do. *It was doing something to them and not with them.*

These early efforts at labor-management cooperation followed the labor relations strategy and had considerably less impact than they might have had if problem identification had led to the involvement of shop-floor employees as partners in the problem-solving process. By retaining problem-solving activity in its traditional, top-down form, as a responsibility and prerogative of management, such groups failed to generate employee commitment to the solutions implemented. Moreover, management left themselves open to harsh criticism from union officials and the rank and file if their solutions failed to match the expectations of labor. In short, the decision to focus cooperative activity upon *communication* and not on *joint problem solving* severely restricts the ability of the labor relations strategy to generate mutual understanding and the effective application of insights. These can only come through directly incorporating the experience of shop-floor workers in the problem-solving process. When this approach is followed, labor never comes to fully realize the complexities and difficulties involved in making business decisions. Conversely, management fails to develop a healthy appreciation for the capacity of workers to generate creative and practical solutions to organizational problems.

Thus, most cooperative efforts that follow a labor relations strategy either suddenly halt under the weight of controversy or gradually die. Union leaders and workers conclude that cooperation is of minimal value because it results in little more than *just talk.* Conversely, management decides that labor-management meetings are nothing more than *"gripe sessions"* in which they regularly are criticized by the union. Still worse, much unwanted work is added to their already busy schedules, and they receive little or no credit for their efforts.

The Traditional OD Strategy:
Labor-Management Boulwareism

A commonly accepted rule of thumb in the world of organization development is to *start from the top*. Typically this means to convert the highest level of management to the OD process and gain their public support for broader intervention efforts. Many years of experience have led OD practitioners to this conclusion, which has nearly become an OD commandment. However, following this kind of strategy—focusing solely upon obtaining the support and sanctioning of upper-level management—can have deadly consequences if the ultimate goal is to create a dynamic labor-management partnership. The problem with this kind of strategy is that it frequently leaves the union entirely out as the recognized and exclusive bargaining agent for employees. The typical strategy is to proceed with building cooperative relations as if the setting were the same as in a non-union work environment—that is, to go directly to the employees without working with or through the union at all.

Such an approach is by no means illegal. Clauses in collective-bargaining agreements almost universally protect management's right to manage the workforce. However, by leaving the union out of the initial strategy formulation and policy development, as well as the ongoing governance of the process, management and consultants essentially create a climate in which it is in the union's best interest to either ignore the effort, or worse, openly attack it as a management ploy for union busting.

Such a reaction on the part of union officials is not surprising. When management follows the traditional OD approach, if success occurs, the union is unlikely to receive any credit for it. In addition, and even worse, officials may come to fear *union busting*. A number of books and articles have been written specifically to promote OD as a means for preventing unionization. Consultants abound who will help install *"positive human resource programs"* to help companies avoid unions or weaken their power. Going around the union to seek out employee interests and gain their acceptance of corporate activities has a long history in collective bargaining, but it is, in fact, illegal.

The practice of circumventing the union and going directly to workers to seek their support for a contract proposal is referred to as "Boulwareism." This term is credited to a former vice president and director of industrial relations at General Electric Corporation (GE), Lemuel Boulware. Under his direction, GE developed an approach to bargaining whereby preliminary survey research was conducted with employees to determine their interests and concerns. From this data, management would formulate the firm's bargaining offer. Once GE established its bargaining proposal, it then held to it as its final, "fair but firm offer."

Management went around the union with an extensive public relations campaign to "sell" the offer directly to employees. Meetings held between the company and the union became strictly *pro forma,* with GE managers refusing to consider alternatives presented by the union negotiating committee. Instead, executives would present prepared lectures on the rightness of the company's position. Eventually, the union filed charges with the National Labor Relations Board (NLRB), claiming that GE was violating Section 8(d) of the National Labor Relations Act (NLRA), in effect, "refusing to bargain in good faith." The NLRB agreed with the union and the company was ordered to cease and desist from its activities.

Specifically, the NLRB found that GE had not only held to a rigid position at the bargaining table, but it had also violated the law by circumventing the union through a widespread publicity campaign to convince employees that the company's offer was the best for them. GE had criticized and ridiculed the union in its literature, and the NLRB held that it was unlawful for the company to make it appear that union representation was superfluous by acting as if no union existed at all. Thus, GE's conduct was held to be a "failure to bargain in good faith" because the totality of conduct, not just a single technique, indicated clearly that it had no intention of bargaining with the union (Feldacker, 1983; Holley and Jennings, 1991).

Even when it does not directly involve contract negotiations, doing labor-management OD, if it looks like Boulwareism, inevitably arouses the antipathy and even the public opposition of union leaders. In fact, rather than creating a climate of cooperation and open communication, this strategy may exacerbate the level of conflict.

A good example of this occurred at Eastern Airlines during the early 1980s, when then chairman Frank Borman attempted to establish shop-floor quality circles in Eastern's maintenance operations. Following the system developed by QC circle consultant William Riker, Eastern implemented quality circles with both its non-union customer-service representatives and its maintenance workers who were organized by the International Association of Machinists and Aerospace Workers (IAM). By 1981 some thirteen QC circles had been established at the company's important Miami Engine Service Center. The employees involved were enthusiastic about the improvements in their work environment and the work process. Union leaders, however, were firmly opposed. In part their opposition stemmed from their on-going conflict with management over trying to end a wage give-back plan in the collective-bargaining agreement. More central to the union's opposition to the QC circle program, however, was management's decision to leave union leaders out of the process and go directly to shop-floor workers, because the union in its proposals was actually promoting employee involvement. Thus, union leaders attempted to halt the QC circle activities through issuing the following IAM Bulletin (1981) "To All Members," urging them to shun circle meetings:

> The history of "Quality Circles" in Japan and Europe has been very good and has carried a commitment from management of job security and a sharing of the benefits and gains accomplished . . .
>
> Unfortunately, "Quality Circles" in this country, without the aggressive participation of union leadership, has generally been doomed to failure and rejection by employees, when management did not offer to share the benefits and used it as a vehicle to create "speed-ups" and discipline, in lieu of the real intent which is to make people work smarter, thereby making the job easier and eliminating obstacles such as parts flow, bad equipment or tooling, poor operations, etc.
>
> Due to the fact that Eastern Airlines has failed to negotiate with your District the proper safeguards and guarantees, we, the Combined Shop Committee, request that the membership not participate in "Quality Circles" until such time as these above mentioned safeguards are met . . .

Machinists' President Charles Bryan was surprised at the members' response to the bulletin. He quickly learned that IAM mechanics were firmly behind the activities in which they had become involved, and some forty-nine machinists from fourteen different departments at the Engine Service Center sent him a letter requesting that he not hold the effort back. The machinists' enthusiasm for the program is illustrated by the following excerpt from a letter they sent to Bryan (Meek, 1988):

> We feel that our participation in the Quality Circle Program has been beneficial to us, the Union, and the Company.
>
> The Program has given us a recognized voice in the Company, which is something we have wanted for a long time. Now, when enthusiasm and motivation for the Program were starting to grow, it is halted by circumstances beyond our control. We fear that if the Circles continues to remain at a standstill all our past efforts and achievements will have been wasted.
>
> We are relying on you to reinstate this Program for the benefit of all concerned before it is too late. [pp. 193–194]

Despite this plea from a small group of workers, the union leadership did not sway from its position, and they continued to issue bulletins ordering members to withdraw. And although the extent of these activities was limited, considering the fact that Eastern had over 40,000 employees at the time with over 12,000 represented by the IAM, they effectively served to exacerbate conflict between union and management, who were in a protracted process of contract negotiations. Finally, after nearly three years of strife over this and other issues, the company was forced to concede to the union's demands, including joint control of employee-participation programs, and the QC circle program was entirely disbanded.

A new program was then instituted under joint union-management control with the title *Employee Involvement*. Eastern had lost three valuable years during which employee participation could have spread widely throughout the company and significantly improved economic performance. The lesson is that virtually all efforts at creating labor-management cooperation are doomed either to experience the same dynamics that occurred at Eastern or to cease altogether if a traditional, management-oriented approach to OD is pursued.

The Results of Project Centered Strategy

Many of us who have experienced the poverty of the labor relations strategy and observed the serious weaknesses inherent in pursuing a traditional OD approach have concluded that the solution to creating successful labor-management cooperative partnerships requires a little bit of both. Thus, interventionists have attempted to refocus their efforts on producing tangible operational results, much like traditional OD, but with the joint support and involvement of top union and management leaders. Again, this rights-oriented approach, which we have chosen to call the *project centered strategy,* eventually proved to be inadequate, but not without first creating some impressive results.

In following a project centered strategy, third-party interventionists brought the parties together to focus first on an issue of importance to both labor and management, something capable of producing visible, material change in the workplace—something that would yield concrete results. Typically in these cases, consultants would draw upon their knowledge of team building, alternative work organization, quality control circle techniques, and gainsharing programs and combine this with the insights and concerns of union and management leaders to identify a key issue or process on which to focus cooperative problem-solving efforts. After selecting a problem or opportunity of sufficient mutual concern, either ad hoc committees, comprised of an organizational cross section of workers, professional staff, and first-line managers, or department-based teams were created to engage in cooperative problem solving. Once these groups were established, all the consultants' energy tended to be focused on ensuring that their efforts would succeed, based on the simple belief that success would increase interest and faith in the value of cooperation, which would, in turn, lead to the spread of more cooperative activities. Little time or energy was invested in developing or maintaining dialogue between top union and management officials beyond discussions about specific problem-solving projects underway. If there were no important developments in these projects, or pressing problems, then joint meetings were simply not held.

In most cases, the potential for short-term success in these projects was high, because the initial joint support of management and union leaders created a stable political climate in which to undertake cooperative problem solving. Moreover, because the union and management members on these problem-solving teams were usually hand picked by the leaders of their respective sides, they typically had the knowledge necessary to address the issues successfully.

Examples of initial successes resulting from following a project centered strategy are numerous, and in some cases, the results are dramatic. An excellent illustration is provided by a northeastern U.S. manufacturer of large metal windows for office buildings, hospitals, and manufacturing facilities. The firm, a subsidiary of a major British conglomerate group, was experiencing serious financial problems due to a decline in business during a recession. One of its plants, which specialized in producing aluminum windows, had been forced to lay off 50 percent of its workforce. After one effort at redesigning the firm's Plant Two, which had to be abandoned due to insufficient funds, the company's marketing department determined that sales of a new, energy-efficient product, the aluminum thermo brake window, could potentially increase by over 50 percent. Although the discontinuation of the first layout redesign project in Plant Two had, as one consultant explained, "left a bad taste in a lot of people's mouths," the employment situation was so desperate that both union leaders and most workers felt that they had no choice but to try anything that might save jobs. Thus, a cooperative Layout Planning Committee was established to find ways to help the company increase the likelihood that it would be able to capitalize upon the projected growth in sales.

This group was comprised of workers, an industrial engineer, a manufacturing engineer, and supervisors from two plants. It was created because it was clear that the firm would be unable to meet its production and sales goals with the existing production system. Production delays were frequent and certain inefficiencies existed, caused by the many interplant transfers that were required to manufacture the product.

In tackling the thermo brake window layout design project, the consultant started out by spending the first month with the problem-solving team engaged in team-building activities. The objective was to help everyone develop a shared appreciation for the task while developing a strategy for tackling it. During this phase, the Layout Planning Committee spent its first few meetings acquiring an orientation to the entire thermo brake production process, the general problems in the process, and the serious obstacle these problems presented to meeting future sales demand. This was truly an enriching experience, as even company sales representatives became deeply involved with the committee. During these first sessions, sales representatives described the firm's past and current record in the aluminum window market and presented a detailed overview of anticipated growth for the thermo brake line.

After their initial team-building, educational, and strategizing activities, the committee members proceeded to identify specific problem areas in the existing production layout. These discussions covered a wide array of issues, ranging from the handling of aluminum extrusions to the wide variety of screws used in final window assembly. Manufacturing engineers acted as a resource to the group during this period. After two months of intensive work, the group finally concluded that the best strategy for improving productivity and meeting increased sales was to consolidate thermo brake production in Plant Three.

During the third month of problem-solving work, the committee undertook its final detailed analysis of the entire production process and the steps required to implement an improved process in a single plant. The problems dealt with in these sessions included relocation of a major aisle in Plant Three, removal of a brick wall to provide the necessary work space, relocation of an entire office, removal of a spray booth, relocation of the plant's entire wrapping and packaging operations, identification of all new equipment required, and specification of all methods of installation of the new equipment and the design of the new layout. In attacking these issues, the committee wisely did not try to arrive at all solutions on their own. Rather, the Layout Planning Committee acted as a coordinating group for all employees and managers affected by the changes.

They began with a comprehensive survey of employee suggestions and concerns related to their very focused task, and with the results of the survey, they developed the redesign plan. Thus, although the redesign was done in a participative way, it was not based on general surveys, which tend to raise expectations that any and all issues that concern employees will be addressed. Then, after the first layout redesign plan was completed, the committee posted a drawing of the plan in a location where it could be studied by all employees. Team members then incorporated the additional concerns and suggestions that followed into the final redesign.

Finally, six months after beginning its task, the Layout Planning Committee's plan, including projected estimates of improvements in production time and efficiency, was presented to corporate management by the company president. Faced with such a meticulously developed plan, and a clear explanation of the potential gains from making this investment, top management almost immediately approved the project. Implementation began that same month. Symbolizing the effort's joint commitment to improving both company profitability and employee job security, implementation began with company workers—rather than an outside construction company—tearing down the brick wall. Involving union members in the construction of the new layout protected a few jobs in difficult economic times, and by the time the project had been completed five months later, many jobs had been saved through the company's expanded capacity to handle increased sales.

In this particular case, redesigning the production layout for one product did not, however, yield sufficient results to bring back all the jobs that had been lost during the recession. The company also had to increase the number of major building construction projects on which its bids were accepted for the production of windows. Thus, encouraged by the success of the thermo brake window project, union and management leaders agreed, with the consultant's urging, to undertake a joint effort at developing bids for new projects.

On the face of it, this seemed a highly risky venture, because workers and management are traditionally at odds in the development of new project bids—that is, workers commonly try to convince management that a job will take considerably more time to produce than is actually required. This happens because factory workers have learned over many years that if management knows how rapidly they can really do a job, there will inevitably be increased pressure for speedup. Furthermore, if a job is completed more quickly than management initially anticipated, it is not unusual to lay workers off in order to cut costs. Consequently, a high level of trust was required for labor and management to jointly develop contract bids.

Following a process similar to that employed in redesigning the thermo brake production process, the Layout Planning Committee next attempted to establish new labor estimates for a major contract. After considerable study and discussion with production workers who would be involved in manufacturing the order, the committee devised a method that eliminated a milling operation. This not only reduced labor costs, but it also made it unnecessary to purchase a new and very expensive milling machine. As result of these efforts, the new contract was successfully secured.

After this first estimating project, a cooperative Job Costing Team was created for Plant Two, the facility that had been so devastated by layoffs. This joint committee acted as a planning, coordinating, and research group. Members of the team went out on the factory floor to ask workers how long it would take to produce and assemble windows for specific projects on which the company planned to enter competitive bids. With employees and supervisors, they discussed alternative production methods, material routing, and materials. Some employees even worked to develop new jigs and tools that could improve productivity, thereby reducing production costs and cutting manufacturing time.

In spite of much hard work—and the surprising cooperation of shop-floor workers—the Job Costing Team was unsuccessful on its first two bids. They did not give up, though, and on the third bidding project they succeeded in securing a subcontract which brought the company $1.5 million in new business. Many laid-off workers were brought back to work, and in time the Plant Two Job Costing Team became a permanent problem-solving group. This decision to maintain the group as a permanent bidding organization was a result of its continued success. Over the next year, the success ratio in obtaining new subcontracts rose dramatically, from 10 percent to 50 percent.

The labor-management cooperative activities just described may sound ideal. Significant operational results accrued from these efforts, and the needs of both labor and management were mutually addressed. Nevertheless, like most project centered strategies, the Job Costing Team eventually stagnated, in part because of its initial, major successes. In all cases where a project centered strategy is pursued, both parties tend to become overly fixated on the specific problem-solving project as an *end* in and of itself rather than as a *means* for developing an ongoing process of organizational change and joint cooperative problem solving. We call this tendency *project fixation,* and it seems to occur whether the initial efforts at cooperation are positive or negative.

If an effort to create a cooperative partnership is successful when a project oriented strategy has been followed, the effort then tends either to stagnate and fail to produce cooperation in other spheres of activity or to be used as a means for addressing new problems and opportunities. This is what happened in the case of the metal window manufacturer described earlier. Once the problems of inadequate sales and employment instability had been addressed through cooperative layout redesign and joint job costing, then both management and union leaders declined to develop new cooperative projects despite continued urging from their consultant. The feeling seemed to be that everything necessary had been accomplished—why take a chance on doing something new and disrupting what had already proven to be successful? The cooperative partnership had, in effect, been defined solely in specific project terms, rather than as an ongoing process. So everyone concerned asked, Why rock the boat?

In cases of dramatic initial failure, the problem of project fixation can be even more serious if a project centered strategy is followed. As is true with successful problem-solving projects, both parties again come to define the project or intervention as *labor-management cooperation.* Thus, when the project fails, and does so dramatically, it is natural for both labor and management to conclude that cooperation is an impractical or failed idea. Even worse, because the experience has been negative, there is a tendency for workers, union leaders, and managers to become extremely cynical about the idea of labor and management working together. Resistance to embarking on any new cooperative ventures therefore hardens, and it becomes extremely difficult to attempt any form of cooperative problem solving, even under conditions of severe crisis. Time and again, we have seen these dynamics occur when a project centered strategy provides the underlying basis for attempting a cooperative partnership.

Conclusion

In this chapter we have outlined some of the early strategies that have been followed in creating a cooperative industrial relations climate. Our description has not been exhaustive in terms of all possible strategies, or combinations of strategies, but our principal goal of illustrating different approaches and their inherent weaknesses has been accomplished. Taking time to describe these failed strategies has not, however, been merely an exercise in selective history.

All of these approaches are still very much alive today. The consulting world abounds with practitioners who enthusiastically sell clients these approaches, along with the usual complement of training programs and handbooks, at a hefty price. We hope that our discussion will discourage potential labor and management customers from investing their time and money in such efforts. Nonetheless, we by no means want to create the impression that developing labor-cooperative partnerships is impossible. We emphatically believe the opposite. Nor is it necessary to adopt a collectivist or authoritarian culture vis à vis Japan and the East Asian NICs to succeed in building a cooperative partnership.

For American cooperative partnerships to bloom and become a permanent approach to both management and industrial relations, it is necessary to build on a firm system of roles, relationships, written agreements, and structures that complement the traditional system of collective bargaining. In the chapters that follow we describe this approach and provide a step-by-step discussion of how to implement it in any organization.

References

Feldacker, Bruce. *Labor Guide to Labor Law* (2d ed.). Reston, VA: Reston Publishing Company, Inc., 1983, pp. 179–181.

Foltman, Felician F. *Labor-Management Cooperation at the Community Level,* Unpublished manuscript. Ithaca, NY: Cornell University.

Holley, William H. Jr., and Jennings, Kenneth M. *The Labor Relations Process* (4th ed.). Chicago, IL: Dryden, 1991, pp. 194–195.

IAM Bulletin. Miami, FL: District 100 IAM, 1981.

Meek, Christopher B. "Labor-Management Committee Outcomes: The Jamestown Case." In Warner P. Woodworth, Christopher Meek, and William Foote Whyte (eds.), *Industrial Democracy: Strategies for Community Revitalization.* Beverly Hills, CA: Sage, 1985, pp. 141–159.

Meek, Christopher B. *Labor-Management Cooperation, Employee Ownership and the Struggle for Control of Eastern Air Lines: The International Association of Machinists and Aerospace Workers at Eastern Air Lines.* Washington, DC: United States Department of Labor, unpublished report, 1988.

National Center for Productivity and Quality of Working Life. *Directory of Labor-Management Committees.* Washington, DC: Government Printing Office, 1978.

O'Dell, Carla S., *Gainsharing: Involvement, Incentives, and Productivity.* New York: AMACOM, 1981.

Whyte, William Foote; Hammer, Tove H; Meek, Christopher B.; Nelson, Reed; and Stern, Robert N. *Worker Participation and Ownership.* Ithaca, NY: ILR Press, 1983.

4

Initiating a True Partnership: Building Upon the Strengths of the Traditional Collective-Bargaining Relationship

Clearly, all of the strategies for creating labor-management cooperation which we discussed in Chapter 3 have inherent contradictions which eventually lead to either total failure or the stagnation of cooperation into a relatively narrow range of programmatic activities. In the volatile world of international competition, these results are hardly satisfactory. The absence of cooperation—or a severely limited sphere of cooperation between organized labor and management—is an inadequate strategy in a world where U.S. corporations face competitors who have evolved broad and continuous forms of institutionalized cooperation at both the enterprise and the workplace levels. Adaptive capacity and the flexibility to change are the minimum organizational requirements for mere survival in today's dynamic world marketplace. To excel requires much more. U.S. corporations must be able to formulate and successfully implement aggressive and comprehensive long-term strategic plans with the full cooperation and support of workers and their unions.

Unfortunately, the traditional system of U.S. industrial relations and the broader legal environment in which it operates are ill-suited to creating such organizational cultures. For example, prior to the Bush Administration's decision to disband the U.S. Department of Labor's Division of Labor-Management Cooperative Services, this small federal think tank developed an extensive agenda for legislative reforms which could have done much to create a legal environment friendly to a democratic free trade union movement but also supportive of the development of formal systems of cooperation between labor and management (Bureau of Labor-Management Relations and Cooperative Programs, 1989; Fetter *et al.*, 1987; Fetter, Reynolds, Etelson, and Levy, 1987; Schlossberg and Fetter, 1986; Schlossberg and Fetter, 1988).

The new Clinton Administration quickly recognized the importance of reversing the dismantling of Labor-Management Cooperative Services. Under the leadership of Labor Secretary Robert Reich a new agency within the U.S. Department of Labor has been established to encourage unions and managers to collaborate, the Office of the American Workplace (OAW). Our objective here, however, is to address change not in terms of public policy but in terms of organizations, and we believe that within the present legal framework for conducting labor-management relations—in spite of its weaknesses—there is still a great deal of room for developing and institutionalizing labor-management cooperative partnerships. Success in building cooperative partnerships requires that the two parties—and the third-party consultants who often help them—neither follow too closely the traditional model of labor-management relations (as in the case of the labor relations strategy) nor totally ignore, or worse, violate the rules of the collective-bargaining relationship (as is the case with the traditional OD or project centered strategies).

Appreciating the Context of Traditional Collective Bargaining

American collective-bargaining contracts are among the longest and most complicated of labor-management agreements in the world. After nearly two hundred years of class struggle played out in the industrial workplace, collective-bargaining agreements have become elaborate documents that provide minutely detailed instructions on such matters as work rules, wages and benefits, job classifications, seniority rights, bumping procedures, and grievance and arbitration processes. All of these regulations serve to severely circumscribe the power and authority of managers to use their own independent judgment in managing a company's human resources. There are specific bureaucratic and legalistic rules and procedures that determine the method and content of managing human resources, and these have developed over many years of negotiating and administering the labor-management agreement. Thus the contract articulates, both explicitly and implicitly, a legally binding philosophy regarding the respective roles of labor and management in the workplace, and then it provides specific rules and procedures for their interaction.

As Kochan, Katz, and McKersie (1986) have noted in *The Transformation of American Industrial Relations,* U.S. managers have never been comfortable with the restrictions on their powers imposed by a collective-bargaining agreement. And the onslaught of heavy union-busting actions, which followed President Ronald Reagan's firing of the air traffic controllers and accompanied the appointment of an anti-union National Labor Relations Board, certainly supported this viewpoint during both the Reagan and Bush Administrations. Nonetheless, managers in unionized work settings have learned how to function within the bounds established by labor-management contracts, although often more slowly and expensively than they would like.

In contrast, most OD professionals tend to have very little understanding of the collective-bargaining process and labor-management agreements. Therefore, as we have already illustrated in Chapters 1 and 3, they typically tend to regard these factors as bureaucratic red tape and a source of inflexibility and ineffectiveness. Even though there may be some truth to this view, if an OD effort is intended to be sustained as a process of ongoing culture change, then it is necessary to build upon the existing cultural and institutional base. The institution of collective bargaining, the labor-management agreement, the methods of administering the contract, the union's organizational structure, and the informal cliques and factions that exist within the union are all part of the deeply embedded assumptions, values, and behavior patterns of the workplace. Such factors can be ignored only at the peril of any cooperative effort. On the other hand, although these conditions may at times be an obstacle to some aspects of cooperation and the realization of systemwide employee involvement, they can also serve as an institutional springboard for launching a cooperative partnership. As a minimum, these factors must be accommodated in the development of any cooperative partnership, or they will eventually work first to frustrate and eventually destroy it.

The Partnership: A Negotiated Process

Just as the collective-bargaining agreement is a negotiated document that specifies the nature and content of the union-management and employer-employee relationship, so also must the framework for a cooperative partnership be developed through a negotiated process between the leadership of both sides. As we have seen in the case of traditional OD or quality-of-working-life approaches to developing labor-management cooperation through employee involvement, management and third-party consultants all too often attempt to introduce these processes exclusively through a top-down, management-directed effort. This approach leaves the union leadership and the existing collective-bargaining structure completely out of the loop, and at the same time it directly addresses questions of productivity and the conditions of work, which under federal law are mandatory issues for bargaining. It is naive to assume that unions will not seek to influence such efforts, and it would probably be suicidal for them not to assume a posture of opposition. Of course, if managers do in fact intend to use techniques of worker participation in problem solving as a means to weaken or even break the union, then they should expect a fight. This book is not intended to assist managers who plan to undertake anti-union campaigns.

Rather, the directions and suggestions here are for both management and union leaders who believe that in today's competitive world they must find ways to work together in pursuit of common goals and interests that benefit shareholders, customers, and workers alike. To succeed jointly, therefore, requires that the leadership of both sides play an equal role in charting the course of the effort. Each side must assume responsibility and receive credit for both success and failure, or ultimately the partnership itself will fail. If either union or management leaders are unprepared to accept both credit and responsibility for successes or mistakes, then the partnership attempt should be abandoned.

Partnership is never easy. For example, one group of managers at a major independent steelmaking company asked us to meet with them to discuss the possibility of developing an employee-involvement program, but when we explained that this would require a collaborative effort with their USWA local, one top executive said:

> You know, we want to improve productivity and effectiveness, and we also want to help our workers realize a higher income and a better work life through making these gains. But I sure don't want to do anything to give workers the idea that the union was instrumental in helping them get these things. I want them to know that these goodies came from management. We sure don't want the union taking any credit for these things.

This manager clearly had the wrong idea about cooperation, and, not surprisingly, our discussions progressed no further beyond this point. Of course, union leaders can also have the same blinders. Since they have become accustomed to reinforcing their importance by emphasizing how they have wrestled improvements in working conditions, wages, and benefits from an unwilling management, it is not unusual for union leaders also to feel uncomfortable giving management any recognition for positive change. As will be noted in Chapter 8, this problem—the inability on the part of both sides to share credit—played a key role in the eventual demise of employee involvement at Eastern Airlines.

Another important step in building authentic cooperation is each party *caucusing* on its own, before engaging in a joint process. This is essential "to sort the smoke from the flame," so to speak, thereby identifying core concerns and problems that each party ranks high on its priority list. Then, when the two groups get together, there is less generalized rhetoric and unproductive positioning.

Developing the Labor-Management Charter Agreement

The negotiation and signing of a written collective-bargaining agreement is the beginning point for any formal company-union relationship. Likewise, it is appropriate that the development and signing of a written document be the beginning of a formal labor-management cooperative partnership. We refer to this statement of cooperation between the parties as a *Labor-Management Charter Agreement.* Such an agreement is developed jointly through discussion and negotiation among the top leaders of both labor and management at the local level. It is often submitted subsequently to all workers for democratic approval at a special union meeting.

The union side should normally include the executive officers of the union, such as the president, vice president, treasurer, and secretary, and also members of the negotiating committee, the chief steward, and division-level stewards. On the management side, the highest-level executive over all directly and indirectly related functions should be involved, including the top general manager or CEO and the top managers of industrial relations/human resources, operations, marketing and sales, and finance. When such agreements are not developed on a company-wide basis, an upper-level representative from corporate management, such as the vice president of industrial relations, and/or a business agent from the international union, should participate directly in the development and signing of the charter agreement.

Although final approval of the labor-management charter involves the signing of this agreement by representatives from both parties, the union and the company, it is best if the agreement is developed through consensual problem-solving processes instead of adversarial negotiations. Indeed, the development of a charter agreement provides an excellent opportunity to educate the leadership of both sides on the philosophy underlying labor-management cooperation, group problem solving, consensus decision making, and employee involvement, while at the same time learning the skills required for implementing these processes. Thus, training and problem solving are combined during this first phase of developing a cooperative partnership.

As a starting point for developing the charter agreement, it is usually necessary to begin with helping both parties to gain an understanding, or redefine their current understanding, of win-lose versus win-win relationships and the importance of interpersonal and intergroup trust for cooperative problem solving. Such simulated experiences as *First Step, Win as Much as You Can,* or *The Prisoner's Dilemma* are especially effective in developing a shared understanding of the limitations and destructive consequences of unfettered competition.

It is more likely that management participants will have already had some experience with these exercises than it is for union representatives. Nonetheless, even if some parties have participated in these exercises before, they usually take on new meaning, as well considerably higher emotional involvement, when considered from a union-management relations perspective. Some of the most dramatic, divisive, and manipulative interaction we have ever witnessed in these simulated experiences has been in the context of forming a new labor-management cooperative partnership.

In one instance, a corporate vice president of operations became so angry at his losing position in an exercise that he threw the pointed end of a pencil at one of us. In another situation, the parties started swearing and threatening each other. Similarly, we have seen spying, lying, bluffing, and all forms of posturing take place during these exercises with union and company leaders. More earnestness seems to exist than is typically seen in contexts where adversarialism is not the foundation for the relationship.

In the short run, such exercises may accentuate competition and conflict, since these exercises are specifically designed to illustrate that everyone loses as win-lose competition and distrust increase. But by the end of the experience, some powerful new lessons have been learned which can be transferred to their relationships in the workplace. It is then easy to illustrate the deleterious consequences of this situation in a highly competitive, international marketplace in which other companies and unions are not playing by the same rules.

Once a shared appreciation of the necessity for labor-management cooperation has been created, the next step in the process requires that the leadership of both parties work together to create a shared vision of the shape their labor-management cooperative partnership will take. After considerable discussion, this shared vision is then synthesized, formalized, and embodied in the written labor-management cooperative charter agreement.

Content of the Charter Agreement

The cooperative charter agreement provides the framework for both implementing and evaluating the labor-management cooperative partnership. In this chapter we will discuss neither the details of the charter agreement nor the subtle points of the reasoning behind them. We would, however, like to provide a brief overview of the basic components of the agreement so that it is clear what is involved in the charter and what range of issues it encompasses. The agreement should include all of the basic provisions we believe are essential in any labor-management charter. In brief, the key elements that must be included in such a charter agreement include:

1. The names of the parties participating in the cooperative partnership.

2. The date and location of the signing of the agreement.

3. A statement of the basic philosophy, values, and beliefs upon which the cooperative partnership is founded.

4. The key ground rules that govern how the cooperative process should be conducted, including the safeguards protecting employees who choose to participate or not participate and the scope of issues that will be considered through the cooperative partnership.

5. The organizational structure of the cooperative partnership, including the different committees involved in the partnership, the role definition of the duties of each subgroup, and the vertical and horizontal relationship between groups, including their respective decision-making powers.

6. The roles and responsibilities of the leadership of the various committees and subcommittees that comprise the structure of the partnership.

7. The rules and procedures for conducting labor-management cooperative meetings, making decisions following the agreed-upon decision-making process, and for fulfilling the reporting relationships and information sharing required between groups.

8. The minimum frequency for holding the meetings of standing committees and subcommittees.

9. The structure and process for filing complaints related to labor-management cooperative activities and appeals on decisions that rejected projects and changes

proposed by labor-management cooperative problem-solving groups.

Although the elements just enumerated above may seem excessively detailed and potentially bureaucratic, over years of experience we have found them all to be necessary to find an appropriate strategy for implementing cooperative partnerships. Each of the nine elements outlined provides an effective and clear cooperative counterpart to the collective-bargaining agreement which is created through adversarial negotiations. The collective-bargaining relationship has forged a culture that depends upon a clearly specified and quasi-legalistic mode of conducting employer-employee relationships. A fundamental goal of cooperative partnerships is to create greater flexibility in responding to needs, problems, and opportunities, but departing entirely from the traditional mode of interaction is risky and threatening to the existing collective-bargaining culture. A labor-management charter agreement provides an effective and acceptable bridge between the adversarial relationship and cooperation.

The Philosophy Statement

The philosophy and ground rules are the foundation upon which the structure and activities of the labor-management partnership are based. Both of these statements are necessary for the smooth development of cooperative processes.

The philosophy statement is especially important because it becomes a joint declaration of the assumptions, values, and beliefs—in other words, the ideology—upon which the partnership is based. Thus, the philosophy provides an ideological map for deciding upon the kinds of projects and programs a cooperative partnership should explore and seriously consider implementing. Cooperative activities are undertaken that are both practically feasible and have the highest potential for realizing the ideals articulated in the philosophy statement.

The statement of philosophy also provides a basis for ongoing monitoring and oversight. That is, the philosophy statement acts as an ideological grid against which either proposed or currently functioning cooperative activities, as well as the independent actions of both the company and the union, can be evaluated. Newly proposed projects and activities that may be inconsistent with the cooperative philosophy can be quickly and easily dropped before vested interests are developed and damage is done. Similarly, as problems arise during the development of the partnership, when the parties independently engage in tactics or adopt practices that are incompatible with cooperation, the philosophy statement can serve as an effective instrument for first evaluating the situation and then, in turn, reaching a resolution that is compatible with the cooperative philosophy.

Repeatedly, we have seen cases where serious problems and even total destruction of cooperative efforts could have been avoided if an initial joint philosophy had first been developed and then used as an active guide for cooperation. For example, at one company where union and management leaders had decided to undertake cooperative activities, top management decided to contract with a management consulting firm to do an efficiency study. In other words, they planned to conduct a factorywide time-study in order to identify jobs that could be eliminated or collapsed or in which productivity standards could be tightened. A time-study team was at work with hidden stopwatches, busily observing workers from behind posts and from dark corners in the factory. At the same time, a labor-management committee was trying to develop a new jointly designed layout for the firm's rolled metal extrusion department. In contrast to the management consultants, the cooperative team's goal was to satisfy both labor and management's needs. The intent behind the cooperative layout redesign was to protect existing jobs through creating a safe and efficient work environment. The overall goal was to meet a growing demand for the department's products, while at the same time realizing the highest possible profitability.

Not surprisingly, when the union caught on to the time-study project, the members felt betrayed and duped. The cooperative effort almost disintegrated as a result of the anger and distrust that was generated. The OD consultants who were responsible for facilitating the cooperative effort were shocked by the stupidity of management in contracting for such services while espousing a desire to build trust and cooperation. However, the company's top management could not understand what the problem was. As they saw it, they were simply exercising their traditional management prerogatives in the way they had always used them.

The careful *joint development* of a cooperative philosophy statement could have at least helped to clarify the attitudes and behaviors consistent with a cooperative partnership. Such a statement, incorporated into a full cooperative charter agreement, would not have guaranteed that management might not have made the same mistakes that were made without it. Still, the chances of implementing two such contradictory programs at the same time would have been reduced. Management would have more clearly understood that what they were undertaking through the cooperative effort was a major departure from *business as usual*. Moreover, even if management had still missed the point, or if they had simply been tempted to stray from the agreement, then a philosophy statement could have helped provide a basis for confronting the problem and realizing the contradictions apparent in management's actions.

In contrast to the preceding case, the partnership between Xerox and Local 14-A of the Amalgamated Clothing and Textile Workers Union (ACTWU) operated in a more open and collaborative fashion. When the company's study of its Webster, New York, plant revealed that millions of dollars could be saved if wire harnesses and other subassemblies were contracted to outside vendors, management informed all its workers of the results. The ACTWU made a counterproposal in which a joint team of union and management representatives would develop an approach to restructure the department and thereby cut operating costs. A philosophy of trust and openness, full authority, and clear guidelines was established. The team eventually succeeded in saving some $3.7 million and retaining 180 threatened jobs (Lazes and Costanza, 1984). Since then, other Xerox-ACTWU have achieved similar results (Klinger and Martin, 1988). Generating agreement on core values through a statement on philosophy provides the critical basis on which partnerships may thrive.

The following cooperative philosophy statement from our typical charter agreements should help to clearly illustrate this point:

> This cooperative partnership is founded upon the fundamental belief that there are many issues, outside of the collective-bargaining agreement, that are of mutual concern and interest to both labor and management and that

can be most effectively addressed through cooperative action. It is our position that the majority of people that are employed at ___(company name)__ are capable and responsible individuals who desire to produce high-quality products for a productive and profitable company. Likewise, it is also our belief that most individuals desire and deserve not only the economic fruits of their labor, but also secure and stable employment and the opportunity for personal growth through contributing the best of their talents and creative abilities in the workplace. The man or woman who serves responsibly as a spouse, parent, and leader in the home and the community does not leave his or her intellect behind when entering the factory or office. If they are treated with the full dignity and respect due them, they will respond with enthusiasm and concern. Lastly, it is a fundamental tenet of this partnership that the people who are doing a job, or are affected by a contemplated change, should be directly involved in the planning, analysis, and design of change and improvements. We believe that those directly in the work area are most likely to have the best and most realistic ideas. They also deserve to be involved in decisions that impact the nature and security of their jobs, as well as the overall quality of their working lives. It is the express role and purpose of this labor-management cooperative partnership to serve as a vehicle for bringing to life the ideals of this philosophy through tangible, concrete action.

Table 4.1 summarizes the critical aspects of an effective, coherent charter statement.

Conclusion

In this chapter we have attempted to illustrate that it is not only necessary but also possible to build a cooperative partnership based on the collective-bargaining relationship and traditions of the past. It is not required to ignore or to directly oppose the traditional culture of the unionized company. In a unionized workplace where strong and coherent systems for communicating with the workforce and mobilizing group action exist, it is possi-

Table 4.1
Elements of an Effective Labor-Management Charter Agreement

Participants:	Top Union/Top Management Representative of Major Areas Equal Numbers (50–50)
Process:	Define the Situation Common Analysis of Problems/Issues Training in Cooperative Problem Solving, Communication, and Consensus Skills Develop Shared Vision of Desired Future

Charter Features:	Names of Key Parties
	Date
	Philosophy Statement: Assumptions,
	   Values, and Beliefs
	Key Ground Rules
	Structure: Committees and Levels
	Roles and Relationships of Groups
	Leadership and Decision Making
	Meetings: Frequency, Minutes, and
	   Reporting
	Mechanics for Handling Complaints and
	   Appeals

ble to build a new culture of employee involvement and participation with great efficiency and depth. To accomplish this end, though, requires that management and labor work together in a true cooperative partnership, on a level playing field for both groups. The beginning strategy for developing such a cooperative effort is the drafting of a *Labor-Management Cooperative Charter Agreement*. The first step to doing this is to create a shared appreciation of the nature and importance of cooperation, supported by a joint statement of philosophy to guide the partnership.

Following the creation of a mutually supported cooperative philosophy, labor and management leaders must next agree upon the ground rules and the organizational structure of the partnership. These topics are the focal point of our discussion in the Chapter 5.

References

Bureau of Labor-Management Relations and Cooperative Programs. *U.S. Labor Law and the Future of Labor-Management Cooperation—Final Report, Bureau of Labor-Management Relations 134.* Washington, DC: U.S. Department of Labor, 1989.

Fetter, Steven M.; Reynolds, Joy K.; Etelson, Jesse; and Levy, Herman. *U.S. Labor Law and the Future of Labor-Management Cooperation—First Interim Report, Bureau of Labor-Management Relations 113.* Washington, DC: U.S. Department of Labor, 1987.

Fetter, Steven M., *et al. U.S. Labor Law and the Future of Labor-Management Cooperation—Second Interim Report, Bureau of Labor-Management Relations 119.* Washington, DC: U.S. Department of Labor, 1987.

Klinger, Sally, and Martin, Ann (eds). *A Fighting Chance: New Strategies to Save Jobs and Reduce Costs.* Ithaca, NY: ILR Press, Cornell University, 1988.

Kochan, Thomas A.; Katz, Harry C.; and McKersie, Robert B. *The Transformation of American Industrial Relations.* New York: Basic Books, 1986.

Lazes, Peter, and Costanza, Tony. "Xerox Cuts Costs Without Layoffs Through Union-Management Collaboration." *Labor-Management Cooperation Brief.* U.S. Department of Labor, Bureau of Labor-Management Relations and Cooperation Programs, July 1984.

Schlossberg, Stephen I., and Fetter, Steven M. *U.S. Labor Law and the Future of Labor-Management Cooperation, Bureau of Labor-Management Relations 104.* Washington, DC: U.S. Department of Labor, 1986.

Schlossberg, Stephen I., and Fetter, Steven M. *U.S. Labor Law and the Future of Labor-Management Cooperation, Bureau of Labor-Management Relations 104.* Washington, DC: U.S. Department of Labor, 1988.

5

Rules, Roles, and Procedures: Structuring the Cooperative Partnership

In Chapter 4 we provided a rationale for using a jointly created charter agreement to initiate labor-management cooperative partnerships. The elements that are essential in any charter agreement were discussed as well as the details of the cooperative philosophy statement. In this chapter, our objective is to help the reader understand the other elements of the cooperative partnership outlined in the charter agreement. Specifically, our emphasis here will be upon the ground rules, leadership roles, and procedures that can help to ensure smooth implementation of cooperative processes.

To some readers, particularly practitioners trained in organization development theory and technique, our approach may seem excessively bureaucratic, rigid, or hierarchical. In response, all we can say is that we have attempted to devise a strategy that is compatible with the existing institution of collective bargaining and the respective organizational structures of union and corporate organizations for dealing with labor-management relationships. Our own research and personal experience, as well as that of others, supports the strength of the strategy we advocate here, and we hope that as this discussion progresses, the reasoning underlying our approach will become clear to those who are either contemplating or are now directly involved in efforts to create cooperative partnerships.

Basic Ground Rules

After jointly developing the basic philosophy upon which a co-operative labor-management partnership will be based, the next step is to establish the basic ground rules that will form the framework within which cooperative activities actually take place. In a sense this is the negative counterpart to the positive role played by the philosophy statement. That is, where the philosophy statement clarifies the broad goals and organizational conditions that labor and management seek to realize through cooperative effort, the ground rules provide a clear set of boundaries within which the partnership will take place. Establishing these boundaries is extremely important, because in their absence tremendous uncertainty will exist. If this uncertainty is not reduced, it will either prevent the parties from engaging wholeheartedly in the cooperative process or else tempt them to use the partnership as a means for achieving a hidden agenda.

Ground Rule 1: Labor-Management Cooperative Activities Shall Be Limited to Addressing Issues of Mutual Concern Outside of the Collective-Bargaining Agreement.

Perhaps the most important and central ground rule, especially when a new cooperative partnership is first being implemented, is an explicit agreement that cooperative problem-solving activities will be limited to addressing issues that are of mutual concern that are not part of the written collective-bargaining contract or *established past practice*. It is not always possible to adhere to this restriction entirely, but in general it is essential if a labor-management cooperative partnership is to be successfully implemented.

After many years of negotiations and ongoing administration of the existing labor-management agreement, few managers, and even fewer labor leaders, are willing to jeopardize hard-won gains and conditions for an experimental effort about which they have not yet become confident or knowledgeable. On the other hand, there are a myriad of highly significant issues and problems that can best be addressed through collaborative problem solving, issues that are not directly part of the contract or past practice.

By declaring the contract generally to be outside the purview of a labor-management partnership's problem-solving and decision-making activities, a *zone of safety* is created. This raises the comfort level for the union leaders because participating in cooperative efforts will not put their gains at risk. Similarly, this ground rule provides management with a clear understanding that the union will not try to use the cooperative partnership as a lever for extracting more concessions from the company or as a tool for eroding the rights of management.

This limitation discourages direct forays upon the collective-bargaining agreement, and, perhaps even more importantly, it restricts indirect efforts to use the cooperative venture as a means for manipulating contractual changes or obtaining favorable decisions in current grievance disputes. This latter problem—using cooperation as a tool to manipulate the other party to obtain a contractual concession—is especially prevalent in the early phases of a cooperative partnership. Managers, for example, frequently agree to participate in labor-management cooperative efforts in hopes of using the process to force a concession at some later date. They frequently try to get the union to agree to either altering or eliminating particular critical contract provisions that have not been accepted through collective bargaining. Using the cooperative forum as a tool for getting results on such *hidden agendas* can be fatal.

As an example, the top management of one of the most distinguished U.S. manufacturers of high-quality office furniture decided to establish a joint labor-management committee with its only union, the International Association of Machinists and Aerospace Workers (IAM). Executives hoped that through the committee, they could convince the union to agree to a change in a companywide seniority policy. For years the company president, and several generations of industrial relations managers, had tried to convince the union to change the seniority clause. It had been incorporated in their first labor-management agreement several decades earlier when the company operated only one manufacturing plant. As the firm's share of the high-end and custom office furniture market grew, two other plants were established with one focused strictly on special-order job shop production. With the ups and downs of the marketplace, and the considerable difference in the skill levels of the workers in the firm's different plants, management found that it was very expensive and extremely detrimental to sustained productivity to maintain the system of interplant bumping and transfers required by the companywide seniority policy.

So when after a prolonged contract dispute a senior business agent from the IAM suggested that the parties form a joint labor-management committee with the company's union local, management immediately began to strategize how they could use the committee to convince the union to sign a new seniority clause based on a separate plant seniority arrangement. Knowing that both union leaders and the general IAM membership were firmly opposed to the idea, however, top management decided to hold back on bringing up the issue. Instead, they planned to first weaken the union's opposition and defenses by supporting several low-cost cooperative programs which they knew both union leaders and workers wanted very badly.

After creating a strong sense of cooperation and positive feelings through the labor-management committee's initial projects, management then proposed that the group form a new subcommittee to study the problems created by bumping and interplant transfers. Although management had expressed openness "to any ideas" developed by the joint subcommittee, they continually pushed for the group to come up with a separate plant seniority policy. Once union leaders realized the firm's intentions, they refused to discuss the issue further. When management continued to push for this policy change in labor-management meetings, the union announced that they would no longer participate if the pressure did not cease.

At this point management finally decided to back off, but periodically thereafter they attempted to reintroduce the issue, claiming that this was really the most significant obstacle to productivity and worker job security. Eventually, when it became clear that they could make no headway on getting the union to agree to the desired changes, management gradually withdrew their support for other cooperative activities by canceling subcommittee and even steering-committee meetings. Eventually, so many meetings were canceled that union leaders announced in writing that they were withdrawing their participation from the partnership and that, as far as they were concerned, the effort was dead.

Fortunately, the aggressive efforts of skilled neutrals revived the partnership, but because management had tried to use cooperation as a tool for leveraging contractual changes, they nearly lost the benefits of their new cooperative relationship. The union ended up more distrustful than when the process had started.

Of course, it is not always possible to avoid running into points of conflict between the existing provisions of a labor-management agreement, which have been developed through the adversarial relationship, and new cooperative systems. For example, it is nearly impossible to avoid having to change long-established job classifications, bumping procedures, or job-based pay rates when developing self-regulating teams. However, regarding a cooperative partnership as primarily a tool for extracting contractual changes or gains is a serious error, which will ultimately undermine any trust that is built, resulting in the eventual demise of the effort. If it does prove necessary to reconsider existing contract provisions or past practice, as it becomes clear that they are in conflict with new cooperative systems, then the best way to confront these problems is to explore them through joint cooperative problem-solving efforts following the guidelines excerpted from a typical sample charter agreement:

> The only exceptions to this rule would be in such instances where the Steering Committee assigns a special study group to research alternatives relevant to issues of contractual concern. In such cases the study group reports its findings, in written form, to the Union's Executive Committee and the Management Bargaining Team for their consideration. In no case is either party in any way obligated by such a study group's efforts to use, accept, or negotiate on the basis of their recommendations.
>
> *Ground Rule 2: All Involvement in Labor-Management Cooperative Partnership Activities, Whether on an Individual or Group Basis, Is Strictly Voluntary. Either Party, Labor or Management, and Any Individual Has the Right to Withdraw or Decline to Participate in Any Program or Activity If and When They so Choose.*

This ground rule is also an important cornerstone for the founding of any new cooperative partnership. The decision to cooperate or withdraw must be a matter of free and informed choice (**Meek,** 1985). Cooperation cannot be forced upon one party by another or, by definition, the outcome is not cooperation. It may be compliance, but it is not cooperation.

Years and years of reinforcement embed the adversarial relationship deeply into the culture of the unionized workplace. Moreover, the behavioral norms and concomitant distrust that naturally evolve from this relationship cannot be reversed by simply issuing an edict requiring that all employees participate in problem-solving groups, regardless of whether they are called quality control circles, total quality teams, action teams, or whatever term is used to name them.

Attempting to make participation or cooperation mandatory, in effect, turns the situation into precisely the opposite of what is intended. The zest and enthusiasm for specific cooperative activities, or eventually for the overall process of cooperation and employee involvement, are the natural outcomes of making conscious, free choices. Indeed, a truly successful cooperative partnership will lead hourly and exempt employees to extend their interest in solving specific problems and to support the cooperative effort outside the realm of traditional working hours.

Over and over again, we have seen workers and managers become so interested in developing solutions to problems that they have decided to tackle through cooperative problem solving that they literally *take the work home*. At Eastern Airlines, for example, when cooperative activities were still popular, some of the jet engine mechanics and other skilled machinists at the Miami Engine Service Center would develop small but important changes in tool-and-jig design in their garages after their shift had ended. Similarly, other employees who were responsible for chairing or facilitating meetings of problem-solving groups would create educational materials and charts on their own after work, rather than expecting to have time off from their normal job so that they could be paid for doing these things. Such motivation and interest drives employees to think about and labor on problem solving after working hours. This serves as a powerful outcome of a truly cooperative partnership built upon a spirit of voluntary initiative and involvement.

Perhaps one of the most surprising examples of this spirit of voluntary action that we have witnessed was the case of a group of women who worked for a custom metal hardware manufacturing company in the northeastern United States. In this plant, a shop steward approached the union president to ask if there was some way that her members could work on improving the shop environment and the productivity of their department. Workers wanted to go beyond the regular labor-management committee meetings because they felt the meetings did not occur frequently enough "to really get things done." Because the firm was experiencing some financial troubles, it was difficult to stop production in order to hold lengthy problem-solving meetings. Realizing this, the union president approached one of us as consultants to inquire if it would be possible to meet with this group of women in the evening once each week for training. They wanted to learn additional problem-solving and measurement skills, as well as to launch their own, independent efforts to improve efficiencies.

This group of five women had many ideas on how to make their work environment safer, produce higher quality products, reduce waste, and improve productivity. They learned how to develop cost estimates for implementing their solutions, and learned methods for documenting the losses and dangers inherent in existing systems or obsolete equipment. They also began to develop numerous proposals for improvements, which they submitted at labor-management meetings.

The problem solving that led to the development of these proposals at first took place during weekly, two-hour meetings held at night after work. Eventually, the women decided that they wanted to solicit input from more department members, so they began also to hold shorter meetings with other workers during lunch breaks. Obviously, this kind of devotion and interest could never be demanded or even directly encouraged by company management or union leaders. Yet we have observed firms like this one receiving literally thousands of hours of unpaid service, which has contributed to improving the bottom line and quality of working life for employees. Ultimately, though, this is the consequence of building a cooperative partnership on a foundation of voluntary involvement and action. That is, workers and managers become so interested and involved in the effort that they cease to turn off their involvement simply because the formal shift is over.

> *Ground Rule 3: In No Case Shall Ideas and Improvements Developed Through Labor-Management Cooperation Result in the Loss of an Individual's Job Whether He/She Be a Member of Labor or Management. In Such Instances Where a Position Is Likely to Be Eliminated, It Is the Firm's Responsibility to Assist the Individual in Finding a Comparable Job at an Equivalent Level of Pay and Skills Elsewhere in the Company.*

In the long run, sustaining cooperative activity becomes impossible if this ground rule is not declared and rigorously followed. Of course, stating that employee suggestions will not result in job loss or compensation reduction has become a fundamental tenet of most major productivity gainsharing plans. It is obvious that very few workers would be willing to develop solutions and plans for improving company profits if they knew that the outcome would be unemployment and/or a reduction in pay for either themselves or their coworkers. Still, it is surprising how many managers and top company leaders hesitate in committing themselves to *no-job-loss* and *no-reduction-in-pay* agreements.

Perhaps their reluctance is a consequence of the insularity of their lives, which removes them from the trials of everyday existence faced by the average worker. Or perhaps some executives, who typically move directly from studies at elite colleges to positions in management, have had too little experience with the world of work and the economic hardships of the working and middle classes. Whatever the case, there is all too often an air of arrogance in the executive suite, which tends either to discount the rationality of workers or to assume that the job insecurity of workers and first-line supervisors is somehow their just reward for not going to college. As one young, upper-level executive with an MBA said when first confronted with the "no-job-loss ground rule":

> Look, what sense does it make to go to all this work to try and save money, and to spend all of this time and money on meetings if we can't eliminate anybody's job? What will we gain if we do that? If these people wanted to have a safe, secure, well-paying job like I've got, they shouldn't have spent all their money on parties and beer when they were young. They shouldn't have got married and had so many kids right out of high school. They should have been

smart, studied hard, and gone to a good college like I did. When you make dumb decisions, you've got to live with the consequences.

The reality is that, without commitment to this ground rule, any cooperative partnership will eventually dissipate and fail. Furthermore, just as workers are not willing to cooperate themselves out of their jobs and current pay levels, supervisors are very likely to undermine and sabotage any cooperative effort that they believe will eliminate either their jobs or the organizational significance of their role.

In fact, supervisory sabotage can happen even when a "no-job-loss rule" is in effect. At a major food-processing firm, for example, where the "no-job-loss ground rule" had been explicitly written into a labor-management charter agreement, serious problems still occurred with first-line supervisors. In this instance, a self-regulating system was developed for an entirely new department and product. This was done specifically to avoid testing the concept by changing the work roles and authority relations in an existing subunit. Nonetheless, supervisors, who were terrified that all supervisory positions would be eliminated if the project was a success, set out secretly to sabotage the project from its inception by instructing the maintenance and supply department supervisors to *always* treat the department's requests as their lowest priority. In effect, this meant that when machines broke down, days would pass before a mechanic would come to the department to fix them.

Similarly, important supplies and materials, which were needed to maintain production, were routinely delivered several hours and even several days late. In one case, a worker had to tie his high school letterman's jacket on the end of a machine to catch the product coming off the line, because the supply department would not deliver the net that was normally used for this purpose. Similarly, workers had to become able to repair their machines themselves in order to meet production goals. Eventually, the sabotage was stopped when the problems were identified and confronted. The "no-job-loss rule" was discussed in detail with supervisors. Without this ground rule, the problems would probably never have ceased, and the self-regulating department would have finally been abandoned.

Individual company and union partnerships may, of course, choose to include a number of other ground rules that they believe will be significant for building and sustaining a cooperative relationship. Each situation has its unique conditions and requirements. Regardless of the particular industry, geographic location, or labor-management relationship, however, it is our opinion that these three basic ground rules are an essential foundation upon which to build any labor-management cooperative partnership. Although some short-term sacrifices may be required in order to adhere to these ground rules, in the long run they can help to ensure that a cooperative partnership will avoid the ills of guarded participation or even sabotage.

Cooperation and the Need for a Parallel Structure

During the 1980s practitioners engaged in the development of employee-involvement programs in both the private and public sectors coined the terms *Big EI* and *Little EI*. Big EI was used to refer to employee-involvement programs and projects that were initiated and directed by an overarching *parallel organization* comprised of representatives from both the union and management leadership. In contrast, Little EI was used to describe spontaneous activities involving worker participation in organizational problem solving that resulted from management adopting a participative style, rather than following traditional, top-down, authoritarian management practices. Invariably, consultants would tell their clients that the ultimate goal of labor-management cooperation was to move from the *artificial system* of Big EI to a fully institutionalized, participative management approach in which managers would naturally involve employees in solving daily and long-term problems. In other words, the long-term goal was *to move from Big EI to Little EI,* resulting in the complete dissolution of the union-management parallel organization.

In our opinion, this viewpoint is severely misguided. It stems from the traditional managerial focus of most organization development/behavioral science consultants who have had little formal training or experience in collective bargaining or union-management relations. For these advocates of employee involvement, who consider Big EI as simply a transition phase on the way to Little EI, there is only one legitimate hierarchy of authority that they recognize, and that is the management hierarchy of the firm. For these consultants, it is as if the union hierarchy and its organizational structure do not exist *or perhaps should not exist.*

The difficulty with this viewpoint is that it ignores the fact that a parallel system *already* exists for conducting the ongoing processes of the adversarial relationship. It involves contract negotiations as well as grievance handling and arbitration. Regardless of how successful a labor-management cooperative effort is in passing on a participative approach and style to first-line and middle managers, the interorganizational structure of industrial reactions will remain. The attendant bargaining and quasi-judicial processes of the adversarial relationship will still continue, no matter how deeply employee involvement becomes embedded in the organization, unless, of course, the actual goal of management is to eliminate the union entirely. Few, if any, union officials will be willing to participate in a program in which the ultimate, although perhaps unstated, goal is to create a new organizational culture in which employees no longer feel that they have a need for union representation.

Union leaders are not suicidal. As we have pointed out earlier, it is an important first step in developing a cooperative partnership for both the union and management to be willing to let the other party, as well as themselves, take credit for organizational improvements that result from cooperative activities. Accepting this condition requires a huge shift in orientation for both labor and management. Unions establish their value and importance to workers by claiming that improvements in wages, hours, and conditions of employment are a direct result of their efforts to force an unwilling management—which is typically characterized by labor as "cold-hearted" and "greedy"—to give in to worker demands.

Managers, if they do not simply resign themselves to being viewed as the greedy "bad guys," would prefer that workers feel that any improvements they receive are the result of company beneficence rather than union intervention. Managers in this situation would like workers to see the union and its leaders as "greedy parasites" who are really only interested collecting dues rather than furthering members' welfare.

Thus, when a cooperative partnership is undertaken, a dramatic shift in attitude and behavior is required of both managers and union representatives. If either side attempts to claim sole credit for improvements realized through cooperative problem solving, the partnership will very rapidly turn sour. Both parties must be willing to let the other side be "good guys." Conversely, the leadership of both sides must not attempt to scapegoat the other when problems arise. With joint credit for success must also come joint responsibility for failure and difficulty.

When the reality that shared credit and responsibility are necessary conditions for a successful, long-term cooperative partnership is acknowledged, it should be apparent that it is impossible to fulfill these conditions through a one-sided, management-initiated and management-maintained system of employee involvement. The adoption and institutionalization of participative management processes, that is, Little EI, represents a significant positive change in the corporate culture of the traditional adversarial workplace, but it is not a substitute or superior replacement for jointly initiated and jointly supervised union-management cooperative problem solving. Rather, Big EI and Little EI should be viewed as complementary and ongoing processes.

Shop-floor employee involvement is a necessary but not a sufficient condition for developing or maintaining a cooperative partnership. Labor-management partnerships are, in fact, formal cooperative alliances between *two complex, formal organizations,* the union and the company. Therefore, they require sustained collaborative activity on an interorganizational basis if cooperation is going to be an institutionalized characteristic of labor-management relations.

In addition to providing a formal counterpart to the collective-bargaining relationship, establishing a cooperative parallel structure provides a vehicle for counteracting and transcending the rigidities and insensitivities that become ingrained in both management and union bureaucracies. Through establishing a separate system for engaging in cooperative problem solving, the parallel organization enables managers and labor leaders to focus specifically on mobilizing the entire organization in improving organizational performance and responding to new environmental demands. Moreover, the union-management parallel system for cooperation also enables labor and management to work together collaboratively in monitoring and managing the diffusion of cooperative activities and the overall change process

(Stein and Kanter, 1980; Woodworth, 1985). As Cohen-Rosenthal and Burton (1987) explain:

> What makes parallel structures work is their provision of a forum for the combination of perspective. Perspective in an organization is often defined by position in the hierarchy. Yet a diversity of perspectives is often needed to solve cross-disciplinary and cross-departmental challenges. The parallel approach implies that all people in an organization can contribute regardless of job title and that they can meet as equals in the parallel setting. At the same time it acknowledges differences in authority in the traditional sphere and does not seek to replace the traditional hierarchy. The outputs of the parallel system are inputs to the formal organization, and a test of its success is the degree of acceptance inside the traditional structure. The traditional hierarchy provides for the maintenance of the system and fulfills the functions of control and continuity. Stein and Kanter state: "The main task of the parallel organization is the continued reexamination of routines, exploration of new options and the development of new tools, procedures and approaches. It seeks to institutionalize change." [p.112]

The Cooperative Parallel Organization: Essential Elements

The heart and pulse of successful cooperative partnerships is a parallel structure that organically grows and changes as a cooperative counterpart to the traditional union-management structure for collective bargaining and grievance handling. Ideally, this parallel structure or *parallel organization* engages union and management representatives in cooperative problem solving and decision making at all levels of their respective organizational hierarchies, while at the same time gradually drawing an ever larger segment of the total workforce, both union and nonunion, into the cooperative process.

A very basic model of this parallel organizational structure is illustrated in Fig. 5.1. These partnership structures can vary considerably in terms of the number of different subgroups that are involved and the actual issues these groups address, but the basic structural elements required for effective governance, coor-

Figure 5.1
*Parallel Organizational Structure: Labor-Management
Cooperative Partnership*

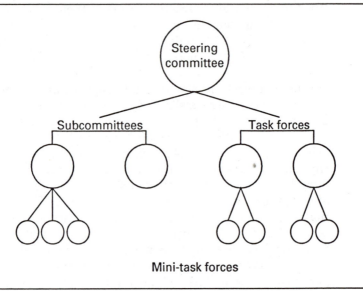

Mini-task forces

dination, and problem solving essential in all labor-management
partnerships are included in the figure.

The Steering Committee

At the top of the partnership hierarchy, or, in other words, in the
leadership position of the cooperative effort, is the *Labor-Management Steering Committee,* which is often referred to as the
Labor-Management Committee or, simply, the *Steering Committee* (Meek, 1985). The role of the steering committee is to serve as
the guiding and governing body for all activities of the cooperative partnership. The steering committee *must be* composed of
the highest level local leaders from both the union and the company. More specifically, the following criteria should be used in
deciding who will represent the company and the union on the
steering committee:

1. The first priority in selecting who will represent labor
   and management on the steering committee is to ensure that the individuals who serve on the committee
   are of sufficient stature and authority to make deci-

sions jointly with the representatives of the other party and to initiate the required actions that flow from these decisions in their respective organizations. Practically, this means that the president and other top union officers, such as the vice president, secretary-treasurer, and chief steward, should all be permanent members of the steering committee. Similarly, the highest level manager at the site and her/his immediate subordinate managers should also be permanent steering committee members. Without such high-level leadership, the steering committee will lack credibility, for every proposal and plan will have to await outside approval. Furthermore, the spirit and practice of cooperation must emanate from the upper echelons of both the union and the company, or, otherwise, middle and lower level managers, as well as rank-and-file workers, will catch the spirit of cooperation, and learn how to realize it in practice, while top managers and union officers undermine the process by strictly interacting as adversaries.

2. The second priority in selecting union and management members of the steering committee is to provide broad functional representation. The steering committee, as a policy-creating and decision-making body for the entire organization, will significantly increase its effectiveness, and general acceptance of its actions, if it has direct support and input from major organizational functions. Steering committee members can serve as effective linking-pins, providing essential information, coordination, and political support between their functional subunits and the committee.

3. The third consideration in recruiting steering committee members is to provide essential interest-group representation. Representativeness in terms of gender, race, and age is not only important for ensuring equity and fairness, but it can also be crucial for ensuring the partnership's success. Similarly, wise union leaders will seek to recruit members of opposing factions to serve on the steering committee, or they may unintentionally open the cooperative process up to unnecessary attacks based solely upon political self-interest.

It may initially seem that the dimensions to consider in constructing a labor-management steering committee are so broad and all encompassing that to follow them would require the formation of an enormous committee. This does not need to be the case. The steering committee, because of its responsibility to act as a truly representative body, is, of course, larger than a typical subcommittee or task force. Nonetheless, it is usually possible to achieve representativeness by selecting and recruiting steering-committee members who have overlapping membership in multiple interest and functional groups.

The steering committee should also be structured so that there is *balanced representation* and *balanced leadership* from both union and management—that is, the steering committee should be composed of equal numbers of management and union representatives. Likewise, the conducting of steering-committee meetings should be rotated regularly, usually on an every-other-meeting basis, between *labor-management cochairs*. Balanced representation and leadership are fundamental requirements if any cooperative effort is going to be successful over the long run.

If either party feels that they are outnumbered, or that steering-committee decisions and actions can be forced or manipulated by one side acting unilaterally in controlling meetings, then feelings of joint responsibility and destiny, essential in any true partnership, will never develop. Instead, the weaker party will become hostile and eventually alienated from the process.

The role of the steering committee, as the name suggests, is to guide the overall labor-management cooperative partnership in much the same manner that a captain controls the rudder guiding a ship. Ideally, this guiding role begins with the creation of the labor-management cooperative charter. A significant number, if not all, of the members of the steering committee should have been instrumental in developing the charter agreement—which clearly articulates the philosophy, structure, policies, and procedures of the cooperative partnership.

The steering committee performs its critical role by adhering to guidelines provided in the charter agreement. The most important activities performed by the steering committee as the partnership's guiding light are:

1. Meeting regularly once each year for an extended session to review the partnership's performance in living

up to the cooperative philosophy as well as more specific goals and objectives that were set for the past year. Based upon this critical analysis of the previous year's performance, structural, policy, and procedural modifications are made to improve the partnership's effectiveness and new goals and objectives are also set for the coming year.

2. Meeting regularly, on at least a monthly basis, to do the following:

   a) Establish new subcommittees and task forces;

   b) Receive programmatic and policy recommendations from existing subcommittees and task forces;

   c) Review and evaluate the work-in-process of existing subcommittees and task forces, and provide these groups with both additional guidance and formal support;

   d) Make major company or facilitywide policy and program decisions and initiate actions necessary for implementation;

   e) Share and discuss the implications of important general information such as monthly performance reports, industry-level data, and policy directives from either the international union or corporate headquarters.

3. Publish, distribute, and post summary minutes of the proceedings of each regular steering committee for the information of all employees.

4. Serve as the final court of appeal for specific employee proposals and complaints that have been rejected at lower levels of the partnership structure.

Through these activities, the steering committee plays both essential task and maintenance roles for the overall partnership, which must be performed on a systemwide basis. By acting in this capacity, the steering committee prevents the partnership from slipping back into the reactive, grievance-process type of dynamics that is characteristic of traditional labor relations. At the same time, it avoids the pitfalls of the project-oriented strategy, which tends to cause cooperation to become fixated on and restricted to an extremely narrow range of cooperative activities. Similarly, the steering committee clearly and operationally establishes and maintains labor-management cooperation as a jointly determined process. In so doing, it overcomes the tendency of traditional OD approaches to turn the effort into a one-sided, management-dominated effort.

Subcommittees, Task Forces, and Mini-Task Forces

The next level of cooperative activity in the partnership structure involves the actual problem-solving and administrative work of subcommittees and task forces. These groups are very important, for it is at this level that most of the actual cooperative work gets done. These joint teams act as the primary mechanisms for cooperation in two respects. First, it is these groups that actually engage in group problem-solving activities aimed at solving specific problems that are either hindering organizational performance or negatively affecting the quality of working life.

Second, subcommittees and task forces play a crucial role in extending both the spirit and the skills of cooperative problem solving by drawing an ever wider circle of employees and managers into the process as direct participants. Where the steering committee gives stability, continuity, and direction to the cooperative partnership, task forces and subcommittees provide the flexibility and action orientation necessary to solve real problems. Both levels of activity are necessary, but neither is sufficient in and of itself for developing and institutionalizing a cooperative partnership.

We have chosen to use the terms *subcommittee* and *task force* to denote the second tier of the cooperative partnership. Our purpose is to differentiate between ongoing, relatively permanent, problem-solving or administrative labor-management activities, which are the responsibility of *subcommittees,* and temporary, ad hoc problem-solving efforts, which tend to be the work of *task forces.* Both kinds of groups are essential to the effective operation of stable but dynamic cooperative partnerships, but their roles are different.

There is, however, nothing sacred about the nomenclature we have chosen to use to denote these two different kinds of cooperative groups and their respective functions. Various companies and unions have called labor-management cooperative problem-solving groups a variety of names, including action teams, quality circles, core groups, departmental teams, total quality teams, and continuous improvement teams. The specific title used to identify them is unimportant, but the functions they perform are crucial.

Subcommittees tend to be standing committees formed to address some particular issue, the needs of a specific subunit, or the administration of a focused program on an ongoing basis. Subcommittees may not be eternal, but they do deal with needs and problems that merit continuous and intense attention over relatively long periods of time. Thus subcommittees are formed as representative, ongoing problem-solving groups for individual departments, as intermediate-level steering bodies for multi-plant operations, as peer-review committees to deal jointly with chronic absenteeism, as auditing committees for administering bonuses for gainsharing programs, and/or committees responsible for directing and administering companywide energy-saving programs.

In contrast to subcommittees, task forces are temporary problem-solving groups that are formed on an ad hoc basis as new needs and problems present themselves to the steering committee. In some instances, such ad hoc problem-solving groups are eventually converted into standing subcommittees, but they always begin with a very specific task to perform, with the clear understanding that their assignment will end as soon as they have proposed a satisfactory solution to the steering committee.

The range of problems that can be assigned to a task force is limited only by the creativity of the steering committee and the willingness of management to enable workers to become involved with issues previously considered the sole domain of management. Such groups have been used to redesign the layouts of existing departments, to develop new products and systems to produce them, to create new technology, to develop bids on subcontracts, and to help design and create new plants. They have worked to launch entire new companies, as occurred in the case of Saturn (see Chapter 2). Any problem for which the solution could be enhanced by including the diverse input of different groups and individuals, directly and indirectly connected, is a likely justification for labor-management task force involvement.

In addition to task forces and subcommittees, there is one more level of group participation, and this is what we have chosen to call *mini-task forces*. Mini-task forces can range in size from two to several individuals, and they are formed in order to increase the effectiveness of subcommittees and task forces. They also provide an opportunity to involve more employees in the larger cooperative problem-solving process.

Task force and subcommittee effectiveness can be significantly enhanced through the delegation of specific, detailed problems to mini-task forces. Effectiveness increases through the use of mini-task forces in at least three respects. First, mini-task forces increase the amount of time that task force members can individually dedicate to addressing their assigned task, thereby shortening the overall time required to develop a solution. At the same time, they also may increase the quality of the solution. It is usually very difficult to set aside sufficient periods of time for holding problem-solving meetings involving all task force and subcommittee members. Coordinating everyone's schedule is an obstacle to holding frequent, lengthy, problem-solving meetings involving the entire group. But an even greater obstacle is the opposition that can arise from coworkers and managers who become frustrated by the disruptions to their daily work schedule that large-group sessions can cause.

When specific problem-solving tasks are broken down into separate subtasks and organized and synthesized in an overall solution for the entire group, then smaller groups of two to three people, and sometimes even single members, can work on each subtask more intensively. This is accomplished without disrupting the daily work schedule or creating ill feelings among masses of coworkers and supervisors. In fact, this delegation of problem-solving tasks tends to encourage employees to spend time working on problems during breaks, and even after work, as they become increasingly absorbed in their own individual tasks.

A second benefit of using mini-task forces as part of the cooperative problem-solving process is that it helps to ensure the active participation of all group members during full subcommittee or task force sessions. When members come to a full-group meeting with a proposal, or a study that they have developed through intensive work by themselves, they tend to participate in the discussion with great interest and enthusiasm. Thus, by delegating the work of task forces and subcommittees to mini-task forces the quality of the overall group process is greatly enhanced and the personal satisfaction of individual members with the co-operative experience is greatly increased.

Last, mini-task forces can also serve as useful mechanisms for widening the circle of employees and managers who become involved directly in cooperative partnership activities. That is, in the process of collecting and analyzing data while studying a particular problem, or gathering additional input to help solve the problem, new employees, who are not members of the formal subcommittee or task force group, can be recruited to assist as mini-task force members. The benefits that can be realized through this broadening of the participant base are tremendous, both directly and indirectly. The direct and most immediate benefit is greater and more specific expertise and relevant experience that can be applied to the issue at hand. Indirectly, mini-task forces also help to spread the spirit of cooperation and the skills of cooperative problem solving throughout the entire organization. This can be done much more rapidly than through formal activities alone, and, as result, organizational effectiveness, as well as responsiveness to employee needs, also increases.

Leadership and Representation

Subcommittees and task forces do a far more effective job of promoting labor-management cooperation if they follow the same basic guidelines for representation and leadership as the steering committee. Management/professional participation on task forces and subcommittees should equal 50 percent of the group and union/worker participation the other 50 percent. Again, this ensures that both parties have equal influence over plans and decisions, while at the same ensuring that there is an equal sharing of the burden of responsibility for the consequences of the group's proposals for action. Similarly, coleadership should also be the norm, and not the exception, for problem-solving teams. Workers will typically want to defer to management to chair and direct subcommittee or task force meetings, and managers will easily slip into assuming the chairperson's role. These temptations should be scrupulously avoided. Following these natural inclinations will at best retard the development of a full and equal partnership and at worst will undermine and destroy a budding cooperative relationship.

On the other hand, rigorously demanding balanced representation and coleadership for mini-task forces would be impractical and counterproductive. Since mini-task forces are extremely informal and temporary, sometimes existing for no more than one meeting, their advantage of speed and flexibility would be greatly diminished by the imposition of formal rules of leadership and representation. Similarly, since a mini-task force can involve as few as one or two people, there is often little need for formally designated leaders. The particular subtask that needs to be performed may involve only workers or only management/ professional personnel, depending on the nature of the task and the information required.

In Fig. 5.2 we summarize the basic rules, roles, and procedures for partnership participation.

Conclusion

In this chapter we have outlined the key structural elements required for the effective development and sustained life of labor-management cooperative partnerships. In today's organizational world, dominated by contingency thinking, some of our discussion may seem extremely normative. Yet we are confident, after years of experience and observation, that the structural elements that we have outlined, as well as the rules and roles related to leadership and procedures that we have discussed, are essential to constructing lasting cooperative partnerships.

In Chapter 6 we will examine the process of implementing this cooperative partnership. More specifically, we will be concerned with helping the reader think clearly about critical issues in selecting a strategy for actually injecting cooperative problem-solving activities into the unionized workplace. Even with a jointly developed philosophy and charter agreement, and with a carefully selected and balanced steering committee in place, long life for the partnership is by no means guaranteed. In moving from formulation to implementation of actual, joint labor-management problem-solving strategies, critical elements need to be considered for long-term success. We will next carefully examine the key factors in the implementation stage of partnership development.

Figure 5.2
Labor-Management Partnership: Mechanisms for Cooperation

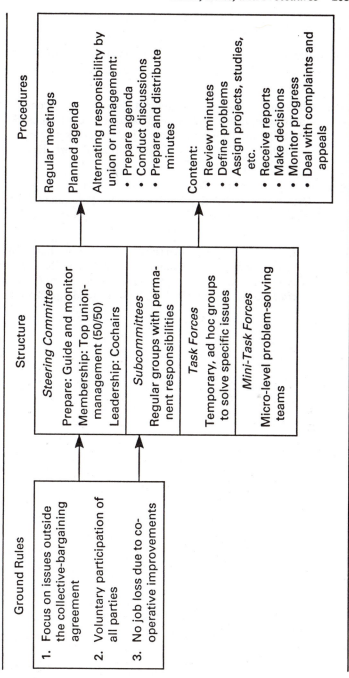

Ground Rules

1. Focus on issues outside the collective-bargaining agreement

2. Voluntary participation of all parties

3. No job loss due to co-operative improvements

Structure

Steering Committee
Prepare: Guide and monitor
Membership: Top union-management (50/50)
Leadership: Cochairs

Subcommittees
Regular groups with perma-nent responsibilities

Task Forces
Temporary, ad hoc groups to solve specific issues

Mini-Task Forces
Micro-level problem-solving teams

Procedures

Regular meetings

Planned agenda

Alternating responsibility by union or management:
• Prepare agenda
• Conduct discussions
• Prepare and distribute minutes

Content:
• Review minutes
• Define problems
• Assign projects, studies, etc.
• Receive reports
• Make decisions
• Monitor progress
• Deal with complaints and appeals

References

Cohen-Rosenthal, Edward, and Burton, Cynthia E. *Mutual Gains: A Guide to Union-Management Cooperation.* New York: Praeger, 1987.

Meek, Christopher. "Labor-Management Committee Outcomes: The Jamestown Case." In Warner Woodworth, Christopher Meek, and William Foote Whyte (eds.), *Industrial Democracy: Strategies for Community Revitalization.* Beverly Hills, CA: Sage, 1985, pp. 141–159.

Stein, Barry, and Kanter, Rosabeth Moss. "Building the Parallel Organization: Creating Mechanisms for Permanent Quality of Work Life." *Journal of Applied Behavioral Science,* Vol. 16, 1980, p. 373.

Woodworth, Warner. "Saving Jobs through Worker Buyouts." In Warner Woodworth, Christopher Meek, and William Foote Whyte (eds.), *Industrial Democracy: Strategies for Community Revitalization.* Beverly Hills, CA: Sage, 1985, pp. 221–241.

6

Important Considerations When Getting Started: The Political Realities of Project Implementation

Selecting an appropriate strategy for initiating and cultivating a cooperative partnership is a matter of great significance, and, as has been the case with many of the issues we have already discussed, an effective strategy in a unionized context often openly conflicts with the commonly accepted "rules of thumb" and popular "folk wisdom" of organization development and the employee-involvement movement. The special dynamics of the unionized workplace—that is, the negotiated and quasi-legal nature of daily management of the employment relationship and the political characteristics of union organizations—present *special conditions* that either do not exist or are of minimal significance in non-union work settings. Attention to these special conditions is essential when first selecting *what kinds* of cooperative problem-solving projects to initially undertake, determining *who* should directly participate in these projects, and deciding upon the appropriate *organizational locations* where cooperative activities should first begin.

From Conflict to Cooperation: Alternative Levels

It is important to realize that a cooperative relationship between union and management may be thought of as a process and not a

Figure 6.1
Labor-Management Relationship Continuum

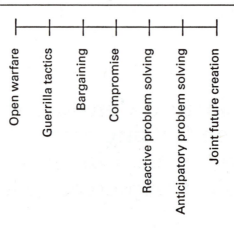

structure. The continuum along which patterns of interaction can be conceptualized is suggested in Fig. 6.1.

On the extreme left is the high conflict end of the continuum, which we have chosen to call *open warfare*. In this case the relationship between the union and the company has deteriorated to the point where each side seeks to force the other to submit to their demands through the use of the most extreme and damaging kinds of economic weapons. Unions typically engage in strikes, corporate campaigns, and boycotts to force concessions from management. Conversely, management may employ such weapons as permanent replacements, lockouts, plant closings, and even bankruptcy to force unions and workers to concede to company demands, a tactic pioneered by Frank Lorenzo at Continental Airlines. Less blatant are the guerrilla tactics, such as work slowdowns by employees at Caterpillar, or the sabotage of equipment used to disrupt factory production at various companies.

At the extreme opposite, or most cooperative end of the continuum, is *joint future creation*, which in many cases involves a total system overhaul. In this case labor and management participate in joint strategizing, planning, and problem solving to create the ideal future state. Of course, engaging in cooperative problem solving for the purpose of creating a mutually desirable future seldom occurs in U.S. companies, but such high-level cooperative partnerships have in fact existed in other countries since as early as the 1960s. Scandinavian trade unions, employers' associations, and national governments decided to create more humane workplaces through the widespread adoption of sociotechnical principles. At SAS, for example, aircraft mechanics worked together with management to create an effective artificial intelligence system which workers now use to perform highly effective aircraft and jet engine maintenance.

Between the extremes of open warfare and joint future creation are several other levels of conflict or cooperation, which are identified in Fig. 6.1. At the center is *compromise,* which in collective bargaining has traditionally been considered the highest level of cooperation or, conversely, the lowest level of conflict practically attainable. We suggest that labor and management should seek a level of cooperative engagement that far exceeds mere compromise. Compromise usually means that each side has reluctantly agreed to concede some of its demands in order to reach an agreement with which neither party is entirely satisfied. This is not a satisfactory cooperative ideal for meeting the turbulent and highly competitive demands of today's international marketplace.

At a minimum, labor and management must learn to engage in what we have chosen to call *reactive problem solving.* At this level of cooperation, when problems arise with the operation of existing systems, or when they emerge during the process of implementing new systems or technology, labor and management need to come together to jointly identify the causes of these problems and then solve them. Actions to raise quality, reduce scrap, improve attendance, or eliminate accidents all tend to be reactive problem-solving activities.

However, if labor and management collaborate in planning and implementing a new system, or totally redesigning an existing system, then they are engaging in what we have chosen to call *anticipatory problem solving.* Proactive examples include redesigning the layout and work systems and developing and introducing productivity gainsharing systems.

Diagnosis: Start-Up Difficulties

In the field of OD, when first trying to decide where to initiate specific interventions, it has become standard practice to begin with a systemwide organizational diagnosis. This can take many forms, ranging from the systematic use of standardized survey feedback instruments administered to everyone in the organization to the use of more qualitative approaches such as culture audits, consultant-conducted ethnographic and ethno-historical studies, or team-based self-studies. These all tend to emphasize the collection of large amounts of data to develop a conceptual picture of the total organization.

It is assumed that formal organizations are complex and composed of a myriad of interdependent relationships. OD practitioners understand that initiating a change in one part of an organization can have repercussions that result in unanticipated consequences throughout the system. To minimize interventional problems, it has become standard in OD practice to begin by collecting massive amounts of data through an organizational diagnosis so that the system can be mapped and the most significant obstacles to change can be identified.

Although OD theory and practice are grounded in values of participation and individual empowerment, it seems that faith in behavioral science has still left a residual orientation from earlier eras. Centuries ago social philosopher Thomas Hobbes envisioned social scientists replacing political and religious leaders as the engineers of a new social order based upon natural law and positive science. Much like the flavor of certain OD texts today, Hobbes's goal was "establishing once and for all the conditions for the correct order of the state and society. . . . " He argued that "the translation of knowledge into practice, the application, is a technical problem." So what is needed is expert calculation of organizational rules and relationships. Thus, "human behavior is therefore to be now considered only as the material for science. The engineers of the correct order can disregard the categories of ethical social discourse and confine themselves to the construction of conditions under which human beings, just like objects within nature, will necessarily behave in a calculable manner" (Habermas, 1973, p. 43).

Although many OD practitioners might wince at Hobbes's social engineering vision, the work of consultants often depends upon extensive diagnostic work which they alone understand and appreciate. In contrast, we suggest that participatory methods, such as team-based joint self-studies, can make this initial intervention much more client-relevant and can significantly reduce consultant-client dependency. However, even self-study efforts can become destructive to the newly forming cooperative partnership if they are initially too extensive. This negative effect stems from the tendency of large-scale diagnoses to generate expectations for dramatic changes systemwide and also from the extensive amount of time required to complete data collection and analysis.

The issues involved are simple. As noted previously, the more employees who are asked questions about organizational conditions and needs for improvement, the more individuals there will be who expect that by providing this information they will soon see major improvements. Of course, the number of issues a joint labor-management committee can practically undertake to solve at the beginning of a partnership is far less than the number that the larger workforce can generate in a systemwide analysis. Usually, when cooperative actions fall short of employees' expectations for change, feelings of disappointment and resentment soon follow.

In non-union firms, where employees lack formal channels for voicing complaints, perhaps the worst thing that happens as a result of unmet expectations is the appearance of employee apathy. But in a unionized setting, where formal channels for employee voice and elected advocates exist, workers are unlikely to accept inaction with quiet resignation. Instead, they tend to begin to voice their dissatisfaction at union meetings and to union stewards, creating strong pressures on union officers to respond. Labor leaders must either get results or else quickly distance themselves from problem-solving activities by blaming management for the lack of action.

To start by making a heavy investment in systemwide employee training can have similar disastrous consequences. Of course, learning new concepts and behavioral skills can help employees make a positive contribution to group processes and problem solving. Many consultants overestimate the importance of this, however, and follow the traditional assumption that everyone in the organization must first gain a basic cognitive and experiential understanding of cooperative processes and decision making in order for joint problem solving to proceed. Some consultants may also be motivated to maximize their income potential by requiring formal training before actual problem solving begins. A substantial income stream can be generated from charge-per-head training fees and the sale of training workbooks, and it was common during the 1980s for cooperative efforts to begin with huge training programs involving all workers and first-line managers. General Motors, for instance, paid the bill for training courses and workbooks for thousands of employees at individual plants before even undertaking a single concrete problem-solving task that would produce visible shop-floor change. Now defunct Eastern Airlines paid approximately $1 million dollars to consultants to provide initial training to workers and supervisors so that shop-floor problem-solving groups could be established.

Training sessions generate initial good feelings, understanding, and increased trust between management and workers, but few visible changes actually occur by training alone. The initial positive effects of training can quickly turn sour without concrete outcomes, which leads to the same kinds of problems that are unintentionally created by starting with an extensive diagnosis.

Key Issues in Deciding Where and How to Begin

Rather than beginning an effort to create a labor-management partnership with a massive investment in systemwide diagnostic research or training programs, it is usually much more prudent and effective to initiate labor-management cooperative problem solving on a smaller scale with a more narrow focus but yet a strategic orientation. Regardless of what particular problem-solving task or tasks a labor-management partnership effort initially undertakes, the first and foremost aim should be to generate a positive experience and initial organizational learning that will serve as a foundation on which to build the partnership through increasingly more complex problem-solving tasks that will encompass an ever-widening range of participants and issues.

Realistically, it must be recognized that in the beginning stages of creating a labor-management partnership, when the parties are first experimenting with cooperation, the dominant dynamics of their relationship may be characterized at worst as open warfare and at best as compromise. Thus, regardless of whether a partnership-building process begins at the tail end of a bitter strike or with parties who seldom engage in open confrontation and typically seek compromise, the starting point for most actual problem solving usually is at the *reactive problem-solving* level.

Of course, developing the initial labor-management charter agreement, with its mission and philosophy statement, involves discussion and consensus building with respect to the ideal joint future that labor and management leaders hope to realize through their partnership. This activity tends to engage the parties at a very general and abstract level. The reference points that managers and labor leaders use as their counterpoints for identifying ideal future conditions are their real-life experiences, but the discussion, while developing the charter agreement, seldom moves beyond the identification of general ideals and values.

Once a charter has been completed and approved, the steering committee moves on to the next phase of organizing problem-solving groups to work on specific problems of mutual interest and concern. This is an extremely important time in the life of a labor-management partnership. The choices that are made at this point tend either to set the stage for the gradual development of trust between the parties and confidence in cooperative action or to start the partnership off on a course that will ultimately lead to increased conflict and the demise of the effort. Thus, the steering committee should proceed with great care when establishing the partnership's initial problem-solving groups, because the experience of these first teams is likely to have a profound and lasting influence on future prospects for labor-management cooperation in the organization.

Specifically, when initiating the partnership's early problem-solving activities, the steering committee, and any consultants advising them, should carefully consider *what* issues or problems should first be addressed, *which part or parts of the organization* should initially be engaged in the process of tackling these matters, and *who* should be recruited to participate as members of the first problem-solving groups. An ill-conceived choice on any of these three dimensions can lead to failure, whereas wisely made decisions can create a solid experiential foundation on which to build more comprehensive and sophisticated partnership activities in the future.

In deciding which issue or issues should first be used as the basis for experimenting with labor-management cooperative problem solving, key considerations should include the following:

1. Does the issue or problem have the potential of providing clear and specific benefits that both parties value?

2. What is the probability that the issue can be effectively solved through joint problem solving and then implemented within a relatively short period of time after the problem has been assigned to a labor-management problem-solving team?

3. What is the present state of union-management relations in terms of the conflict–cooperation continuum, and given this state of joint relations, how threatening will specific problems be to either party?

4. Given the internal political composition and dynamics of both union and management organizations, what is the probability that specific proposed issues for problem solving will become fodder for internal political strife?

Joint Action for Joint Benefit

Edward Cohen-Rosenthal and Cynthia E. Burton (1987) in their book *Mutual Gains* point out most emphatically that initial joint problem-solving activities taken on by union and management groups should involve issues that are recognized as important by both parties. They explain:

> Cooperation should do something worthwhile or it should not be done at all. The basis of cooperation is to attain important goals and objectives. If a cooperative program is entered into only to appease or solely to get along, then soon it will have to answer uncomfortable questions about what it has really accomplished. The rule of thumb is that the closer the goals and objectives are to the central goals and objectives of the union and management partners, the more likely the program is to maintain itself and result in positive accomplishments. [pp. 140–141]

This is a very important point because the leadership and rank and file on both sides of the fence tend to look upon cooperative action very narrowly in terms of how well it can meet their own group's interests and needs. Consequently, if a problem-solving project effectively solves a problem or addresses a need that is valued by one party only, it will not be considered an example of success by the other party. An issue addressed and resolved that makes only the workers and union officials happy—such as better rest room and break facilities or on-site day care—can easily be viewed by managers as just another example of how the union has manipulated them to get more without any clear economic return on the expenditure. Conversely, a project that improves labor productivity or reduces the waste of raw materials, for example, but does not improve the working environment can be easily interpreted by union leaders and the workforce as another instance of how the banner of cooperation has been used by management to "squeeze" more out of the worker. Of course, it can be argued that over the long run workers' positive attitudes will lead to smoother labor-management relations and greater efficiency, thereby creating more profits and a more healthy corporation. This may be true, but such arguments are too vague and abstract to have much influence, especially during the initial stages of cooperation when distrust between the parties is high and experience with cooperative action is limited.

It is much safer and wiser, therefore, to select initial joint problem-solving projects that can yield clear and tangible benefits to both parties. This is especially true if the steering committee decides to limit the first cooperative efforts to a serial pattern of one-project-at-a-time action. If multiple projects are undertaken, then a sort of quid-pro-quo arrangement can be used in which one effort provides more clear and tangible gains for the company while a simultaneously undertaken project generates greater immediate benefits to labor. If this latter approach is adopted, however, it is important for management to give equal priority to both types of problem-solving projects when it comes to implementation because the company ultimately controls the purse strings and the time schedule for action. A situation in which company-oriented programs are implemented almost immediately while employee-oriented programs take months or even years to get off the ground does not constitute a viable quid-pro-quo arrangement. Thus, ideally, especially during the first phases of cooperative-relationship development, it is best if any project undertaken has clear and mutually beneficial outcomes for both parties. Improved productivity should also produce clear gains for labor in terms of greater job security, a more efficient work system or layout should also create safer and less physically demanding working conditions, and enhanced product quality should likewise result in greater employee discretion and autonomy.

Intimately linked to the issue of "perceived mutual benefit" is the question of problem or project difficulty and complexity. On this point Cohen-Rosenthal and Burton state:

> Tangential issues do not get the time and attention that central issues receive. Even if tangential issues are pursued "successfully" many do not care about the results. Some argue that cooperation should be built first upon accomplishing something easy. This is generally wrong. All this proves is that cooperation can tackle the unimportant or facile issues and does not breed respect for the process or the desire to use it. [p. 141]

Cohen-Rosenthal and Burton are certainly right in arguing that solving problems of low perceived value and relevance is a poor foundation on which to try and build a cooperative relationship. However, we tend to disagree with this viewpoint if it does not also entail some initial assessment of the chances of success in actually reaching the stage of implementation. Projects undertaken that are vague or that involve broad organizational goals and objectives that will take many months to complete are a poor choice for initiating a cooperative relationship. Similarly, programs and projects that will require massive amounts of capital to implement are also usually a poor choice, because in the best case they will require months if not years to implement, and in the worst case—after a prolonged period of analysis and evaluation—they may prove to be too expensive and thus may result in no tangible change whatsoever. Thus, it is always wise to begin with cooperative endeavors that are both within the technical grasp of the problem-solving team and the financial means of the organization, and that can result in tangible action in the workplace during the first six months of the partnership.

In the beginning, many individuals on both sides will be skeptical about the potential value of cooperative action, and some will even be antagonistic to the concept of union-management cooperation. For union antagonists, cooperation is just a euphemism for "selling out"; and for management antagonists, cooperation means giving up important management prerogatives which they have spent years trying to protect from worker encroachment. Such skeptics and antagonists will hardly be patient participants in or observers of the unfolding cooperative process. Rather, they will actually have a vested interest in seeing the cooperative partnership fail. They will delight in seeing difficulties develop, and they may consciously or unconsciously create obstacles to ensure that labor-management cooperation does in fact fail.

Antagonistic participants and observers will be especially interested in seeing cooperation fail. They have invested many years of effort in building up an image of the other party that they have used effectively to protect themselves from direct criticism and personal accountability. For union antagonists, workers suffer and the company fails to earn profits because of incompetent and callous management; and for management antagonists, it is always the union that is the root cause of worker dissatisfaction, low productivity, poor quality, and unsatisfactory profit-and-loss statements. Thus, launching a cooperative partnership with extremely complex, time-consuming, and expensive problem-solving projects is a very risky venture, no matter how important and mutually valued these endeavors may be. A less dramatic project with a high probability of resulting in a joint solution that can be implemented in reasonable period of time is much more appropriate during a partnership's infancy.

Avoiding Political Turmoil

Whenever participation and planned change are undertaken in the unionized workplace, one of the consultant's and the participants' most important considerations should be the avoidance of political conflicts. This is especially true when the foundation of trust and cooperative experience is thin and likely to be short-lived at the upper levels of the union and management hierarchies. Therefore, in deciding which cooperative problem-solving projects to undertake—especially during the early phases of the partnership—it is important for both parties to assess carefully whether any of the options under consideration will generate extraordinary political turmoil between the parties or inside each party's respective organization—or possibly both. Projects with a high potential for exacerbating severe and long-term conflict between the parties should be avoided until a solid and broad-based foundation of cooperative experience has been developed. Similarly, issues that can potentially be used by different political factions within the company and union to malign and undermine the current leadership, or that could exacerbate conflicts between competing factions, should also be avoided.

Issues that are central to ongoing conflicts and negotiation disputes between the union and the company are certainly very important to both sides. Unfortunately, they also tend to be very difficult to resolve, because they may require contractual changes and because both sides always have a very strong emotional commitment to their own positions. Moreover, issues that have been a major point of contention between labor and management over the course of several years almost inevitably lead to incidents of character assassination and scapegoating as the conflict escalates. Consequently, it is extremely difficult for either party to adopt an open-minded and problem-solving attitude when tackling these kinds of problems or implementing solutions to them.

An approach to organizational change and renewal that has become very popular in recent years, and that provides an excellent example of the kinds of political problems that can arise when cooperative projects are selected without careful consideration of the political risks involved, is the adoption of team-based or self-regulating work systems. Stories and literature abound concerning the problem of first-line and middle-management resistance to the introduction of autonomous work teams. Such opposition is not surprising, given the threat that self-management poses to supervisors and managers in terms of their job security, role responsibilities, and decision-making authority. In the unionized workplace, similar problems arise, and they can be compounded by the unique political context of a union environment.

In companies where conflict and distrust have become the dominant characteristics of union-management relations, the continual addition of new managers to first-line supervision is a common phenomenon. As the ranks of supervision grow and the style of shop-floor management becomes increasingly autocratic and punitive, distrust further intensifies between the parties, with managers watching closely to ensure that workers are on the line at their jobs and the workforce responding by finding every opportunity to avoid working.

This situation thus becomes a classic vicious circle in which more supervisors are added and more disciplinary warnings are issued to workers for even the most minor infractions. In turn, workers strike back at management with increasing frequency through slowdowns, sabotage, and absenteeism, which, of course, leads to the hiring of more supervisors and the issuing of even more warning slips at the slightest provocation. As this process progresses and the relationship deteriorates, the union begins to blame the company's inevitable financial problems on too much management overhead and incompetent supervisors. Management, on the other hand, claims that the company's problems are caused by lazy, dishonest, and even malevolent workers who would not do any work at all if someone were not constantly monitoring and directing their actions.

Clearly, in such cases the reduced overhead costs, greater worker motivation, and increased flexibility that come with socio-technical design could do a great deal to improve working conditions while simultaneously reducing production costs. And such actions may eventually be necessary for company survival. Attempting to undertake these kinds of radical changes as the starting point for a labor-management partnership can be extremely risky, however. On the one hand, union leaders and workers may try to use the project as a means for undertaking what becomes in essence a witch-hunt in which they attempt to prove that first-line supervisors are unnecessary and a waste of money and that certain supervisors, who are particularly resented, really are as incompetent as the union has been claiming over the years. So the project, instead of proceeding from a problem-solving orientation, becomes a sort of purge in which the union's goal is to "throw the bums out." On the other hand, first-line supervisors and middle managers may approach the effort with the attitude that they must defend their ranks from destruction by proving once and for all that workers are lazy, untrustworthy, and unable to do anything at all without close supervision. We have seen these kind of dynamics at work under many circumstances, but they are especially common when self-regulating or semiautonomous work systems become an early and principal thrust for a new labor-management partnership.

The case of one food-processing firm with which we consulted for several years provides an excellent example of how these problems can arise and spiral into virtual warfare. In this instance, the company and the union decided that one of the first projects they wanted to undertake was the development of a new product, including the design and implementation of the new department that would produce it. In the process of developing the new product and exploring different equipment and work-methods options, the problem-solving team that had been assigned the project became attracted to the idea of self-management. They visited two firms that had been experimenting with the concept for several years, and as a result of these experiences became convinced that a self-regulating system would be ideal for producing the new product. However, labor relations at this company, and especially at the plant where the new product was to be made, had historically been extremely adversarial. Further complicating the situation was a long-term condition of competition and win-lose conflict that had developed between the firm's Production and Marketing/Sales Divisions.

Marketing and sales managers had taken the lead management role on the problem-solving team, because the adoption of a new product line requires extensive marketing research. In the process, they had also become advocates with the union for a self-managed work system. Unfortunately, the Marketing and Sales Division also had a hidden agenda: They chose to use the project as an unique opportunity to get even with the Production Division by proving once and for all that incompetent production management was at the heart of the company's financial problems. The union had its hidden agenda as well, which was that the project would finally prove that the company did in fact have too many supervisors.

Not surprisingly, as production management became aware of these other agendas their inherent aversion to self-management increased to become essentially a fortress mentality. Production managers adopted a "no-holds-barred" approach to preventing the introduction and success of the new product, even though the product was essential to the company's survival because of its high volume and value-added potential. At first the vice president of Operations, and virtually every production manager under him, argued aggressively against the new work system, and when that didn't work, they attempted to prove that the product was not really viable either. When this effort failed to stop other top managers and the board of directors from moving ahead with the new product, production management then attempted to sabotage the implementation of the project.

Their sabotage effort began with an attempt to ensure that the wrong kind of workers would be recruited into the new department. As a union operation, the company was required to abide by traditional job-bidding procedures, which gave everyone a chance to bid for jobs in the new department with the most senior applicants actually winning the bid. The bidding notices explained that the new jobs would involve rotation with all the production positions in the department as well as performance of the administrative duties traditionally handled by a departmental supervisor and clerk. To subvert the system, however, plant personnel and production managers actively recruited some of the older employees for the new jobs knowing that they would get the positions if they bid. They told these workers to ignore the job-rotation requirements, because they weren't really going to have to do these things anyway, and they also told them not to worry about the administrative work, because they really were going to have a supervisor for the department. Production management assured these older workers that, as usual, the most senior applicants would be able to stake their claim on the better jobs in the department. Furthermore, they pointed out that the new department would pay some of the highest rates in the plant and that production standards would be much looser than normal because it would take some time for everyone to learn the new jobs and for the new product to become viable in the marketplace.

This first attempt to sabotage the project almost succeeded. An intensive classroom training program was scheduled for all new department employees before actually beginning production. We were assigned the job of conducting some of the early training sessions in which the group was to be introduced to the general principles of job enrichment and socio-technical design, as well as the specific work system they would implement in the new department. As an initial exercise to help everyone become acquainted, and hopefully build enthusiasm for this pioneering work system, we started out by going around the room asking each employee to tell their name, to describe their work experience at the plant, and also to explain why they had bid into the new department. To our surprise, the first worker explained:

> Well the reason I'm here today is because I've got twenty years' seniority, the jobs in this department pay the highest production wages in this here plant, and I know it's going be gravy for a long time to come 'cause this is a new department and a new product so management can't really push efficiency too much.

We were shocked and disappointed to hear this explanation, but our anxiety really became intense as we went from worker to worker and one-by-one they all basically said the same thing, until the twelfth and last person spoke. She was the only female employee who had bid into the department, and she said:

> I sure didn't come here for the same reason that you fellows did. I have worked for the company more than twenty years, but I didn't bid into this new department because I thought we were going to have gravy jobs. Didn't you read the job description? It said we are all going to be paid the high rate because we are going to learn all the jobs, we're going to trade-off doing them, and we're also going to be our own managers. There isn't going to be any supervisor. I don't know about you, but I'm sick and tired after all these years of getting stuck on the same boring jobs where I do the same thing all day long, day in and day out. I'm also tired of having a supervisor breathing down my neck and telling me what to do like I was a little child even though I know more than him and I've been here a heck of a lot longer, too.

We were relieved to find at least one worker who actually understood how the new department was going to work and who also wanted to be there because of the new system. But our relief was short-lived. The reactions of the other workers to this woman's comments were explosive. The first worker to react said:

> What are you talking about? I'll be damned if I'm gonna rotate jobs with anybody. I've got the most seniority of

anyone in this room so I got a right to the best job, and there ain't nobody gonna push me off of it to do somethin' else. And all that stuff about us being our own boss—that's bull. The superintendent told me that wasn't gonna really happen. That man over there (he pointed to a supervisor who had been listening from the doorway)—he's gonna be our foreman, he's my man. You must be crazy, woman!

Many of the other workers joined in making essentially the same comments, and the whole meeting was in an uproar. Not surprisingly, the supervisor who had been watching from the doorway, and the shift superintendent who also appeared, were almost rolling on the floor laughing. At a loss as to how to proceed, we quickly called a fifteen-minute break and ran to the telephone to call the union's chief steward, who was also the steering committee's labor cochairperson. We also tried to reach the vice president of Marketing and Sales, who was the management cochair, but he was not available. Fortunately, we were able to contact the chief steward, and he quickly rushed to the classroom to explain to the group that what they had heard about the new work system was exactly right. He said:

What you guys read in the bid announcement was right. You're going to have to learn all the jobs in the department and you're also going to have to rotate with each other on a regular basis. This will make your jobs less boring, it will make sure that you can cover for each other if one of you needs to leave the department or is sick, and it will also prevent injuries from using the same muscles all day long in the same pattern. And I don't know what you're talking about saying you've got to have a supervisor. All these years most of you guys have been complaining about how there's too many supervisors around here and how you don't need them. Now you have the chance to prove it and you're crying you got to have a boss. Look, this department is not going to have a supervisor. You guys are going to have to supervise yourselves. The reason we were able to negotiate such a high pay grade for the jobs in this department is because you're not going to need supervision and because you're also going to have to learn all the jobs and rotate doing them. If you don't want to follow the program then you might as well get the hell out of here right now cause we don't want you in here!

Later, when the vice president of Sales and Marketing found out what had happened, he did not hesitate to attack the production side for trying to kill the program, pointing out that this was just another example of how they were working against the company's best interests. Despite this initial setback, the new department and its system of self-management proceeded as planned. Some of employees who had initially bid into the new department followed the chief steward's advice and left immediately. Most of the workers stayed, though, and they actually became advocates of the new work system. Unfortunately, production management remained hostile toward the project, and they attempted to sabotage it through other means. Specifically, they concluded they could kill the new system if they could just prove that it was disorganized and unproductive. They set out to ensure that it would be by instructing all support departments to treat any orders or requests made by the new department as their lowest priority. Thus, when the new department ordered supplies, they routinely arrived days or even weeks behind schedule. Moreover, the Maintenance Department was instructed to forgo regularly scheduled maintenance checks, and when machinery broke down, the department frequently had to wait several hours or days longer than normal for a mechanic or electrician to arrive to perform the needed repairs.

Fortunately, this new strategy for destroying the project also failed, because as the self-managed work team encountered these obstacles the members simply became even more strongly committed to succeeding. When supplies did not arrive, the team members went out and bought what was needed with money out of their own pockets. When a net for catching the product off the end of the line didn't arrive—because the shift superintendent had held up the order—one of the workers used his high school letterman's jacket to rig a temporary net so production would not be halted. Other workers, who had some skill in mechanical or electrical work, studied the documentation available on the department's equipment and started fixing it themselves. As a result, departmental output and productivity continued to rise, far surpassing the learning curve that had been initially projected by engineering, and eventually, as it became evident that many problems were the result of sabotage, managers were reprimanded and some were even dismissed.

This outcome was simply a matter of luck, however. Given all the conflict and political infighting generated by this effort, it could just as easily have failed, destroying the entire partnership with it. And despite the eventual institutionalization of the new work system, many bad feelings and deep-seated grudges were generated. Of course, such conflict might just as likely have occurred after several years of tackling less politically sensitive issues, but it probably would have been far less manipulative and much more openly confronted.

The point of this example is not to attack the introduction of self-managing systems in the initial stages of forming a new labor-management partnership. In some cases, this may be the most appropriate first step to take, and under certain economic circumstances, it may be essential for survival. What we want to make clear is that careful consideration of the short- and long-term political implications of a particular project or program choice is essential at any time, and it is even more important during the first stages of trying to get a new partnership started. In our example, the labor-management project served not only to exacerbate already existing conflicts between the union and the company, but it also fed a very destructive competitive relationship between Sales and Production. These problems could have been foreseen and either the project could have been delayed or the conflicts could have been addressed directly from the start.

Who Should Participate and Where to Start

Just as important as deciding which issues to tackle first are the questions of who should participate in a partnership's early problem-solving activities and where in the organization these efforts should begin. These decisions are inextricably linked, and they are extremely critical in terms of their potential impact on the long- and short-term development of support for cooperation. Again, when making these choices, political considerations abound.

It is essential to point out that the suggestions made in this section are especially important during the early stages of a developing cooperative partnership. Nonetheless, even in a well-advanced partnership, one that has been in existence for several years, these questions are still important, particularly when a decision is made to tackle a politically sensitive issue through cooperative action. Poor choices on these matters can essentially determine the success or failure of a problem-solving effort, especially when it concerns problems that have deep and profound political implications.

On this dimension, once again, the logic appropriate for selecting the participants in initial problem-solving projects and the organizational location where these efforts should begin is often different in the unionized setting than the reasoning traditionally employed by consultants and participants involved in OD, Employee Involvement, and QC/Continuous Improvement programs in non-union workplaces. Unfortunately, in many instances experts have tended to extrapolate from their non-union experiences to unionized settings, and the consequences have been disastrous. Two of the most troublesome—and also most universally accepted—assumptions about participant and project selection are:

1. The younger members of the workforce are the best and most highly motivated candidates for becoming involved in participatory activities because they are more flexible, creative, and anxious to participate. Younger workers are more interested than older employees in participation because they have not been desensitized by years of meaningless, mind-numbing work, and because they are generally more highly educated than older employees.

2. It is always best to select first projects that involve issues and organizational processes that are within the scope of direct influence and action of existing organizational subunits. Top priority should first be given to problem solving that departments can handle with their own resources without attempting to bring about changes in other departments or divisions. In other words, "Seek first to clean up your own house before attempting to change others."

When combined, these two assumptions result in a bias toward building a cooperative spirit and problem-solving capacity upon a foundation of young, enthusiastic workers with a particular focus on change at the departmental or subunit level first. If this bias becomes the basis for building cooperation in the unionized work setting, the results can be disastrous.

Although younger workers may indeed be the most open-minded, the most flexible, and the most highly motivated to participate of all employee groups in most workplaces, they are by far the weakest base on which to build a cooperative program in a unionized setting. The youngest workers are also the employees who have the least seniority, and therefore they are almost always the least influential members of most unions. Younger employees are usually also the employees who feel the least sense of loyalty and commitment to the union and the philosophy of unionism. Since they have not participated in numerous contract negotiations, and they have not observed the role that the union has played in obtaining the superior wages, benefits, and job rights that they enjoy, most younger workers do not attribute these conditions to the union or union intervention on their behalf. These realities therefore present a serious problem when any labor-management partnership attempts to use younger workers as a key force for change by heavily involving them in the initial attempts at cooperative problem solving.

In short, by primarily involving younger and therefore low-seniority workers first in major problem-solving activities, and empowering them to make decisions on issues in which labor has never been consulted by management in the past, the traditional power structure of the union can easily become threatened. Ironically, the more successful a young-worker-led problem-solving activity actually proves to be in addressing the task it is assigned, the higher the probability that over the long run this activity will ultimately prove to be a liability because of the threat it has posed to the union's traditional power structure.

A very successful project that results in significant changes in the workplace invariably increases the plant and even the companywide visibility of the employees that participated in the problem-solving team. If most of the team members are young, low-seniority employees, this can automatically incite fear and anger in older, more senior members of the workforce, especially if they have not been consulted by the younger employees during the cooperative problem-solving process. Furthermore, since the younger employees who participate in cooperative problem solving are likely to become emotionally and intellectually energized by this empowering experience, they will invariably volunteer enthusiastically for future cooperative projects, and they may even decide to become more directly active in union politics and programs. Given the fact that under normal circumstances these younger workers would have little or no interest in trying to influence union decisions, their new activism becomes immediately apparent and again may cause senior employees to fear that these workers, and by association the labor-management partnership which seems to have brought them out of the woodwork, are a serious and imminent threat to the existing power structure.

Not surprisingly, when younger employees begin to become more active and vocal in union issues, perhaps even running for union offices, older employees react almost instinctively by turning against the cooperative programs for which these younger workers have become the most ardent advocates, or they may simply respond by rebuffing and ridiculing the young activists. Either reaction can be destructive to the development of a newly formed labor-management partnership. The ridicule and disdain that may be heaped upon these young workers by their more senior colleagues may encourage them to respond in kind either by becoming vocal critics of the local union or, if they are unusually aggressive, by forming a coalition which eventually attempts to take over the union's leadership. Either of these reactions will in turn immediately convince the more senior employees, who are also the most powerful members of the local union, that the cooperative partnership is really just a covert attempt by management to "bust the union" by tearing it apart from within. Once political turmoil within the union has reached this level of conflict, the demise of the partnership is at hand.

Emphasizing subunit- or departmental-based change when first experimenting with cooperative problem solving can produce similar problems. This is not only because of the high potential these efforts have for producing the threat of power shifts within the union organization; these dynamics can also apply to the management structure.

In any organization, a variety of factors can play a critical role in determining which individuals and subunits have the greatest degree of power and influence over others. Tradition, differential skill levels, resource dependency, or the role a subunit plays in helping other units deal with external and internal sources of uncertainty and/or the mobilization of resources of other groups for action are all important determinants of just how much influence any group or individual may have and how they can use this influence in the organization. Moreover, since it is the natural inclination of any group or individual to protect and even attempt to expand the power and influence which they enjoy, no matter how little or how great, it is natural for them to react negatively to any activity or change that may alter the existing balance of power. In the unionized workplace, focusing change efforts first at the level of single subunits, which are part of the traditional bureaucratic structure of the organization, runs a great risk of again posing a considerable threat to the existing power structure.

Articles about organizational change have emphasized for many years the significance of this particular organizational problem, which is frequently called "encapsulation." Very simply, whenever new and more intense attention is devoted to organizational change and improvement within one subunit, regardless of whether the subunit is an individual, a department, a division, or even an entire plant within a larger company, almost immediately a hostile reaction is evoked from the other subunits that are not directly involved with the change. Certainly this results in part from a sense of jealousy, but equally important is the increasing degree of influence the subunit begins to exercise within the organization, which may seem to result in their becoming the recipients of rewards and benefits to which others do not have access or that under traditional circumstances the subunit would not be entitled to receive. Suddenly, the existing power structure and the normal paths to organizational rewards are altered, and this threatens other groups and individuals that have achieved their power and status through playing by the rules of the past.

Key socio-technical design and redesign programs of the late 1970s and 1980s particularly suffered from this problem. For example, in one of the first and most highly publicized U.S. cases of using socio-technical design principles to develop a greenfield site operation, the Gaines Dog Food plant in Topeka, Kansas, all of the key managers who pioneered this innovative effort were eventually driven out of the company by other company managers who felt threatened and therefore opposed the system of self-regulating teams. In the case of OD and Employee Involvement efforts, these dynamics are particularly acute because the emphasis on teamwork and cooperation in each subunit only serves to accentuate the "us-versus-them" dynamic.

In the unionized workplace, there is an even greater potential for these kinds of problems arising when subunit-based change becomes the principal thrust of the initial labor-management problem-solving activity. This is because the dynamics of power are not only played out through the formal management structure, or even just through the formal structure and what the Human Relations Movement used to call the "informal system." Union power relationships must also be incorporated into this picture, especially as they relate to the status and influence that different groups, positions, and individuals have over daily life and key decisions in the workplace. Craft employees have a higher pay scale than semiskilled and unskilled workers, senior employees have first rights to higher paying and less physically demanding jobs, union leaders and shop stewards have seniority in the case of layoffs, craft workers do not cross over craft lines and do the work of other crafts, supervisors are not supposed to do the work of bargaining-unit employees, certain departments or employee groups may traditionally be the leaders of the union, and some departments and jobs are considered "gravy," or the best places to work, and therefore are the preserve of only the most senior and influential members of the union. These are only a few examples of the kinds of status and power relationships that are characteristic of the unionized workplace. It may be impossible to undertake any meaningful change activity without conflicting with some aspects of these status-quo conditions, but obviously it would be very unwise to challenge several of these "sacred cows" at the same time. Unfortunately, focusing cooperative problem solving primarily upon change within existing subunits can inadvertently result in just that as a particular department, group, or position is raised to a position of unusual and special attention compared to the past and compared to the rest of the organization. When this happens, and when it is combined with an emphasis on involving younger, highly motivated and energetic employees, the chances of long-term failure increase significantly. This will be more clearly illustrated by the case study described in the next section.

Sowing Failure from Success: A Case Study

The story of this particular cooperative partnership took place at a manufacturing facility owned by one of America's major manufacturers of medical equipment. This particular plant, which was located in the Great Lakes region of the United States, although small with a total of only slightly more than 200 employees, was a very important operation because of the high skill level of its unionized workforce and the technical flexibility of the plant. A job and small-batch manufacturing unit, this plant typically designed and manufactured difficult-to-make custom orders for all kinds of equipment and storage units used for sterilization and food handling in hospital settings. The hourly workforce were all members of the International Association of Machinists and Aerospace Workers (IAM).

Top management and union leaders at this operation decided to try and develop a labor-management cooperative partnership as a result of encouragement from the district leadership of the IAM and several discussions with a third-party consultant who was paid with federal government funds to assist with such efforts. A labor-management committee was formed at the plant with essentially equal representation from labor and management. Top union officers and the negotiating committee served as the union side, and the plant manager, his top management staff, and engineering and first-line supervisors served as the management representatives. After several meetings and some basic training provided by the consultant, the labor-management committee decided, at the consultant's suggestion, to move forward with a real problem-solving project, which in this case involved the development of a prototype to be sent to an industry convention in hopes of generating some badly needed new business. The plant manager, who we will call Henry Anderson, explains how the project got started:

> I don't know precisely what our consultant looked at when he came here, but he was looking for a common thread somewhere in the organization through which we could both experience winning, I believe, rather than either one or both of us experiencing losing as we had in the past.
>
> At that time we had a new product that was going to be produced here, and we were having engineering problems. We were under severe time constraints to produce a prototype to get to a convention so that this product could be made. And I believe that short period was about 2½ months. . . . That was unheard of considering the complexity of the type of thing we were trying to build, but what happened was that the union people got involved and we

set up a subcommittee to follow this and mini-task forces as it progressed down through the factory.

The idea for this came from our consultant. He was very active here at the time. He laid out the program and followed its progress each day, but, of course, he discussed with us the problems and how we could anticipate solving them mutually, and lo and behold, at the end of 2½ months we had a finished unit sitting on the shipping dock.

The committees were formed. This shop is a sheet-metal factory, and it pretty much goes like: "I shear the material, I punch the material, I bend it, I weld it, I clean it, I grind it, I assemble it, I test it, I ship it." Now you have to remember that there are four or five hundred different part numbers in this so it wasn't like making one part number of each. Those people accepted the responsibility of seeing that that thing progressed through their own department, made the people in the next department aware of what they had, and then the next department would pick it up. It moved right down through the factory with that communication thing going on out there without it being directed or supervised by the planning department or production or inventory control.

Thus, through cooperative problem solving and action, and with the help of their third-party consultant, labor and management succeeded in working together to produce a prototype for showing at the industry's major market convention, and they accomplished this in a time frame that would have been considered absolutely impossible prior to this effort. Unfortunately, although the unit was completed, it failed to function properly in testing because of several critical engineering design errors, and therefore it was not shown at the convention. The plant manager explained:

They pretty much picked that thing up and followed it and built it in 2½ months. . . . That was super! One thing that wasn't super, though, was that it was built to the engineering prints, and because of that engineering documentation the unit didn't really function properly, and so it didn't get to the show. But we did do it collectively as we had set out to do, and so that was certainly no loss.

Although Henry Anderson felt that actually completing a prototype through cooperative effort was a positive result which far outweighed the fact that the model never did get to the convention, in reality this incident created some very bad feelings, which in the end helped to undermine the overall partnership. The distrust created by the incident was especially severe. Management was so embarrassed about what had happened that they never actually told the union's leaders or the general membership that the prototype never reached the market convention, much less why it was not sent. Eventually, however, union leaders and the rank and file discovered through the grapevine what had happened, and predictably they were both angry and disappointed.

In spite of the bad feelings, the effort to create a cooperative partnership did not stop, and six months later the labor-management committee approved the conversion of an existing department to a self-managing work team. The decision to support this conversion was strongly motivated by the traditional union objective of trying to protect members' jobs. In December, plant manager Anderson announced to the labor-management committee and their consultant that the company had decided to introduce some new machinery into the plant's Sink-Polishing Department. He explained that this new equipment would eliminate three jobs unless some alternative and necessary work could be identified for the individuals who would be displaced by this change. Anderson offered to keep these people on if a viable solution could be proposed by the labor-management committee.

To the consultant, this offer presented a unique opportunity to get the labor-management committee interested and involved in a very serious transition to worker participation. He suggested that the department be essentially reformed into a self-managing work team. The consultant explained that this change would result in greater productivity and that it would also expand the job duties of all department members. Everyone would be capable of performing all departmental tasks, including the work of the supervisor, thus reducing overhead costs. The department seemed especially appropriate for this kind of intervention. Because it involved the dirtiest and least-skilled jobs in the plant, it was a prime area for job enrichment and participation. Furthermore, most of the workers were young and open to experimenting with new ideas and methods. The union, willing to do anything that might protect the jobs of its members, enthusiastically agreed to support the consultant's recommendation. The plant manager promised full support and cooperation from the management side.

One month later, the team concept was presented directly to the members of the Polishing Department as a group. Sixteen of the department's eighteen employees enthusiastically volunteered to participate in the conversion. The two employees who did not volunteer were the department's most senior and most skilled employees. These individuals were considerably older than the rest of the group. All of the following month of February was devoted to finalizing the formal project proposal and gaining the support of all union members. Finally, in March, the new, self-managing team was actually implemented as a pilot project, which would be evaluated and reviewed after an initial six-month trial period. Before implementation, the team members received extensive training in the new system, group problem solving and decision making, and, of course, all of the department's jobs, including the duties of the supervisor.

As the months passed, in most respects the Polishing Department improved significantly in its ability to operate as a self-managed team. Both productivity and quality improved dramatically, with rework and scrap reduced to almost nothing. Furthermore, turnover was reduced to almost zero. This was a major surprise, given the fact that the department was considered the least desirable place to work because of its dirty surroundings and heavy demands for physical exertion. Traditionally, the department had been the province of newly hired workers who bid out of the department as soon as they acquired enough seniority. This situation changed, however, and all but one of the sixteen original members of the self-managing team became firmly committed to the team concept. Even the two senior employees who had initially chosen not to participate eventually decided to join the team. These positive changes became particularly apparent when new labor-management problem-solving projects made requests for volunteers; the Polishing-Department team members applied for every new project that the labor-management committee initiated.

New attitudes toward work became evident beyond the case of cooperative activities. Several members of the Polishing Department had been notorious for their record of filing grievances and harassing supervisors. The dramatic turnaround in their behavior and attitudes surprised everyone. Instead of constantly complaining and overloading the grievance process with new grievances, these employees began focusing their energy on developing suggestions and ideas for improving departmental and plant performance. In short, the members of the Polishing Department became extraordinarily energized by their experience with self-management. When the six-month trial period was up they immediately requested a three-month extension, and when that period ended they again rallied for an additional three months. This second extension turned out to be their last, however, because of the intense internal union conflict the experiment eventually generated.

In spite of their strong performance on operational grounds and the enthusiasm of the Polishing-Department members for self-management, by the end of their first and only year of existence the team had garnered considerable ill will among their fellow employees and the plant's supervisors. In part, they had become victims of their own success and rather vocal enthusiasm, but there were also several other factors and conditions that ultimately helped lead to their demise. For example, from the beginning, employees in other departments believed that the Polishing Department was the recipient of undeserved "special treatment." This resentment began when a $10-per-week bonus was granted to all team members because they had learned all of the department's jobs and were willing to perform them on a rotating basis. Initially, plant manager Anderson had balked at the idea of the bonus because he feared that it might create "political problems" and "jealousy." The consultant, however, explained that the principle of payment for knowledge was central to the concept of a team-based work system, and that certainly an amount as small as $10 would not cause trouble. Small or not, the bonus produced an incredible amount of rancor among the rank and file. One Polishing-Department member explained:

> The bonus was pretty much like a sliver that started as just a little pain but gradually worked its way in with other irritations and then finally festered into a big sore.

If the $10 bonus had been the only source of irritation, perhaps the sore would have eventually healed. Unfortunately, it was just the first of several factors that generated ill will toward the self-managed team, and as the team proceeded to make various mistakes, the bonus only served to act as a constant reminder that the Polishing Department was getting something that nobody else had. One of the team's biggest errors was to occasionally engage in activities that others considered an abuse of freedom, and, even worse, team members tended to engage in these abuses in a manner that was public and visible to the rest of the plant.

For example, on one very hot summer day, several Polishing-Department members decided to have some fun and cool off by shooting water at each other. Although it started out small, this incident eventually grew to involve nearly the entire team, and a couple of employees even went so far in their "horseplay" as to shoot fire extinguishers at each other. By the time the "water fight" had ended, nearly everyone in the plant had heard and seen what was going on, and they were not impressed. Even worse, what happened afterward only served to further reinforce the impression that the Polishing Department was getting special privileges. Under normal circumstances, the employees involved would have been issued warning slips or possibly even suspended on the spot because of the serious safety hazard they had created. In this case, however, because there was no supervisor and because virtually everyone had been involved in the horseplay, there was no one capable of or interested in taking disciplinary action. Not surprisingly, this incident and several similar events deeply angered senior union members as well as plant supervisors, who were also seriously worried that the team system might eliminate their jobs.

Management's response did nothing to help mitigate the negative reactions created by the incident. Plant manager Anderson felt that he should act, but he was unsure what to do because fundamentally he was a strong supporter of self-management and he also did not want to do anything that might squelch the team's enthusiasm. He explained:

> We took a department . . . and we tried to condition those people to be self-managing without the benefit of any form of supervision. Here's one of the things where I think we made a mistake. I don't disagree with that philosophy, but I do disagree with the total philosophy of no supervisor. We put union people in a position where we wanted them

to make decisions, but they were not willing to make all their own decisions. Some of their decisions made it impossible to live with their own peers. And I am talking about the decision of having to write a man a warning slip for poor performance or for not being at work consistently— which was a serious problem with one employee before we started the project and got worse during its duration.

By the way, we still have a union contract, okay. So if a team member violates that contract, you can't expect those people to blow the whistle on themselves. So at least in the area of discipline, and maybe some others, there has to be some supervision around; not in the classic sense that we may all understand it—a guy stands back there and watches over your shoulder all day long—but some form of supervision to do those things that those people are not willing to do, or that they could not possibly do, because we have a union contract.

I still agree with the philosophy that people should have some control over their destiny each day and make some decisions but not all. . . . One of the problems that we had in particular . . . with the department is that it happens to be one of the most undesirable jobs in this factory; because not only is it strenuous, but it is also dirty and noisy too. You find that people with lesser seniority wind up in that department, and a few older people who seem to disregard the noise and dirt and have decided they like the job. So what we did is turn a bunch of young guys loose on a few older employees, and we started to generate so much interest and energy out of the younger people that they completely disregarded the needs of the older people. And they completely took over the department without any formal announcement that they had the authority to do this or even the ability to do it in some people's minds.

So I wound up with a terrible safety problem. They were down there feeling they could do anything they wanted to do. They were riding wheels around and hanging dirty pictures on the wall and all kinds of nutsy things that you know young people will do. You can expect it, I guess I just never anticipated it.

So we had a situation where a lot of people felt that the self-managing department was acting pretty peculiarly, and they were saying, "Why the hell does the company put up with that bunch of screwballs down there?" We weren't blind, we knew what was going on there too, but we thought it was a natural progression in these kinds of things. Okay, we didn't like what was going on there totally, but we thought it was just kind of natural.

What with our consultant being in and out of here so much he probably didn't know exactly what was going on down there either. . . . I recognized more than he did because I was here all the time, but I was negligent enough not to say, "Something awful crazy is happening, we have got to stop it whatever it is."

In addition to the problems that the Polishing-Department team created for itself as a result of occasional horseplay and its inability to deal with disciplinary issues, they also generated hostility because of their zealousness for improving and sustaining high levels of departmental productivity. The consultant explained:

The members of the self-managing team really developed a lot of enthusiasm for their work, and they were seriously concerned about keeping up the Polishing Department's productivity. Unfortunately, their enthusiasm sometimes led to some pretty obnoxious behavior. You see, when the team would get ahead in their work they would sometimes leave their work stations and go and badger the people in other departments that were feeding them work. And they weren't very diplomatic. They would say things like: "What's the matter with you? You're holding us up!"

You can imagine the kind of trouble that created. I told them to cut it out, but I don't think they really took me seriously.

Not surprisingly, reading the "riot act" to their peers in other departments gained the Polishing Department several new enemies in addition to those created by the disciplinary problems and the $10 weekly bonus. Thus, as time passed and the group moved through each new extension, it also became progressively more alienated from the rest of the plant. The consultant had anticipated that this problem of alienation, or encapsulation, would arise, although he probably didn't anticipate the reasons for it, and therefore, only a month after the Polishing Department became self-managed, he proposed converting two more departments—the Brake Department and the Stockroom—to the new system. The union, however, turned this proposal down because of upcoming contract negotiations. Nearly a year later, the consultant again attempted to diffuse the team system into new areas, and this time he proposed that a self-managing-team approach be adopted in the Paint Department. By this time, however, the Polishing Department had generated many enemies and had become a tremendous source of political turmoil. The department steward therefore firmly opposed the proposal, and self-management never progressed beyond the Polishing Department.

By the close of the Polishing Department's first year of functioning as a self-managed unit they had become so alienated from their peers that the situation was beyond repair. The oldest and most powerful union members were especially hostile toward the group and therefore the concept of self-management. Thus, when a third request for extension of the team system was proposed at the monthly lodge meeting of the local union, a bitter and heated argument ensued. Polishing-Department members made an impassioned plea for the extension, but the majority of union members attending opposed the proposal with a nearly unanimous negative vote. One former team member described the dynamics of this meeting:

> I will say there was a lot of jealousy. . . . It got so bad that we had a union meeting on Monday night, and the radicals who were against the project got a group together to make sure it didn't go on. They said something like, "The labor-management pilot project is over. The time limit for this pilot project has expired. You were only supposed to get six months, and then you got three more, and after that expired you got three months more extension. It's been a whole year and you guys are still going with this dumb project. . . . It's over, and we want it stopped! As of tomorrow morning, there's not going to be any more pilot project. You guys are supposed to have a boss, and there will be a boss!"
>
> They really hated the idea of us telling ourselves what to do instead of having a foreman. . . . It was so stupid and immature. You couldn't pound it into their heads with a

20-pound sledge hammer. They told us, "Tomorrow morning you guys will go down there and stand around until the foreman comes and tells you what to do!"

Thus, the self-managing work team was formally dissolved. Yet, in spite of this action, the system continued on an informal basis with a supervisor mainly serving as a coordinator and occasionally as an authority to take disciplinary action. Institutionally, though, self-managing work teams were dead and the very idea of them was anathema throughout the plant. Labor-management cooperation was also severely damaged, but it was still not quite dead. Other projects had kept the project alive in spite of the political conflict generated by the Polishing Department.

One cooperative problem-solving strategy that proved particularly beneficial to all parties involved was "cooperative job costing," or the combined effort of engineers, managers, and shop-floor workers in the development of cost estimates for subcontract bids. Approximately one year after the initial formation of the partnership, plant manager Anderson received a memo from corporate headquarters stating that the company was willing to manufacture a number of products in-house that had previously been contracted to outside suppliers. Enclosed was a list of twenty-five different items, and the memo indicated that any of the firm's many plants could produce any of these items if they could demonstrate that they could do so at a lower price than either outside suppliers or internal competitors. This was an interesting offer, but, like the prototype project, it had to be acted upon in a very short time frame. Anderson knew that struggling to meet this deadline would severely strain the plant's management and industrial engineering staff, but he was hesitant to pass up the opportunity because business had slowed markedly and he knew he would have to lay off a large number of workers if new orders were not secured very soon.

The consultant suggested that the plant try to develop a bid for only one item, but to do it well using the resources of the labor-management committee. After considering this proposal, Anderson asked the union to recruit several factory workers to help with the project by working directly with the industrial engineering estimating team. He explained:

> We needed work pretty badly. Our market was starting to drop off. I was afraid that our costs were going up. So I

took a look around this corporation for a product that we could do here, and I found one that was being produced by a vendor. I went to the union and told them that what I would like them to do is take a look at these charts—there was about a million and a half dollars worth of sales in there—and have them give me a quote for the corporation. And if the quote was equal to or better than the existing costs, then I'd get the product for them. So what we did was ask for six volunteers from the factory to work as industrial engineers for whatever period was required to complete that piece of work. I took one of my most astute I.E. people and put him in a room with them, and we taught them what they needed to know to do.this piece of work. How to put the weldings on the piece of paper, what the machine numbers were. In the area of standards, which we had to have, we gave them permission to go out on the floor to ask questions and query how long it would take.

The six-person team worked for an entire month to produce a complete package of material and labor cost estimates for the potential new in-house product, which was called the "transfer loading car" (a stainless-steel cabinet on wheels used for delivering meals in hospitals). Several members of the Sink-Polishing Department's self-managed team volunteered for the project along with about an equal number of volunteers from other parts of the plant. This highly motivated group worked aggressively, moving back and forth between collecting data from their peers and vendors and then analyzing and compiling it. Having been released from their normal duties to work full-time on this project, the Job Costing Task Force became deeply immersed in the task, as Henry Anderson explains:

> What happened was those guys were so energetic. . . . I'm telling you that I couldn't stay out of that conference room or keep myself from wanting to get involved after I saw the way they were working. I'd go in there and they'd be talking, and I'd see them go down to get a cup of coffee past my office and they weren't talking about football, they were talking about that damn car. In fact, I really first realized just how serious they were about the project when a very funny incident took place. One day I popped my head in

the door and one guy started to say, "That S.O.B. . . . " and then they saw me and he shut up and didn't say anything more. So I said, "Ah, come on now, you can say anything in front of me. What were you talking about?" So the guy said, "Okay I'll tell you. You see I was out in the welding area, and I asked this one guy what the standard was for a certain job and he gave me a bad standard. . . . So I asked him a second time in a different way and then two more times after that. He was still giving me a bad standard, and I knew it. I finally got pretty frustrated and said, 'Is this the proper standard?' He still insisted it was, so what I started to say was, 'If that S.O.B. doesn't care about bringing this work into the shop, then we're just going to have to contract it out!' "

That really surprised me. You know, if you want to get into a real pow-wow with the union all that you have to do is go out and start talking about subcontracting out work, and you'll have a pretty terrible thing on your hands. But they were really seeing how that can happen at that time. I think that project was really a high point in our whole labor-management program.

After a month of intensive work, the Job Costing Task Force had completed their assignment, and the job of selling the bid to the corporation was passed on to the plant manager. He explained:

And from that piece of work we came up with a standard that could save the corporation about $90,000 a year. So I kept my end of the bargain and went out and lobbied hard to get those cars in here, but with a $90,000 egg in my pocket, I really didn't have much of a problem.

Thus, as a result of cooperative problem solving the transfer loading car became an ongoing part of the plant's regular production for a minimum of three years. The $90,000 savings gave the corporation a 15-percent cost reduction, and forty jobs were saved because of the $1.5 million in new business that this new product brought to the plant.

Because of the unquestionable success of this problem-solving project, the labor-management committee became a permanent part of the costing out of other products and orders.

Substantial new business was brought to the plant as a result of this new cooperative strategy for subcontract bidding, and therefore the job security of the plant's workers was greatly enhanced, even though this took place during a period of economic recession. Unfortunately, despite the undisputed success of this partnership activity and its clearly beneficial effects for both labor and management, even this effort eventually contributed to the partnership's demise. In subsequent job-costing projects, the same employees continued to be the principal participants in the process, and because several of these individuals were also members of the Polishing-Department team, many employees came to view these costing efforts as just one more example of the "junior employees" taking over the self-managed team. They believed it was a case of "the tail wagging the dog."

This perception, and the ill feelings that had evolved over nearly two years of labor-management cooperative programs and projects, finally contributed to the complete dissolution of the partnership some two years after it had first been formed. Ironically, it was an aggressive initiative to try and protect workers' jobs from an imminent cutback, much like the situation that had prompted the union to support creation of a self-managing team, that this time precipitated the downfall of cooperation. By this point, however, the prospect of continued and even heightened internal political conflict caused union members to choose to let people be laid off rather than endure more turmoil.

In this case, plant manager Anderson, when faced with a significant downturn in orders and the possible layoff of a significant portion of the workforce, proposed that twelve workers be retained out of the total that would normally have been laid off. He called the alternative that he proposed "Employment Maintenance," and it involved having the twelve employees function as full-time facilitators and members of cooperative problem-solving groups that would work on a long list of items that the labor-management committee had identified as top priority for joint action. Through these efforts it was hoped that the jobs of these twelve workers would be retained and that through their efforts orders could also be increased making it possible to bring back the employees who had been laid off, thus increasing the job security of everyone. What Anderson did not realize was that his proposal also had the potential of significantly exacerbating the internal political schisms that the partnership had already helped to create within the union. It was not long after he brought the plan before the labor-management committee that this situation became apparent. He explained:

> The marketing forecast for the facility had decayed pretty badly. . . . We had received one very large order a year and a half ago . . . and that had caused us to hire a whole bunch of people to do this thing in January, February, and March. But after that our conventional products—those that would normally support this organization—were dropping off pretty dramatically, and we were going to have a pretty damn bad layoff. So I went to the union in hopes that we could get more involvement . . .
>
> I approached them in this fashion: "Gentlemen, we are going to have a layoff, and it's going to be pretty severe." I think thirty-some people were going to be laid off, which at least at this place is pretty severe. I told the union, "We are willing to retain some of these people on what I prefer to call project work."
>
> They seemed to think that was a pretty good idea. As union representatives, they felt that it was their job to help keep jobs here and to stabilize employment. . . . And so what we did was we sat down as a committee, and we made a list of what turned out to be thirty-seven items that we felt needed to be done. Some of these were mine, some of them were theirs, some were quite involved, and some were pretty superficial. . . . What I wanted to do was get a lot of different people involved from outside of that department (you know, the Sink-Polishing department) so that a lot of people could experience all of this. We wanted to do a welding program, for example. There were lots of things that would have got lots of people involved.
>
> So what we did was we finally boiled it down to where I felt I had an obligation to retain people who had four or more years' seniority but not the whole group that had come in on that special order. That came down to twelve people. That's a lot of money on a yearly basis. We also had to agree on who was going to work and not going to work as coordinators for these projects, and we really got into a hassle over this.

What we had was thirty-seven projects and twelve people from the factory to work on them with some guidance from the rest of the factory. So there were more projects than people to go around. So we tried to prioritize them and say that the twelve people would be absorbed in these three projects for the next three months, and after that we may pick twelve more and do it like that. But when the union went back to make their presentation to the membership, they got into an argument over who would do this work.

The most senior man in some cases would say, "Hey, I want to go into the office and do that, and I have the most seniority, so I should be permitted to do that." And in other cases the most senior man would say, "Hey, I want to stay out here and run my machine. It should be the least senior man that should do that." So here I was . . . saying, "If we've got a five-man team working on welding, I've got to have at least one experienced welder on it or I'm going to have to teach the whole group to weld before we can even start." So the intermingling of these philosophies caused the union to ask for a special meeting. . . . The union president came into my office and asked for the meeting at 2:00 P.M. They had the largest turn-out for a union meeting they had ever had, even for the ratification of a contract. In fact, everybody was there . . .

Just before the meeting the union president came in and talked with me and told me what he was going to do. I didn't want to be giving this fellow advice, but when I heard what he planned, it really scared me. He and his committee had fallen into a great deal of disfavor because they were totally dedicated to this concept of cooperation. Just a month before this big vote we'd put him, his entire committee, and some members of the self-managing team on an airplane and flew them to Philadelphia where they did a dog-and-pony show on what we'd been doing. They had also flown to Washington, D.C., to talk at a conference. . . . A lot of union folks were pretty jealous about these trips, and so I was pretty worried when the union president came in and told me, "I'm going to put this proposal before the whole body, and if they don't accept it, I am going to resign." That was just what he did. He got up in the union meeting and basically said these words, "I have a proposal to put in front of you, and if you don't agree with me, then you're voting down labor-management altogether, and I'm going to resign." And what with him being in disfavor anyway, everybody clapped and then they voted everything out the door in one big sweep—him, the idea of employment maintenance, and the whole labor-management program.

Conclusion

In this chapter we have presented some of the conditions that are unique to the unionized workplace that must be under constant consideration whenever a company decides to embark upon joint problem-solving activity. As can be seen, the potential pitfalls are many, but ignoring these issues can be perilous, as the last case study illustrates.

In the next chapter we will focus more specifically on the strategies and techniques that can be employed in initiating and managing cooperative projects and programs. Against the backdrop of political and social dynamics discussed in this chapter, the logic underlying the approaches we will suggest for project implementation should be far more clear and their importance immediately apparent.

References

Cohen-Rosenthal, Edward, and Burton, Cynthia E. *Mutual Gains: A Guide to Union-Management Cooperation.* Westport, CN: Praeger, 1987.

Habermas, Jurgen. *Theory and Practice.* Boston: Beacon Press, 1973.

7

The Nuts and Bolts of Project Implementation and Management

At this point we hope that the reader has not decided in despair that unionized workplaces are just so complex and filled with political intrigue and conflict that it is far too risky to try to undertake the development of a cooperative partnership in these environments. We realize that confronting the realities of the unionized workplace can be intimidating, but developing a successful labor-management partnership is not an impossible task. It can be done, and there are strategies and techniques that can be used to make the job much easier and less prone to the kinds of problems that were described in Chapter 6. In this chapter our emphasis will be upon these positive actions that can be used to build an effective and enduring cooperative relationship.

Project Selection

As we pointed out in Chapter 6, determining the right project or projects for starting a partnership involves selecting those issues that both the union and the company have a vested interest in resolving, while at the same time carefully avoiding problems that have a high potential for inflaming existing political tensions or creating new ones. The key group responsible for this task is the steering committee. Other groups and individuals can also be tapped for opinions and preferences, but during the early phases of developing a cooperative partnership it is usually wiser to seek this input *after* the projects have been selected and the range of issues has been carefully reduced to a more narrowly defined problem-solving task. As the partnership grows in experience and maturity and the number of direct participants increases, collecting opinions from large numbers of employees on a wide variety of issues involves much less risk.

There are many techniques that can be used to generate a list of items that are worthy of joint problem-solving attention, ranging from simple procedures like group brainstorming to more involved processes such as the nominal group technique. Whatever techniques are chosen, however, they should in all cases facilitate the accomplishment of two very important process goals. First, this should be an exercise in working together. It should enable the members from both sides to share their opinions and to experience areas of commonality as well as difference. Therefore, it is wise to break the steering committee up into small mixed groups of union and management representatives, at different points during the process, to generate ideas, alternatives, and preferences.

On the other hand, it is also important to respect the existing system by allowing union and management members of the steering committee sufficient time to discuss the issues and proposals under consideration in private, strictly among themselves. This latter point is particularly important when it comes to weighing the political risks involved with one course of action as opposed to another. It is very difficult and risky for either the union or management to openly discuss their own internal political problems and vulnerabilities in front of the other party. Thus, if in the name of cooperation the steering committee attempts to consider all matters strictly through open joint discussion, it is very likely that important political considerations will either be completely ignored or that the two parties will automatically entirely remove certain issues from the realm of cooperative discussion.

In the beginning, it is especially important to link problem-solving projects directly to the philosophy statement that was incorporated into the written Labor-Management Charter Agreement. One simple technique for doing this is for the group to select one or two of the goals or values that they have identified as central to the partnership, such as "creating a more productive workplace" or "increasing employee job security," and then, using a simple "force-field analysis," to identify those positive factors in the workplace that are acting as *driving forces* as well as those negative factors that are acting as *inhibiting forces* in relation to achieving the desired goal or state. Of course, more complex and sophisticated approaches can be used to accomplish this task, but the emphasis should be on generating data and creating a shared appreciation without too much complexity. And because this is an open-ended and low-risk task, it is an early and very good point for breaking into smaller mixed labor-management subgroups to generate several analyses. How and when to break into small mixed subgroups depends, of course, on the particular situation, but this is usually a good time and a safe way in which to start.

From the several subgroup-developed force-field analyses, which are presented to the entire group by each labor-management team, a larger analysis for the entire steering committee can be generated. Once the group has reached this point, it can begin to prioritize or assign weights to the negative or inhibiting forces that need to be removed.

The reason for focusing on the negative factors that need to be removed flows from the overall logic of force-field analysis. Inhibiting, or negative, forces tend to behave like springs. If positive forces are increased, or more pressures toward achieving the desired state are added, then the inhibiting forces do not disappear. They tend, rather, to intensify, similar to metal springs being compressed, and they may eventually push back with even greater force, negating the new driving forces. The use of disciplinary intervention to deal with behavioral problems is probably the classic example of these dynamics.

One example of this phenomenon is illustrated by the case of a large oil refinery located in southern California. Over the years, this refinery has developed a chronic situation in which its maintenance workers quit work earlier and earlier each day so that they can be at the head of the line racing to their cars to go home as soon as the whistle blows marking the change of shift. This problem typically runs in six-month cycles, with workers at the beginning of the period following the rules and stopping for clean-up just ten minutes before the shift change. As time progresses, however, quitting time becomes increasingly early, until the majority of workers, who are within walking distance of the refinery gate, stand at the entrance about thirty minutes before the whistle blows. At this point, management traditionally responds by positioning supervisors behind oil and fuel tanks to wait for the first workers who head for the gate and catch them by surprise. They then issue warning slips and suspensions. After a few surprise attacks, made on random days, the workforce again becomes sufficiently fearful of losing pay, or even their jobs, that they return to obeying the rules and quitting for clean-up at the official time. By the time another six-month period passes, the same process is repeated. The change is never sustained because it is too costly for management to maintain constant surveillance of the workers, and, in accordance with the logic of force-field analysis, employees simply find new ways to get out of work. For a change to last, it would first be necessary to remove the negative factors that cause workers to want to escape from the workplace as early as possible and that prevent them from experiencing their daily work as interesting and meaningful.

Since most labor-management partnerships begin with reactive problem solving, it is wise to start by trying to remove the factors that prevent the parties from realizing some of the goals and values that they have jointly defined as official for the partnership. Actually deciding which issue or issues to tackle requires evaluating them in terms of all of the key points that were discussed in Chapter 6 including:

1. How significant is this factor in terms of preventing us from reaching our desired state or goal? Will removing this obstacle really make a difference?

2. How important is it to each party to resolve the problem or problems associated with this factor?

3. Where does this issue rank in terms of how simple or complex it will be to tackle?

4. How expensive is it likely to be to solve this problem, and how long and complicated will the process be for securing the funds required to solve it?

5. Given the present maturity of the partnership, how significant are the political risks involved with this issue in terms of the internal dynamics of the union and management organizations and the relationship between the parties?

Evaluating issues in light of these dimensions requires the input and joint decision making of both parties, but the initial evaluations can probably be most productively handled by breaking the group into separate union and management meetings. That is, the representatives from each side meet together privately, in a different room or even a different building, and they then evaluate each of the items in terms of all of the dimensions cited above.

These separately held meetings are called *caucuses,* and they are an approach mediators commonly use in collective bargaining by to help the parties clearly identify their most important points of disagreement and agreement and then move toward developing alternative positions they are willing to accept. The caucus is an extremely valuable technique because it is a practice with which both parties are familiar and comfortable, and it is also a relatively *safe environment* in which the members of each organization, the union and the company, can openly air their internal differences and then resolve them so that they can present a united front to the other party. In this context, both parties can more freely discuss the political problems associated with any particular issue, and they can then decide whether or not it is worth the risk to confront these particular problems or perhaps wiser to set them aside for future action.

Although the caucus is a valuable and effective tool, OD consultants sometimes feel very uncomfortable with it because it seems to reinforce the system of secrecy that already shrouds the collective-bargaining process, breeding distrust and encouraging manipulation. Caucuses may seem to prevent the parties from engaging in the open and honest dialogue that is necessary to solve the problems that confront them. To some extent this may be true, but, as we have illustrated, it is far more dangerous to move forward with a course of action without carefully weighing the political risks to either party. We have found that the frequent and creative use of separate union and management caucuses can be a valuable tool for addressing these problems and ensuring the long-term success of cooperative activities.

Again, many different techniques have been devised for comparing and evaluating alternative choices. Any of these methods are probably adequate for performing the task, depending upon how much time is available to devote to this part of the analysis. For example, one approach to developing an evaluation could be to have every member rank each inhibiting factor raised through the force-field analysis in terms of the five dimensions that we have recommended, and then through group discussion a common evaluation for use in identifying the most through the least preferred issue for joint action can be generated. Another approach could be to have every participant rate individual factors on a Likert scale in terms of key dimensions. In other words, each possible issue for cooperative action would be rated from 1 to 5 in terms of Very Important to Very Unimportant, or High Political Risk to Low Political Risk, etc. Whatever approach is used to accomplish this task, it should be remembered that the principal objective is to get honest and complete information out in the open within each caucus group so that they can collectively evaluate the best and worst avenues for joint action from their respective positions.

Once the issues have been evaluated and prioritized for action by both of the parties in separate caucuses, then each group's ranking and evaluation should be shared in a joint session of the steering committee. Each side should show the other its evaluation and explain the reasoning behind it. As one party presents its evaluation, the other should freely ask for clarification on items that are confusing, but argument and debate should be avoided until both sides have presented their analyses. Even seeking information for greater understanding and clarification should be handled with some degree of reserve and respect for the other party's need for confidentiality, particularly in terms of discussions related to evaluations of political risk. If either side feels that a particular item involves too much political risk from their perspective, then this concern should be respected, and the group should not be forced to publicly reveal its internal problems beyond what it feels comfortable sharing. As time passes and the leaders of both sides work together on more and more issues and trust increases, open discussion of political concerns will become more frequent and natural. In the beginning, these matters must be handled with sensitivity and care.

Once the evaluation of issues has been shared by both management and the union, the steering-committee members must work together to determine which issues they wish to tackle first through cooperative problem solving. This can be accomplished through open discussion and debate, or any appropriate group-process intervention can be used to help them move toward closure. If the group is fortunate, they will discover that their evaluations are surprisingly similar. If they find that this is not the case, then a lot of discussion—and some creative use of group-process techniques—may be necessary. In either case, it is best for the group to reach their decision through consensus decision making. If they have not yet become fully familiar with consensus decision-making processes, then it might be advisable for them to acquire some training before trying to reach a group decision on what items to tackle first. Many simulation exercises on group decision making are available.

Deciding Where to Begin

Once the steering committee has reached a consensus on those issues that they wish to tackle through cooperative problem solving, the next step is to select the organizational location or locations where the problem-solving activity should first begin. As we have illustrated in Chapter 6, this is an extremely important decision, and it should be made carefully through joint discussion and decision making.

Tackling an issue on a plantwide or even a companywide basis, unless the plant or company is very small, can be risky because projects are frequently complex and a very long period of time may transpire between the project's inception and the final realization of visible change in the workplace. On the other hand, as we have seen from the examples in Chapter 6, it can also be risky to begin a process of cooperative problem solving and organizational change in a single subunit, such as a department or section, because such efforts so frequently become isolated from the rest of the organization and end up as the objects of jealousy and ridicule. Thus, if starting very big or very small can both be problematic, then where is the best place to begin?

The question of site or location selection interacts to some extent with the question of issue selection. An issue that can engage representatives from several departments and that is focused and concrete also helps determine where in the organization the partnership should begin its problem-solving efforts. In other words, an ideal place to begin is with an issue that can result in tangible change, that both workers and managers value, in two or more subunits that are either directly or indirectly related to each other.

By bringing representatives from several departments together to solve a problem of common concern or interest, cooperation is generated between labor and management and also between organizational subunits that are either directly or indirectly interdependent. Most importantly, the likelihood of the project becoming "encapsulated" and generating political conflict becomes severely, if not entirely, curtailed. Departments or sections that normally would become critical of each other and jealous or resentful if only one group had been singled out as the focus of cooperative activity instead become linked together in a common effort. This is the ideal context in which to pursue any labor-management problem-solving endeavor, but *it is especially important in the case of a newly forming partnership.*

Which issues may fit this context depend on the particular workplace in which the partnership is being formed, but certainly such opportunities abound in any organization. The prototype project described in Chapter 6, for example, certainly had the potential for creating cooperation and unity at many levels. This was a very specific and narrowly defined task that actually involved everyone in the organization pulling together to accomplish a common goal that required everyone's input and cooperation. Unfortunately, in this case, the Engineering Department worked too independently in developing the design specifications, and as a result, the prototype failed to operate properly and could not be shown at the industry trade show. This problem was, in turn, further complicated by management's failure to respond honestly and openly by telling the union and workers what had happened. The prototype project did not fail, however, because it was too complex, too expensive, or too time consuming, and therefore, we can state that it did in fact very successfully meet the requirement: The task was narrow enough in scope so that it could be completed and implemented in a reasonable period of time, and it was broad enough in terms of the range of departments involved so that encapsulation and political conflict could be avoided.

Although the prototype project was ideal because of its narrow scope and broad-based participation, it is by no means mandatory to begin a labor-management partnership with problem-solving efforts that encompass an entire organization. It is wise, though, to focus on an activity that will require the input of least two subunits and that will also directly benefit more than one of these groups in some tangible way upon completion. Again, there are many opportunities to identify these kinds of problem-solving tasks in any organization. As an example, the labor-management steering committee at one small metal-fabricating company where we consulted identified a problem-solving project that had the potential for removing inhibiting forces that were preventing the realization of at least three of the partnership's key goals:

1. Stable employment and working hours.
2. Efficient utilization of labor.
3. Maximum utilization of capital equipment.

The operation employed a highly skilled workforce and had many expensive machines that were used for cutting, bending, shaping, molding, and welding metal into a variety of shapes and forms. Because the company received many small and unique orders, ranging from large applications such as machinery housings for power-generation equipment to small applications such as filing cabinets for U.S. Navy ships, it was constantly required to design and make new and unique tooling in terms of dies and molds.

As tooling had accumulated over the years, the company had failed to expand its storage facilities for these tools, and it had never created a system for monitoring and recording their disposition and location. Consequently, tools were laying all over the shop, and there was no particular logic to their placement. The end result was that machine operators were often standing at their machines with no work to do while they waited for highly skilled and expensive set-up workers, who were spending their time looking for tools (an average of two to three hours per day) instead of setting up the machines. Moreover, this had repercussions throughout the factory, both for the departments ahead that were feeding the machines that were idle and for the departments that were waiting for work. Feeding departments became jammed with piles of cut or bent metal that was waiting to go to the next operation to be further bent and shaped, and sometimes departments down the line had to quit work early because they weren't getting all the parts they needed to complete welding, assembling, or packing orders. In short, the situation was intolerable. The problem had become expensive to the company, and it threatened the workers' job security and income. Likewise, the situation, directly or indirectly, had a negative impact on nearly everyone in the factory at one time or another.

The steering committee realized that solving this problem would benefit a wide range of groups and individuals. At the same time, the problem itself was narrow enough in scope—in effect, designing and implementing a storage, cataloguing, and security system for tools—that it could be resolved in a period of months, at a reasonable cost, and with an end result that would be visible to everyone. It is this kind of project that is ideal for forging a spirit of cooperation, especially during the formative stages of a labor-management partnership.

Who Should Participate

Once the issue or issues to be tackled through cooperative problem solving have been defined and the organizational locations where the effort should begin have been selected, the individuals who will participate must be recruited. This too is an extremely important decision, and it is less straightforward than simply finding those individuals who have the technical expertise and experience required to solve the problem selected. Generating commitment to the solution among those employees who will actually have to implement it, contributing process learning to the steering committee, and avoiding political conflict are all equally important considerations when it comes to recruiting the participants.

Table 7.1 provides an illustration of a tool that can be employed to ensure that all of these considerations are given weight when recruiting task force members. We call this tool a *task force recruiting chart,* and it is very simple to use. Across the top of the chart are listed all the departments, skills, and functions that should be represented on the problem-solving team. In other words, the categories that are entered across the top for each column represent all of the technical knowledge and experience that are necessary to handle the task that has been selected and also the departments that will be directly and indirectly involved in implementing the final solution. Across the left-hand side of the chart is a list of categories that are important in terms of social and political considerations. In this case, the categories listed include those groups or classes of employees who should be involved in order to preclude such future adverse consequences as political conflict, misunderstanding between groups, or discriminatory impact on certain employee groups such as female and minority workers and managers.

Table 7.1
Task Force Recruiting Chart: Technical and Political Considerations

Political Considerations	Technical Considerations					E.D.P.		
	Setup Person	Machine Operator	Sub-assembly Welding	Industrial Engineer	Maintenance-Construction	Inventory Data	Purchasing	Stores
Senior workers	x						x	
Senior managers				x	x			
Junior workers		x						x
Junior managers			x					
Female employees			x			x		
Minority employees	x			x				
Professional office staff						x		
Competing union faction		x						
First-line supervisors			x					
Steering committee				x				

Table 7.1 illustrates how this selection process worked in solving the tool-storage and inventory problem described in the previous section. In this case, the group first identified eight functions, skills, and departments that should be represented in the group in terms of technical and implementation considerations. They next listed all of the categories that they felt should be included to prevent the development of political and social problems. In this case, they identified ten categories that they believed were important. Once all of these categories had been identified, the steering committee recruited individuals whose qualifications cut across all of the criteria that were considered important. As can be seen from Table 7.1, the group was able to fill all of the cells with recruits from the key technical and implementation categories that they had identified without adding other members to meet their social and political criteria. As a result of taking these initial actions to ensure that all important groups were recruited, both the problem-solving and the implementation processes proceeded smoothly, without encountering any obstacles arising from a lack of technical ability or from internal conflict between management levels, departments, or union factions.

The actual selection of the representatives on a task force or subcommittee follows the same process that was employed for organizing the steering committee. Management is responsible for selecting the managerial and professional employees who will represent the company. Likewise, the union has full responsibility and freedom to select and recruit its representatives. It can be useful, however, for the two groups, or at least the management and union cochairpersons, to discuss their choices before actually recruiting the participants.

Although each side has sole responsibility and authority for deciding who their representatives will be, and the other party has no power to reverse this decision, there may be some instances when one party's choice presents either political or technical problems for the other side. For example, management may select a supervisor who is strongly disliked by employees. The company may feel that the individual is just misunderstood or that he or she could benefit from participating in labor-management problem solving by learning how to work cooperatively. These are both valid reasons for selecting such a person, especially if that person has special skills or technical knowledge that will be critical in solving the assigned problem. But if this choice makes it almost impossible for the union to recruit anyone to work on the group, then it might be wise for management to reconsider its choice.

Conversely, the union may want to recruit a participant whose skills and duties are so critical that it would negatively affect the work flow if this employee had to leave the job to attend frequent meetings. In such a case, perhaps the union should reconsider its choice in light of its potential impact on daily operations. Of course, once an offer has been extended, it is extremely difficult to reverse, and this is why we recommend that the union and management get together to discuss their choices before recruiting begins. By jointly consulting before approaching potential task force or subcommittee participants, the two sides can discuss any points of difficulty as well as determine whether their combined choices do indeed satisfy all of the technical, political, and social considerations.

Vague Objectives and Insufficient Guidance: Sources of Failure

Launching a new task force or subcommittee on its assigned task and ensuring that the group satisfactorily accomplishes what it has been assigned are among the key responsibilities of the steering committee and its union and management cochairpersons. A bad start can almost certainly ensure the failure of many task forces and subcommittees, whereas a well-structured and well-thought-out directive from the steering committee can go a long way toward guaranteeing that even a weak group will succeed. Effective management of the problem-solving process by the cochairpersons and the steering committee can also play a very significant role in helping task forces and subcommittees to stay on track and remain highly motivated in performing their task.

Most of the time, however, labor-management partnerships either ignore or inadequately handle the processes of proper initiation, management, and support of task force and subcommittee activities. Time and again, we have seen management and union leaders intentionally avoid giving clear directives or abstain from intervening directly in the activities of the problem-solving teams that they have initiated. When we have asked them why they adopted this "hands-off" policy, the answer is invariably the same. As one manager explained:

We don't want to squelch the group's creativity or prevent a real feeling of participation by getting too actively involved in what they are doing. They should feel free to make their own decisions and to follow their own ideas and instincts.

In the abstract, this strategy for dealing with problem-solving activities may seem reasonable. In the real world, however, this approach seldom works as it was intended, and often the consequences are frustration—for both the steering committee and the problem-solving group—and even total failure for the entire effort. What was intended to produce a sense of empowerment and personal responsibility instead seems to create confusion, leaving the problem-solving team members wondering what they are *really* supposed to be doing. Thus, rather than feeling empowered to act according to their own intuition and on their own initiative, problem-solving groups in these situations tend to behave very cautiously and conservatively.

In effect, what seems to develop is an attitude very much like that of students in a new class in which the professor or teacher provides no syllabus or guide describing the expected course study schedule and grading procedures. In these situations, the teacher usually tells the students that he or she wants to have an atmosphere of equality and freedom in the classroom, and that they, the students, should feel free to speak frankly and openly about their opinions and feelings. The students are told it is up to them to decide what they are going to learn and how they want to go about learning it. To some students, this declaration of democracy in the classroom may sound wonderful, but for average students, who are concerned about their final grade or who have had this kind of experience before, frustration and cynicism usually develop. The students know that they are not equal to the professor or teacher in the classroom or in the larger system, and they also know that ultimately it will be the faculty member who will decide whether or not they have done a good job by determining their final grade. Thus, instead of developing a sense of freedom and participation, the students behave very cautiously, either playing a "cat-and-mouse game" with the faculty member, trying to figure out what the teacher really wants, or becoming engaged in a prolonged process of haggling over every detail of the workload and grading procedure in an attempt to get the best conditions possible for an "easy A" and to protect themselves from the chance of future cavalier actions on the part of the instructor. In our own college, for example, several professors who joined together to team teach a special seminar on advanced topics for graduate students attempted to create this kind of student-empowered classroom. In this case, although the students had already experienced a considerable degree of freedom in their program, they still used up nearly a third of the semester trying to decide such matters as what topics they would study, who would have to present how much material, and how they would eventually be graded.

Very similar dynamics seem to take place when a labor-management subcommittee or task force is created without the provision of a clearly defined problem-solving task and the ongoing support and direction of union and management leaders. For example, at one 800-employee firm where we consulted and conducted research for several years, and where an effort to create a labor-management partnership had already been underway for about one year when we first became involved, a plantwide "productivity-improvement" subcommittee had been established by the steering committee some seven months earlier.

The members of this group had been carefully selected, and participating in this effort was a good cross section of the entire plant, including different political factions and age groups as well as female and minority-group employees. However, the union and management cochairpersons of the steering committee asked for consulting assistance to this group because even after seven months of weekly or biweekly meetings, the productivity subcommittee still said it was not ready to propose any concrete actions to the steering committee. Sitting in on this group's meetings was both a surprise and a disappointment.

Although they had received some initial training in group problem solving and meeting effectiveness, the members seemed to wander from topic to topic with little direction or purpose. A long list of problems had been generated by the group, some clearly related to labor productivity and some apparently unrelated to this issue, and throughout the meeting different individuals would suggest that they begin trying to work on one item or another. In response, other group members would either agree or give reasons why the issue suggested was not appropriate. Frequently, subcommittee members would say things like, "I don't

think that's what the steering committee *really* had in mind."
Then they would give a long list of reasons why this item was not
what the steering committee *really wanted them to do*. On several occasions, they would also turn to their new consultants and
say, "Do you know if this is the kind of problem that the steering
committee *really* wants us to be working on?" Curious about
these dynamics, we inquired about the subcommittee's life and
experience thus far, and we learned that when they were first organized, the only direction they received was the instruction to
"feel free to tackle any subject or problem you feel is important."
We also learned that throughout the entire seven months, they
had never had a formal reporting meeting with the steering committee or cochairpersons and no leader had ever sat in on any of
their meetings to offer advice or guidance or even just to observe
their activities. When asked if they thought the steering committee did not really mean that they were free to work on any issue
that they wanted to address, everyone seemed to agree with the
following response that was given by a supervisor who had been
assigned to the subcommittee:

> Oh, come on now. You've got to be kidding! They're the
> bosses and union big shots around here. They know what
> they want done and what they don't want done, but they
> won't tell us exactly what's on their minds. I mean if we
> stick our noses into some area they really don't want us
> to, or if we step on somebody's toes without knowing it,
> then, you know, we're all gonna be in hot water. This is a
> big plant. There's all kinds of things around here that are
> hurting our productivity. How are we supposed to know
> what they *really* want us to work on, and how are we sup-
> posed to know what things we shouldn't stick our noses
> into? All we can do is guess. So we just sit here in these
> meetings every week and go around in circles trying to
> figure out what the steering committee really wants from
> us.

When we heard this, we asked the group if they had asked
the steering committee or cochairpersons what they thought they
should be doing. Another employee responded by saying:

> We tried that several times at first, but all they said to us
> was the same thing, "That's up to you to decide. Do what-

ever you guys think is best. It's your decision." So we gave up asking, and ever since we've been trying to figure out what we're supposed to do.

In effect, this labor-management group had become paralyzed by both the immensity of potential problems that they could possibly tackle—the issue was too broad—and the uncertainty they faced regarding the true interests and agenda of their leaders. When we asked the company and union presidents why they had not given the group more initial direction regarding their task or provided clarification and direction later on in the process, they both said:

> We didn't want to influence what they did too much. This is supposed to be all about cooperation and participation. We thought that if we got too much involved in what they were doing, then they would just do what we thought and not do what they really thought was best.

So despite both the company and union leadership's good intentions, they had created a situation that was the opposite of what they actually desired. Rather than inhibiting a group's effectiveness and the degree of individual participation, a clear task definition and set of objectives, as well as continuous communication and guidance from the steering committee, can actually free group members from confusion and uncertainty, thereby enabling them to participate freely and actively in the problem-solving process.

Effective Initiation, Guidance, and Support of Problem Solving

The problems discussed in the foregoing section we have seen repeatedly in case after case over several years. In a misguided attempt to avoid "over managing" and "over directing" the cooperative process, management and labor leaders create an atmosphere of uncertainty and distrust—conditions that they are trying to eliminate—and the net result is inaction. The solution is to send new problem-solving groups off to work on their assigned task with a clear and specific set of objectives and task definitions, and then, after the group has begun working, to provide ongoing guidance and support to the effort.

Before creating a new subcommittee or task force, the steering committee must first define for itself the specific goals or problems that it wants the new group to address. The problem-solving team should not even be established until all members of the steering committee clearly understand what they are assigning the new group to do and have reached a consensus on what the group's task and objectives will be. If the steering committee fails to reach a consensus on the specifics of the new group's task before the team is actually formed, then the group will find itself caught in the middle between opposing interests and praised by one for its efforts while condemned by the other for the same activities. The end result can be nothing but destructive, both to the problem-solving group and to the overall partnership effort.

Once the members of the steering committee have reached an agreement concerning the specifics of the problem-solving group's assignment and the members of the team have been recruited, then ideally subcommittee or task force members should receive their assignment and directions at a meeting of the steering committee. This ritual, if it is followed routinely with the beginning of each new group, can have a tremendous positive impact on a new team's commitment and motivation. Meeting with the entire steering committee to receive an assignment instills in members a strong feeling of responsibility to do their job and to do it well for both the partnership's leaders and all employees. Such a meeting signals to team members that what they are being asked to do is highly valued by both company and union officials. It also provides members of the group with an opportunity to raise questions and seek clarification of their specific assignment.

Although the meeting, and the give-and-take of discussion that occurs there, are very important in setting a new group off on the right course, the details of their assignment should also be given to them in writing, with a copy for each member of the group. Included in this written statement, which should be jointly presented by both labor and management spokespersons, should be:

1. A clear and specific statement of the problem or issue that the group is supposed to address. This instruction should describe the kinds of data and details that the steering committee expects to be in the group's final report or proposal, including such things as a detailed analysis of the causes of the problem, a list of specific

actions that should be taken, a proposed timetable for taking action, and an itemized cost estimate for the project.

2. A description of the resources that the group can draw upon to assist it in tackling its assignment, including where it can meet, how frequently it can meet, the maximum time period it can normally meet for each session, support services that are available to it in developing its estimates and analyses, a budget for photocopying, clerical help, materials and tools, consulting assistance, and so forth. A clear explanation should also be provided so that if the problem-solving group finds it needs additional resources or assistance beyond what the steering committee initially anticipated, the members will know how and to whom they should make this request.

3. A basic timetable that the group is expected to follow in performing its assigned duties, including target dates for completion of subtasks of the overall project, an end date for completing the entire project (or the first major phase of the effort), and times for interim reports on the group's experience and progress to the entire steering committee.

4. Brief biographical descriptions of all of the group's members to help them to get to know each other more quickly and to highlight the kinds of knowledge, experience, information, and contacts each team member can potentially provide.

Rather than inhibiting a new task force or subcommittee, this kind of information and clarity of instruction will resolve any anxiety and doubt and enable the group to begin their work almost immediately. Moreover, knowing what resources are available helps to speed up the process because it eliminates the waste of time so frequently caused by attempting to "reinvent the wheel" and agonizing over what is or is not appropriate to request. Also, providing a basic timetable for presenting interim and final reports helps to create a sense of urgency about getting to work on the problem-solving task at hand.

Nevertheless, before beginning work on their problem-solving assignment, it is wise, if time and money permit, to start new groups off with some basic general and specialized problem-solving and meeting-effectiveness training. With a specific assignment in mind, individual and group motivation for learning new skills and concepts is much higher. In the case of the first few waves of problem-solving groups created in a new labor-management partnership effort, it is also best if members of the steering committee participate in these sessions as well. All too frequently, steering-committee members lose, or in some cases never even experience, direct involvement in the problem-solving process.

By participating in training sessions with new task force and subcommittee members, the steering committee can gain a more direct appreciation for the values and processes that are being developed through the partnership's activities. Although the majority of their meetings are devoted primarily to governance processes, it is still possible for the steering committee to employ many of the problem-solving and meeting-effectiveness techniques taught in the classroom within the confines of the steering committee's operations.

Learning can be even more strongly increased at the steering-committee level by placing one steering-committee member in each new problem-solving group as a participant. Such experiences are very important to the overall growth and development of the partnership. Without these kinds of experiences, steering-committee members can fail to gain an understanding of the kinds of transformations in attitudes, feelings, and behaviors that are developing between managers and workers who are actively involved in cooperative problem solving on the shop floor. It is far too easy for the steering committee to continue to operate in a mode that becomes not altogether different from traditional negotiations, with the union sometimes getting its way and the company sometimes getting its way, through a process that lacks the intensity and the sense of equality that accompany cooperative problem solving.

These differences in experience are probably most clearly evident when a long-standing labor-management partnership fails. At this point, the feeling of loss is far more deeply experienced by shop-floor workers and first-line supervisors than it is by upper-level managers and union officials who served solely on the steering committee.

For example, when Eastern Airlines CEO Frank Borman decided to suspend management's involvement in all cooperative activities, from the corporate level down to shop-floor teams, the top union leaders were angry primarily because Borman was reasserting unilateral management decision-making authority. Top management officials at the vice-president level showed little emotional reaction to Borman's decision, although some privately expressed fear of union retaliation while others applauded it as an attempt to "get the union out of business where it didn't belong." The reaction on the shop floor—and even among some middle managers—was dramatically different. As researchers, we saw workers, shop stewards, and supervisors who had been actively involved in cooperative problem solving actually become tearful about the return to the old system of strict adversarialism. They described with anguish the old style of shop-floor relations, where workers constantly tried to outsmart managers and supervisors by working according to time-consuming, detailed work rules. Some even sabotaged operations, and managers retaliated through such punitive actions as suspensions and the withdrawal of traditional privileges. Everyone was concerned about the long-term future of the company and their jobs—a reaction that in retrospect was clearly warranted. They were also deeply saddened by the awareness that they would have to return to being enemies with people they had come to like and respect as both friends and colleagues. If high-level managers and union leaders had also participated intensively in the cooperative problem-solving process, they would no doubt have found it far more difficult to give it up and return to warfare.

Placing steering-committee members on task forces and subcommittees as direct participants is beneficial not only from the standpoint of increasing the steering committee's depth of appreciation and understanding for cooperation, these representatives also can serve as linking pins to the steering committee, providing ongoing communication and support for problem-solving activities. In this role, the participating steering-committee members can informally report on the progress of their respective problem-solving groups, and they can also request additional resources and technical support at steering-committee meetings. Providing such a linking and communications function can help greatly in smoothing out the problem-solving process and in ensuring that task forces and subcommittees have all the resources they need to get the job done correctly and on time.

Coordination and support should not, however, be limited solely to the linking-pin function provided by individuals who are jointly serving as members of both the steering committee and specific problem-solving groups. Providing coordination, communication, and guidance is also a significant role of the steering committee's union and management cochairpersons. Together, the cochairpersons should meet regularly with their counterparts from the task forces and subcommittees currently in operation. The purpose of these meetings is to discuss the experience and needs of these groups in dealing with the problems or tasks that have been assigned to them and to review their progress in terms of keeping to the timetable initially established. Thus, if problems in pursuing the original assignment arise, or if special needs for technical or material resources become apparent, they can be addressed quickly, thereby minimizing frustration and delays. Furthermore, if a task force or subcommittee seems to have misunderstood its original assignment, or if it has digressed from what it is supposed to accomplish, the cochairpersons can provide some direction and guidance so that the group can get back on the right track.

Giving problem-solving groups additional guidance and direction while they are still in the process of data collection, problem analysis, and solution development is also an important function served by periodic interim reports to the steering committee. Such reports should be scheduled in advance so that these meetings coincide with key events during the problem-solving process. Ideally, the entire task force or subcommittee should participate in the presentation of interim and final reports. If this is impossible, the report should be presented by the group's union and management cochairpersons together. Of course, as a labor-management partnership grows and the number of groups engaged in problem-solving activities becomes large, such reporting to the entire steering committee may become impracticable. In the early phase of a cooperative partnership these sessions can be extremely important. Again, these meetings reinforce the importance of each task force and subcommittee's particular assignment and thereby enhance the participants' interest and motivation. Equally important, these meetings help to ensure that problem-solving groups ultimately do reach the stage of proposing solutions that the steering committee can in fact pursue and support. Reaching this point is much more difficult if a task force or subcommittee meets only twice with the steering committee, once to receive its assignment and a second time to submit its final report and proposal.

In many instances, we have seen labor-management problem-solving teams meet together for several months in a joint effort only to find when they made their final report to the steering committee that they had solved the wrong problem or pursued the development of a course of action that the company, the union, or both groups could not support. In some cases, this became apparent during the subcommittee or task force's report, and they were told that they would have to go back to the beginning and start all over again. In others, the groups were politely thanked for their efforts, but they never heard anything more about the issue or their proposal from the either the company or the union.

After many hours of collective work, this is hardly the way a joint problem-solving project should end, and in the long term such a situation will seriously damage the development of the partnership. Individuals who have already invested a great deal of time, emotional energy, and intellectual effort into solving a problem are unlikely to return to the task with the same level of enthusiasm if they are told to go back to the beginning and start over after submitting a report and proposal for action that they thought was complete. In these cases, we have seen labor and management participants simply refuse to participate any further in cooperative problem solving. Similarly, quietly hoping that everyone will forget about the issue and the problem-solving effort by never getting back to a subcommittee or task force on its report is an equally ineffective course of action. Such tactics undermine the credibility of the partnership. They breed distrust for the leadership of both groups and cynicism about the process as a whole.

It is much easier and less painful to alter the course of a joint problem-solving group while its work is still in process than after the entire effort has been completed. Again, we have found that the failure to manage cooperative problem solving in this way is often not a matter of disorganization or lack of rigor on the part of many cooperative partnerships. Frequently, steering committees and cochairpersons avoid becoming involved in the ongoing efforts of their problem-solving groups because, again, they do not want to inhibit free and open discussion or the ingenuity of the team. This approach would be fine if the company and union leaders were willing to accept any proposal that a subcommittee or task force submitted, even if it was related to a different issue than the one the steering committee initially intended. Since this is not the case, however, it is much wiser to provide gentle but specific guidance and counsel while a problem-solving group is still in the process of doing its job.

Building Momentum and Ownership Through Feedback

Although we recommend that new labor-management partnerships limit the extent to which they open up the floodgates of employee opinions concerning areas for change and improvement, we are by no means suggesting that the partnership should operate in a closed or secretive manner. Staying focused and avoiding raising employee expectations that cannot be met does not mean that workers and managers should be kept in the dark about what the partnership has done or plans to do in the future. Secrecy breeds distrust, and distrust leads to rumors that invariably reflect everyone's worst nightmares about what might be happening—*the union has sold out to management* or *top management has sold its supervisors down the river to keep peace with the union.* In fact, the more everyone is kept apprised of what is happening, the more healthy the relationship will be and the more rapidly it will grow and spread throughout the workplace.

As we noted in Chapter 5, an important function of the steering committee is to share with the entire workforce its progress by posting copies of the minutes of its meetings on bulletin boards and at frequently visited spots, such as the cafeteria and break areas, throughout the workplace. Accompanying steering-committee minutes should be the progress and final reports of subcommittees and task forces. Important data related to organizational performance should also be supplied to the workforce by the steering committee. Of course, management could post such information independent of the partnership, but if it does come from the steering committee the credibility of the data is higher and the point is made that this is information that is of importance to the workers and not just for management and shareholders.

Performance data that are shared regularly, on a weekly, monthly, or quarterly basis, should be easy to read. Usually the graphic form is most useful, because employees are less likely to become lost in a mass of numbers and because trends can be shown that make it clear where performance is getting better or worse. Ideally, the entire workforce should be introduced to this regularly posted information, both steering-committee minutes and performance data, through face-to-face meetings with all employees in their work groups. In these meetings, employees can learn what kinds of information are being posted, why it is being posted, and how to interpret the charts and graphs.

Later on, these initial oral presentations and discussions should be followed by other *regularly scheduled* progress reports and "question-and-answer" sessions with members of the steering committee on a quarterly, semiannual, or, at a minimum, annual basis. These face-to-face discussions can help to draw in the members of the workforce and management who have not directly participated in partnership problem-solving activities. Through these sessions, the meaning and purpose of cooperative efforts becomes clarified, rumors regarding problems and questionable behavior can be addressed and halted, and everyone begins to feel part of the partnership-building process.

Whether such meetings are held with departments, with entire shifts, or with the whole workforce depends on the particular work setting and the goals of the steering committee. Meetings with large groups are beneficial in that they create a strong sense of unity across the entire organization, but they tend to be impersonal and to leave little room for discussion. Smaller group meetings provide more time for individual input and questions, but they only reinforce a feeling of cooperation with the larger group in a very abstract manner. Combinations of both kinds of informational meetings are therefore probably the best approach, but this is not always possible in environments where employees are widely dispersed geographically or when machinery and equipment cannot be left unattended. Thus, each organization must work out for itself which approach is technically feasible and best for them.

Conclusion

In this chapter we have attempted to provide in detail the basic approaches that we have found most effective and appropriate when first initiating, and then building, labor-management cooperative problem solving in the workplace. We have focused most intensively on the techniques and processes involved in this stage of partnership building because they are most crucial in determining whether a labor-management cooperative partnership will succeed in any specific work setting. As time progresses and the partnership grows stronger with more and more employees participating in problem-solving activities, the room for mistakes becomes much greater. A few errors or even serious political problems will probably not threaten the continued existence of a mature and active partnership. During the infancy and early stages of growth and development, though, the same mistakes can be fatal. This means that when both parties have the least sophistication and experience in dealing with labor-management cooperation they are both under pressure to be far more careful and thoughtful in the planning and execution than will be necessary after a few years of cooperative activity. We hope that the foregoing discussion will help both union and management officials to embark upon this process with greater ease and safety.

In the next chapter, to help illustrate the points we have made in a more holistic and complete manner, we will describe two cases in which dramatic results were achieved through labor-management cooperation. In one instance, the effort succeeded over the long run, and in the second, the partnership, and eventually the entire organization, died. We hope that these examples will prove enlightening and that they will serve as useful mental exercises in developing labor-management partnerships.

8

Dissecting Two Cases: An Analysis of Success and Failure

This chapter reviews two company-union attempts to develop cooperative partnerships, one successful and the other ending in failure. The examples are drawn from New United Motor Manufacturing, Inc. (NUMMI) and Eastern Airlines. After describing the course of events in each case, we analyze why Eastern failed while NUMMI succeeded.

The purpose of this chapter is to enable the reader to see and understand how the many recommendations made in previous sections of the book fit together. This analysis also will help us understand how the neglect of even a few considerations can prove fatal. Turning first to NUMMI and then to Eastern, the thrust of these cases is to demonstrate the integration of the various tactics and tools described throughout the earlier chapters.

New United Motor Manufacturing, Inc.

Located in Fremont, California, the auto factory was originally constructed by GM in 1962, and it produced the Chevrolet Malibu, Buick Century, and GMC trucks. Throughout its first twenty years, the plant was the site of major battles between company executives and the UAW, Local 2244. Workers considered management as stereotypically authoritarian and inflexible, and company officials considered the union antagonistic and out of control. Every few years there would be a work stoppage, caused by a "sick-in" or strike. Absenteeism was around 20 percent, which occasionally resulted in a forced halt of the production line, especially at start-up time. Eventually, in 1982, GM shut the plant down, declaring that it was confrontational relations with the union—and not technological obsolescence—that had made the factory unprofitable. Fremont was dead last in production of all GM facilities, and it was facing an increasingly competitive, global market. When the gates were padlocked shut, there was a backlog of over a thousand formal grievances, sixty disputed firings, and 5000 workers without jobs.

Within a year, the plant began preparing to reopen, this time based on a joint venture between GM and Toyota Motor Corporation of Japan. A key provision of this venture was that Toyota would assume management of the plant and would implement a management style similar to that seen in its Japanese facilities. For Toyota, the agreement would provide a manufacturing presence in the United States, which management hoped would help to defuse the growing trade tension between Japan and the United States. Toyota would also gain experience with U.S. trade unions and suppliers. For GM, the agreement offered a chance to reverse public criticism of the Fremont shutdown and to develop a high-quality but inexpensive car, the Nova, which would be marketed through the Chevrolet division. GM would also benefit by learning first-hand the Japanese approach to manufacturing, which was significantly more cost-effective and efficient than the approach taken by American industry. Finally, the state of California as a whole would benefit because the number of auto-assembly plants had fallen from five to only one and unemployment was a major concern.

The UAW was brought into the process early, but its local leaders opposed the new venture and filed a lawsuit to block the deal. Over time, opposition diminished, and the UAW signed a letter of intent with the two companies in 1983. The union agreed not to be bound by traditional job classifications and rigid rules, and management committed to hire the majority of employees from the laid-off workforce. Former collective-bargaining agreements would not apply to the new venture, but workers would be paid the prevailing auto-industry wages and benefits. Rather than the individualistic shop-floor system used in most U.S. factories, the reopened Fremont plant was to be structured around a team concept.

Amazingly, the union and the new company functioned according to the principles of this brief 1983 letter of intent for some twenty-two months while production was planned and the plant was refurbished. The first collective-bargaining agreement was finalized in 1985, recognizing that the company and the union had a common goal to "build the highest quality automobile in the world at the lowest possible cost to the consumer" (Agreement Between NUMMI and the UAW, 1985).

The financial commitments from GM and Toyota each totaled $100 million—GM providing the old plant, and Toyota providing $100 million in cash. Additional financing was arranged through the new firm, NUMMI, and its lenders. The total investment in upgrading the original plant, additional new construction start-up, and initial operating capital was approximately $450 million (New United Motor Manufacturing, Inc., 1992).

NUMMI had to overcome other hurdles besides new capitalization and an antagonistic history. The Ford Motor Company rigorously opposed the joint venture, and Chrysler went so far as to sue NUMMI. The U.S. Federal Trade Commission conducted an extensive fifteen-month investigation to determine whether the antitrust laws would be violated. In the end, the FTC narrowly voted to approve the plant, but numerous conditions were imposed, including a production ceiling of 250,000 GM vehicles annually. By April 4, 1985, everything was ready to go and dedicatory services were held for opening the factory to full production. They were officiated by Roger Smith, GM Chairman; Eiji Toyoda, Chairman of Toyota; UAW leaders; and officials from both countries' governments. Speakers hailed the resurrection of the Fremont facility as an innovative step in labor-management cooperation and an expansion of the worldwide auto industry. This creative partnership between executives and UAW Local 2244 was promoted as the beginning of a nonadversarial relationship that would enable the new company to produce superior products at minimal cost.

Table 8.1 shows the evolution of auto types for General Motors and Toyota, along with the number of vehicles built each year at NUMMI.

According to numerous independent evaluations, the Nova, distributed through Chevrolet dealers, compared favorably with Toyota's Corolla, which was built in Japan. *Consumer Re-*

Table 8.1
Annual Production

	Nova	Corolla FX	Geo Prizm	Toyota Corolla	Toyota truck	Total
1985	64,766	0				64,766
1986	191,536	14,318				205,854
1987	143,652	43,726				187,378
1988	71,117	40,912	1,827	14,575		128,431
1989	0	0	112,342	80,129		192,471
1990	0	0	101,957	103,330		205,287
1991	0	0	94,994	111,143	2,527	208,664
1992	0	0	75,493	105,407	75,271	256,171
1993	0	0	85,257	121,719	116,061	323,037
TOTAL	471,071	98,956	471,870	536,303	193,859	1,772,059

ports, *Car and Driver,* and other evaluators extolled the quality and safety of NUMMI products. Researchers documented that by late 1986, NUMMI's productivity figures were double those of GM Fremont's previous twenty years (Krafcik, 1986). Later, as market conditions shifted, Fremont built Corollas, Geo Prizms, and Toyota pickup trucks, dropping the production of older cars in favor of hot-selling, higher-demand vehicles. At each of these major milestones in new product lines, a cherry tree was planted in front of the Fremont facility to symbolize the firm's roots and long-term future.

By early 1991, the plant had built a million cars. Later that year, NUMMI began operating a new, $350 million truck facility. Currently, the plant consists of 4 million square feet and employs 3500 hourly and 750 salaried workers. Investment has totaled $1.5 billion and factory capacity is now 125,000 pickups and 220,000 cars annually. A new 1991 paint plant, just-in-time inventory systems, a body shop with 210 welding robots, support from over 300 U.S. parts suppliers—all make for an impressive manufacturing operation. The quality of work life is also much improved. The grease and grime of the old GM environment are gone, and the refurbished NUMMI is clean, well-lighted, and quiet. Today the domestic content of NUMMI production for Toyota trucks is approximately 60 percent, and 75 percent for Prizms and Corollas. The company's 1993 sales included $377 million in parts exports to Canada and Japan. The Geo Prizm and Toyota Corolla were ranked on the "Best Built Small Cars" list, and the Toyota pickup was listed in "Best Built Trucks in North America" by J.D. Power & Associates.

The Cooperative Partnership

In our view, the labor-management system at NUMMI is a unique blend of Japanese and American features. To expedite the early learning process, some 450 team leaders and group coordinators hired at Fremont were sent in small groups to the Takaoka, Japan, plant of Toyota over a month before NUMMI opened. They studied in classes and received on-the-job shop-floor training. They learned total quality management, continuous improvement, team building, and labor-management cooperative practices. Each person worked side-by-side with a Japanese trainer on the Takaoka assembly line. When NUMMI employees returned to California, they then served as trainers for new hires at NUMMI, sharing skills, concepts, goals, and methods. This process took place throughout most of 1984. It was a critical step in creating a culture change: Formerly militant UAW workers were being socialized into a cooperative system with very different norms and values. Applicants for the new jobs were required to participate in a three-day assessment center which provided factory simulations, group discussions, written tests, and personal interviews. Ultimately, more than 80 percent of the candidates who received job offers were former GM employees at Fremont.

Initial production of the Nova was launched at the end of 1984 by the roughly 400 workers hired and trained by that time. From then on, new people were added each week and then trained extensively before being assigned to a shop team. The foundation of NUMMI's human relations philosophy was mutual trust and respect.

Artifacts of the old GM plant culture of elitism were abolished in the new factory: There were no executive parking lots and no management lunchroom. Even office walls were no longer a barrier as supervisors spent their time and held their meetings on the shop floor. Everybody, from CEO to custodian, wore a NUMMI uniform rather than management in white shirt and tie and workers in blue-collar. The traditional lines of demarcation between boss and worker were blurred socially and psychologically.

Under GM, the original plant was termed the "battleship" by blue-collar workers. Confrontation was the norm. A previous president of Local 2244 often declared that union leaders had been trained to fight management, and vice versa: GM managers were trained to fight the UAW. Both parties were quite adept at doing battle. The NUMMI system, however, was premised on a very different logic, that of collaboration. Of course, not all workers accepted the changed relationship, as Chethik's (1987) series of interviews and articles in an area newspaper indicates.

The following list captures the essence of this new philosophy of labor-management interaction. These items are excerpted from the collective-bargaining *Agreement Between NUMMI and the UAW* (1991):

> The company . . . accepts Union organizing and collective bargaining as an essential and constructive force in our democratic society.

The Union's primary objective is to improve the quality of life. . . . It recognizes, however, the necessity of increasing productivity.

The parties are (both) committed to:

* Maintaining a prosperous business organization.
* Providing workers a voice in their own destiny.
* Working together as a team.
* Promoting full communication.
* Resolving employee concerns through procedures using problem-solving and nonadversarial techniques that are based on consensus instead of confrontation. [pp. 1–2]

The Japanese Influence

As noted earlier, Toyota has managerial responsibility for running the NUMMI organization. Japanese executives were appointed to the top two management positions at Fremont. Eiji Toyoda, Chairman of the Board of Toyota Worldwide, appointed his son, Tatsuro, as CEO of NUMMI. Chief Operating Officer was Kan Higashi, also from Japan. Their goal was to develop a unique management style that would synthesize the best practices of the U.S. auto industry and those of Japan.

The key dimensions of this new leadership model were (1) stable and cooperative relationships, (2) built-in quality assurance, (3) a positive image of the firm in the community, and (4) long-term agreements with suppliers. Objectives are established for each year by every team and reviewed periodically to measure accomplishments. Decision making is passed down through the plant's structure. Consensus makes for more acceptable results and greater commitment to implementation. Joint decisions tend to succeed only if team members have adequate knowledge of the whole company's situation. Thus there are regular forums held for educating everyone at NUMMI as to market conditions, production results, company finances, and overall objectives and policies.

Various Japanese techniques are used to enhance organizational results, including the following (*New United Motor Manufacturing, Inc.*, 1992):

Ringi-sho: A document that circulates among key parties, reporting a brief survey of a specific problem or situation, proposed solution, and costs. The various teams involved may discuss, offer reactions, and, as agreement is obtained, sign off on the *ringi-sho*.

Kaizen: The continuous search for cost reductions at NUMMI. Individual team members and the group as a whole have the obligation to seek ways of reducing material use, cutting production and labor costs, and improving quality and efficiency. The basic objective of this very important process is to keep surpluses at a minimum, whether they are steel, energy, or time. During the first year, the *kaizen* spirit of continuous improvement averaged some 220 worker suggestions per month, greatly improving efficiencies (*Inside Track,* 1986).

Jidoka: The principle of quality assurance requires that defective products and/or parts be prevented from passing from one work station to the next. It may require stopping the assembly line, preventing equipment breakdowns, and other techniques to ensure 100-percent quality throughout the process of building of a new car.

Just-in-Time: This concept is used to keep inventory at the right amount at all times, so that the correct part gets to the right place in the right amount at the key point in time. Instead of excess inventory, with its associated costs, just-in-time provides needed parts with precision.

Kanban: This procedure enables NUMMI to avoid overproduction. It is a replenishment process which provides needed manufactured parts through each step of production, but in reverse order.

Both management and the UAW are trained in the use of these various techniques, but, more than that, they share strong commitment to employ them in their day-to-day operations. From the outset, Local 2244 and NUMMI management agreed that the company would consult with the union in advance of all key business decisions. Instead of secret meetings by top managers in the executive suite, labor leaders are brought in for open dialogue about new developments and requirements that might necessitate a change in the production schedule, or new product development.

Worker Empowerment

Workers have the right to stop the production line if there is a problem, and management agrees by contract to seek no disciplinary action. Declared the UAW's international representative, Joel Smith: "Workers now have the authority to help clean up the glitches along the assembly line, as they occur. . . . We've finally got the chance to make decisions and solve problems, something we never had before" (Smith, 1986).

If a worker is not performing at the expected level, or if an employee violates company policy and is facing suspension, there is a joint management-union review of the circumstances before anyone is discharged. The outcome of these joint reviews is that the task of managing becomes a shared process of leadership, rather than being the exclusive domain of a few MBA-trained, white-collar executives.

The first line of authority is an hourly team leader, not a salaried supervisor. The team leader coordinates the efforts of six to eight peers into a working unit. The group as a whole is responsible for the amount and quality of production as well as safety and costs. Team members and coordinators are all UAW members, and every four teams make up a work group led by a company supervisor. There are only four organizational levels from the shop floor to NUMMI CEO. And the difference from the traditional structure seen in most U.S. auto plants is striking: Instead of confining workers' activities within a narrow, rigid sphere (as assembler, electrician, for example), NUMMI team members are encouraged to become involved in all aspects of the shop floor and jobs are rotated on a regular basis. Under the system that prevailed at GM between 1962 and 1982, there were over 100 job classifications. At NUMMI there is just one classification for all production workers and there are a mere three different groupings among the highly refined, skilled trades. This dramatic drop from 100 classifications to 4 offers genuine flexibility, and this is a major factor in NUMMI's ability to do more and do it faster and more safely than ever before.

These new, simple classifications release workers' creativity and make the jobs themselves more varied and more meaningful. A worker in the body shop, for example, described the positive aspects of performing different work, in his case nine jobs in less than a year's time: "You don't get bored that way. It can't compare with the old system" (Stansbury, 1985, p. 14).

Under the old system, monotony and boredom reigned on the factory floor as workers moved robotlike within the narrow confines of a specific role. The system reflected Frederick Winslow Taylor's (1911) vision of de-skilled, disempowered workers split up into "a scientific division of labor," in which manufacturing is broken up into the smallest of steps. Under the tutelage of industrial engineers who were influenced by time-and-motion studies, workers became automatons, mere cogs in the machine. The old structure was well in place during GM's first two decades at Fremont, and its results were costly: absenteeism, rebellion, and abominable production.

In contrast, it seems to us that the new Fremont system was intended to liberate workers' potential. Instead of dreading the battleground, NUMMI factory workers actually began to enjoy going to work. *Newsweek* referred to the new system as "a model of industrial tranquility" (Raine, 1986, p. 43). The first collective-bargaining contract was approved by 92 percent of Local 2244's members, a dramatic attitudinal turnaround. The agreement not only made workers more accountable and joint consultation a reality, it also provided the strongest job-security protection of any UAW contract in the nation. Management was required to cut its own salaries before a shopworker could be laid off. This commitment to a stable workforce was tested severely when Nova sales slowed to the point that only 60 percent of the assembly-line capacity was needed. In a typical U.S. factory, this would have meant 300 layoffs, but not at NUMMI. Instead, the 300 workers kept showing up, kept getting their paychecks—and were trained in new methods of problem solving. Equality of sacrifice was born—a much-needed system of reciprocity in U.S. industry. And through the crisis, the new NUMMI culture was clearly manifest—this NUMMI kept commitments. It became known as a company with a heart.

Absenteeism, which under the old system reached a level of 20 percent, was reduced to 2 percent, a plant record, in NUMMI's first year. Unexcused absences were less than half of a percentage point. With respect to union complaints, only twenty formal grievances were filed during the first year, and of those, all but one were settled before reaching arbitration. After three full years, only four grievances actually went to arbitration. No wonder Bill Usery, former U.S. Secretary of Labor, hailed the significance of NUMMI's cooperation, citing it as the beginning of "new ideas in labor relations" in America (Walsh, 1985, p. 9). The historic lose-lose relationship, which had decimated 5000 jobs, was recast into a new win-win partnership, providing an impressive paradigm for other troubled industries across America.

In the new NUMMI culture, roles changed significantly. For example, instead of expending the majority of their time and energy handling grievances, or fostering conflicts, union stewards became facilitators of change, as well as trainers and educators. And shop-floor supervisors, rather than focusing on their own power and authority, took on the new role of channeling information to the workers and providing support, tools, and other assistance.

Perhaps the experience of Local 2244 president Tony De-Jesus best captures the spirit of the NUMMI partnership. In 1977, he had led a wildcat strike at Fremont. With the Toyota-GM joint venture starting up, he was invited to help select supervisors for the new company. The invitation came as a total shock to him. At first, he rejected the idea, but then he realized that this gave him an opportunity to address major problems of incompetence and worker abuse. So he offered his views, and management accepted the union suggestions. From that point on, DeJesus accepted the idea that if and when supervisory problems arose, the union bore some responsibility (Chethik, 1987).

As the new organization developed, several UAW members were hired into management jobs within the department of human resources. Joel Smith, the union's international representative over the Bay area, played such an important role in the early years of NUMMI that he was finally offered a job as a company vice president of Rockwell International.

Perhaps the words of Douglas Fraser (1985) best sum up the changing labor relations at NUMMI. After returning from a visit to the company, he commented to us, "I just can't believe those are the same militant guys of Local 2244 a decade ago. It is now an incredibly positive environment and a successful producer of cars." He, and many outside observers, were rightly amazed. Toyota had taken a radical, much-maligned group of UAW workers and transformed them into a high-commitment, high-performance team. They were able to meet and, in most cases, exceed industry standards. A plant that employed over 3000 workers was able to reverse two decades of decline and escape a factory death knell. They succeeded in matching the productivity of their rivals in Japan, including NUMMI's sister plant in Takaoka. Amazingly, the Fremont plant, which had been at the bottom of GM operations, was now at the very top. NUMMI was building some 200,000 vehicles annually—a sharp contrast to the disastrous decade of 1972–1982. By the end of 1991, NUMMI had built over a million cars and was beginning to produce Toyota trucks.

Quality also drastically improved, putting NUMMI on a par with the rest of Toyota, the auto-industry leader. This meant lower warranty-repair costs and increased sales (Smith and Childs, 1987). Surveys in *Consumer Reports* reported Nova owners to be the most positive in terms of customer satisfaction. The result was $40 million in profits over NUMMI's first two years.

Table 8.2 highlights the contrasts between the historic conflict system of GM and the new labor-management system of collaboration at NUMMI.

Of course, NUMMI is not a workplace utopia. In June 1993 the UAW local voted down a management proposal to allow three-person crews in the stamping plant. The move was part of a company plan to begin a new bumper operation that would lead to hundreds of new jobs. Many NUMMI workers in the stamping facility were working so much overtime that their wages were nearly doubled. A small group of union dissidents fueled fears that overtime would disappear, but management argued the proposed system was being used in other auto plants and workers still enjoyed ample overtime.

After several weeks of union study and further discussion on the proposal, workers voted by a 2-to-1 margin in favor of the new crews. It enabled NUMMI to operate the stamping plant 120

Table 8.2
Key Features of the NUMMI Case

Old Adversarial System	New Labor-Management Partnership
Strikes, sick-ins	No strikes or slowdowns
Declining productivity	Increasing productivity
Low quality	High quality, TQM
Individualistic culture	Team-based culture
100 job classifications	4 job classifications
20 percent absenteeism	2 percent or lower absenteeism
Primary investment in new technology	Primary investment in human capital
Numerous firings	Stable workforce
Emphasis on quantity	Emphasis on quality
Authoritarian management style	Participatory management
Union militancy	Union as partner
Bare-bones training	Extensive training and selection process
Hundreds of grievances annually	20 or fewer grievances annually
High-cost automobiles	Low-cost automobiles
GM culture and management	Toyota culture and Japanese management
Managerial perks and elitism	Equality and commonality
Rigid labor contracts	Flexible arrangements
Insecurity, layoffs, and fear	Job security, growing employment, and trust
Managerial domination/union insubordination	Joint decision making by both parties

hours per week rather than the average 80 hours. The company also broke ground on a new plastic bumper facility, allowing more parts production for export. Truck production is increasing by an additional 25,000 pickups, and NUMMI is planning to start production of a new four-wheel-drive truck as well as possibly a compact sport utility vehicle for 1995 (Staff Reporter, 1993).

Eastern Airlines

In Chapter 1 we briefly described the devastating labor-management conflict at Eastern Airlines (EAL). This section describes just how the company's collapse occurred, a collapse that was preceded by an expensive and complex system of labor-management cooperation.

Eastern Airlines began operation in 1926, and one of its first leaders was Eddie Rickenbacker, a World War I pilot. During the three decades he ran the company he referred to himself as "the captain," and his workers as "privates." The military metaphor dominated management thinking and company human relations during those years, and the result was a sequence of strikes, pickets, and slowdowns. But no matter what happened, as long as the Civil Aeronautics Board controlled the industry, management enjoyed sufficient reserves to keep the industry stable and profitable. Labor costs were simply passed on to the customer, and all airlines enjoyed similar guidelines.

Three major unions represented Eastern workers: Pilots belonged to Airline Pilots Association (ALPA); flight attendants were members of the Transportation Workers Union (TWU); and shop-floor employees were under the umbrella of the International Association of Machinists (IAM). Together these groups totaled some 37,500 workers.

In 1975, former Apollo astronaut Frank Borman was appointed head of EAL. Under his leadership the military model was continued. His West Point training and NASA nickname, "the colonel," reinforced the company's historic reliance on authority and control.

Conflict in the Air

In the 1970s the 10,000-member International Association of Machinists (IAM), District 100, grew in power as a formidable negotiator with Eastern. It ran a slate of candidates for the airline's

Miami credit union board of directors and won, ousting management seats which had controlled the $100 million credit union since its inception. This event emboldened the IAM and it became an important precedent for future IAM power struggles with Eastern's management. When Congress deregulated the airline industry in 1978, Eastern and its competitors found themselves competing against new start-up firms and confronted with higher fuel costs and deep recessions. The result was a series of economic crises for Eastern during the years that followed.

In the mid-1970s the union had agreed to layoffs of 2000 workers and a one-year pay freeze, saving Eastern $80 million. Sensing that a one-year giveback would not be enough, Eastern executives came up with a five-year proposal called the "Variable Earnings Program" (VEP). It would have workers give up 3.5 percent of each year's wages in return for Eastern profit sharing of any amount over 2 percent of gross earnings. Billed as worker investment in the airline, the VEP was a concessionary tactic of management, which ended up costing union members another $100 million by 1982. Workers felt betrayed and began to press for full disclosure of corporate financial information.

Chairman Frank Borman hired the Wall Street firm of Lehman Brothers Kuhn Loeb to advise the airline on how to change labor practices and reduce costs. A report was prepared entitled *The Goose That Laid the Golden Egg* (Joedicke, 1981). It put the blame for Eastern's problems on company workers and unions and called for production speedups, the creation of more pay grades, further wage concessions, and the use of so-called profit-sharing and labor-management cooperation programs to strengthen the company's labor relations policies and practices.

The report, kept secret at the time, fueled management's efforts to use employee-involvement methods to manipulate naive workers. The company claimed inflated contributions to worker pension funds, when in reality Eastern was paying less than other airlines (Barber, 1984). A new VEP was proposed during collective-bargaining talks in late 1981, but the union opposed any more VEP as damaging to worker interests. EAL, as we noted in Chapter 3, installed quality circles and used them not only to obtain cost-cutting ideas, but to encourage workers to bypass union stewards on the shop floor and deal directly with first-line supervisors who led the QC circles. The IAM believed that such programs weakened the union's role at Eastern and called for a boycott of such practices. District 100's new leader, Charles Bryan, proposed instead that worker participation be set up at all levels of Eastern decision making, giving the union significant new power. A steering committee would be created to consider people's ideas and to coordinate various team efforts. No layoffs were to occur because of involvement programs, and Bryan proposed that the money saved be split equally between Eastern and its workers.

Needless to say, Borman and top management rejected the IAM's plan, all the while working behind the scenes to implement the Lehman Brothers recommendations. The company began strict enforcement of coffee breaks in its Miami maintenance shops. Historically, while everyone had a fifteen-minute break, it was taken on a staggered basis on completion of a mid-morning job. Now, Eastern insisted that all machinists break at the same time, forcing long lines to just get a beverage. Many would not even get their cup of coffee before the fifteen minutes were over.

On one occasion, a worker spilled water on a foreman during break time. Twelve minutes of pay was deducted from hundreds of employee paychecks as punishment. Angry trade unionists began issuing bulletins and press releases in protest. Some wore "Free the EAL Hostages" buttons. Under mounting pressure, the company finally restored the pay deductions, but hostility continued to grow on both sides.

The union hired its own experts to consult on wage and pension issues, and the outsiders' investigation revealed startling information. While the union had contributed hundreds of millions of dollars to keep Eastern afloat and had made the company more competitive with so-called "more successful" non-union airlines like Delta, the reality was that Eastern had achieved a degree of success. For example, with fewer planes than United, it carried 6.6 million more passengers. It ranked three companies better than Delta in on-time performance. It had only 154 employees per aircraft as compared to Delta's 178, making Eastern the number-one U.S. airline in terms of productivity. Of twenty-five major airlines in the Western world, Eastern was first in total passengers carried. Its annual operating expense per aircraft was $1.6 million below that of Delta.

As these facts began to be published, Bryan grew increasingly critical of management's complaints about workers and calls for further concessions. The company borrowed millions of dollars to finance the purchase of seventy-seven new planes, at a cost of over $2 billion, the largest jet purchase in history. The heavy debt load made Eastern finances worse, blocking any profit sharing for employees. Being the military-minded strategist he was, Borman put his faith in technology and the power of the machine. His underlying premise was that new, fuel-efficient jets would save Eastern money, but he erred. Instead of rising further, gasoline prices plummeted. All of these activities took place as the U.S. economy foundered in the midst of economic recession and high interest rates. Fear grew that bank representatives on Eastern's board were encouraging loans to line the lenders' pockets (Locker and Abrecht, 1984).

District 100 next launched information meetings for its Miami members, and dissension intensified. Flight attendants from the transport workers union also began attending these meetings. Borman countered with his own information campaign, inundating workers with newsletters, videos, company PR, and Miami press coverage. In April 1982, over 4000 IAM supporters marched the streets of Miami, protesting Eastern management for its incompetence and aggressiveness.

The demonstration exponentially heightened national interest in the IAM's complaints. Ethical questions began to flood the media. A group of workers were sent to EAL's April 1982 board meeting in New York, protesting company demands for concessions and calling for labor to have a greater voice in the firm's decisions. Contract negotiations in the following months were more vitriolic as the IAM president of Local 702 documents it (Urra, 1984). The union called for an end to the VEP and requested seats on the board of directors. By late 1982, 95 percent of the union voted to strike if an agreement could not be reached.

Game playing accelerated as the union and EAL fought for the hearts of workers. Borman tried to pressure employees by proposing a decrease in job security and the use of part-time workers. Old work rules were eliminated in new proposals. The VEP program was redefined, but still seemed to promise more pay cuts. In fact, a rough estimate of the new wage agreement was 8.3 percent over three years, but the reality was a $6000–$10,000 loss for each machinist, compared to peers at other airlines.

At the last minute, on March 24, 1983, Eastern agreed to alter its "final" offer and offered a pay proposal similar to the airline industry standard: 17 percent over the next three years with a 21-percent retroactive increase going back that year to January 1. The agreement also specified continuance of old work rules, increased job security, and equal control regarding worker participation programs of the future. The IAM voted 90 percent in favor of the new contract.

New Labor-Management Cooperation

Both before and after the 1983 bargaining efforts, Eastern and the IAM engaged various consultants—Florida International University faculty, Washington, D.C., pension experts, labor and Wall Street financial professionals, and the organizational consulting services of a former U.S. Secretary of Labor. These and other private consultants from Texas charged over $10 million in fees to create a partnership between management and Eastern unions. The challenge of changing the traditional pattern of hostility at EAL was formidable. A television program, *Firing Line* (1989), documented the extent of the problem over the previous decade. Referring to "the wars," one IAM member said, "I lived and breathed fighting management at Eastern Airlines," and an associate acknowledged that he seldom did one hour's work during an eight-hour shift. Declared Jeff Callahan, manager of labor relations: "I remember terminating four people in a day, that's how calloused we were. . . . Constantly we were at each other's throats. . . . You had to look at the culture of this corporation to know that the only success you as a person were going to find was by being the meanest, nastiest, toughest guy on the block. . . ." Our research and involvement over several years at Eastern tends to validate those perceptions.

While many thought the March 1983 agreement would put Eastern's problems behind them, other events overtook the company and its unions. By June of that year, a cash crisis exacerbated EAL's problems, pushing Borman and his lieutenants to call for a new, 20-percent cut in workers' pay. Additional cuts would be made in vacation, health-care benefits, and changes in work rules, totaling over $360 million. If the cuts were not forthcoming, Borman threatened to file Chapter 11 bankruptcy, the same tactic that had recently been used by Continental Airlines head Frank Lorenzo. By December, Borman had his wishes. The new settlement included putting 18–22 percent of wages into a new Wage Investment Program, giving workers 25 percent of the company's common stock and four seats on the board of directors (Salpukas, 1983). The one-year agreement also included some 3 million shares of preferred stock valued at $260 million, which was to function as an interest-free loan to EAL, guaranteed by a promise that the firm would pay it back through 20 percent of future profits. The contract also called for a projected EAL savings of $75 million through new productivity systems based on a labor-management partnership that was yet to be created.

It was hoped that all these changes would reverse the $103.7 million loss of 1983. Various observers hailed the plan as a rebirth, with Eastern perhaps coming out of bankruptcy and the IAM as midwife. *The Wall Street Journal* described the pact as "A New Era for Eastern's Unions." Borman referred to it as a "beginning," and EAL's vice president of human resources reported there is an "awareness of belonging and participating." The company's financial vice president declared, "We had a civil war going on and we had to make peace with ourselves" (all cited in Salpukas, 1984, pp. D-1 and D-2).

Successfully building a new labor-management partnership in order to increase productivity required genuine workers' participation. Instead of tight management authority and a culture of conflict between the parties, the new system gave employees the right to monitor executive performance and review monthly business plans before each meeting of the board of directors. Proposed decisions could be appealed by the unions, and labor gained access to pertinent company information such as capital expenditures.

Joint labor-management teams were established to solve specific problems at Eastern. Early results led to a restructuring of the company's new hub in Kansas City, a more efficient operation, a reduction of grievances, and the elimination of certain management positions.

Both management and labor committed to stronger job security so that productivity improvements would not lead to worker layoffs. Instead, an ad hoc team of management and union members would attempt to bring tasks that had been contracted outside back inside, thereby increasing jobs for EAL workers in specific areas who had been laid off since the 1970s.

Earlier practices centered around management control through costly overhead and rigid work rules. Workers recalled the days when three ramp personnel had been used to unload a plane while three superiors watched from a nearby van. In the maintenance shops at Eastern, managers would sit in their offices spying on the factory floor with binoculars in order to monitor and record an employee's every move. Distrust was rampant. Workers harassed superiors, filed thousands of costly grievances, and took the company to court. Often, the IAM would react to management pressure by doing the most punishing thing it could—going by the book. Instead of laboring quickly and efficiently to repair a jet engine in three to four hours, a worker would follow every step in the manufacturer's manual, sometimes taking three full days to do the job.

Such hostile practices, poor quality work, and inefficiencies—combined with high interest rates on huge new aircraft acquisitions and non-union competing airlines—spelled disaster for Eastern. According to various annual reports, the company lost $95.6 million in 1975, broke even for several years, and made a small profit in 1979. But it lost $17.4 million in 1980, about $70 million in 1981, $74.9 in 1982, and $183.7 million in 1983. Interest alone began eating up 5 percent of gross revenues, compared to less than 1 percent at other firms. The $2 billion debt for new aircraft was equal to 63 percent of Eastern's assets.

So while the IAM called the VEP "extortion" and complained that Borman was "crying wolf" (Bryan, 1982), the union and its advisers overlooked the fact that there were structural aspects to Eastern's problems that would be difficult to circumvent by mere labor-management collaboration. The big question was whether the new strategy of joint decision making and open sharing of company information would turn EAL around.

The impact was felt almost immediately. The first half of 1984 saw a dramatic cut in losses, and a small profit was obtained in the next quarter. During the first three months of 1985 a huge $107 million operating profit was earned, leaving a net amount after profit sharing of $24 million. In the next quarter a similar net was achieved, making that six-month period the most profitable in Eastern's history. By autumn, even *The Wall Street Journal* claimed the turnover "seemed to be succeeding" (Cohn, 1984, p. 1).

A more flexible interpretation of work rules led to greater efficiency. Hourly "lead persons" from the IAM gained the authority to assign peers their work, allowing for the elimination of some sixty first-line supervisor positions. Many tasks traditionally done by management—such as certifying attendance, filling out flight paperwork, and checking flight weight—were now assigned to blue-collar workers. Eastern operations in Los Angeles and Boston even eliminated time clocks and time cards. Absenteeism dropped 41 percent from the previous year, and passenger traffic rose 8 percent (Arnold and Dubin, 1985).

Teams were trained and managers developed a new, more participatory leadership style. A quality-of-working-life program, called "Program for Positive Action," set off a series of power-sharing activities. Ideas were implemented that perhaps had been under consideration for years, but only now were workers willing to share them. Also, it was only at this time that EAL was willing to listen and respond. The outcomes were impressive:

- The lining of each RB 211 jet engine contains eighteen heat shields, costing nearly $380 apiece. Some 4000 used shields had been junked in the scrap room, motivating a group of workers to propose that they be welded and reused. The annual savings was $304,000.

- Another machinist proposed that the company buy a different hydraulic fluid, saving $240 per barrel. The result cut costs by $177,000 in 1984.

- Worn-down fan blades from engines were tossed in a scrap heap after extensive use. A new blade costs $164. Workers came up with the idea of remachining the used blades at a cost of only $19 each, netting annual savings of $306,000.

Various teams came up with innovative proposals which were debated and then implemented (Cohn, 1984). One idea was to repair air-conditioning units internally rather than spend a quarter million dollars by contracting the work outside. At machinists' suggestions, EAL expanded its print shop and began to print all its own forms and written material, saving an estimated $250,000. Instead of outside maintenance contracts, machinists were trained to repair Eastern computers, modems, and screens, developing new expertise among the IAM while saving several million dollars. Instead of shipping jet engine cores to United Airlines for rebuilding, Eastern mechanics proposed that they do the work themselves, and they saved over $640,000 in a six-month period. Other teams of stock clerks investigated long-standing suspicions that certain suppliers were overcharging EAL, and their audits uncovered cost excesses as great as four to eight times the market rate for numerous items. They also uncovered "sweetheart" deals between suppliers and certain EAL purchasing managers, which had led to higher costs and illegal payments. Complaints concerning baggage handling also declined by 35 percent during 1984 (Simmons, 1985).

Eastern's Collapse

If all these changes sound too good to be true, it turns out that they were. By late 1984, the honeymoon was showing signs of wear and the touted one year of sacrifice was beginning to appear permanent. Cynics in the IAM began to predict that Borman would not restore the concessionary wages that had been lost. Bryan and his IAM leaders began complaining about management's "lies." Consultants argued that Eastern's improved performance should justify raising wages by half the earlier cuts, which would have required the firm to pay another $11 million each month (Kuttner, 1985).

While EAL's labor costs had dropped significantly, from 43 percent to 35 percent, new competitors such as People Express were spending only about 18 percent. Management pushed for a cheaper labor agreement but the IAM was adamantly opposed. The company's loans soon began to default, and Borman announced that he was going to extend the original one-year contract through 1985. Bryan sued, claiming this unilateral action violated the old agreement, and he told readers of *The Wall Street Journal* that Eastern's chairman had committed "an act of insanity" (Cohn, 1985, p. 2). At that point, Borman again threatened to invoke Chapter 11.

Meanwhile, as hostilities exploded, Eastern's suppliers became concerned and began to demand cash for goods and services. Passengers booked flights with other airlines, and travel agents, also became jittery. The crisis grew until February 1985 when the parties finally reached the basis of a new accord, restoring 5 percent of sacrificed wages and a degree of profit sharing. Additional management slots were cut, and although prospects improved, the fragile peace and trust were both damaged (Arnold and Dubin, 1985). Thus, when the IAM voted to ratify the new contract, it was initially defeated by a mere 300 of 7000 IAM ballots cast. After more explanation and debate, a vote in May won by a 2:1 margin.

Eastern's stock value soared as the three-year contract was finally settled. The company regained passengers and new flights were added. Strikes at other airlines helped Eastern weather the 1985 turbulence, and the cooperative efforts continued to reduce labor costs. The reduction of the "them versus us" conflicts of the previous decades seemed to suggest the promise of survival over the long haul.

In spite of these positive trends, the reality is that by mid-1985, Eastern was operating on two levels. On the surface, things were going well. The airline began to bounce back from $380 million in losses over the previous five years. In the first quarter of 1985, the company posted $53.2 million in profits, $29 million of which was set aside for workers' profit sharing. The company projected that it would earn $83 million by year end on sales of $4.8 billion. Stock prices rose from 4¼ to 8 within several months.

EAL launched new, aggressive marketing strategies, won a new route from Miami to London, added more competitive air freight space and no-frills late-night flights. Optimism was pervasive. Borman declared, "This airline is going to be enormously profitable," while the head of a major competitor suggested that Eastern was becoming "truly formidable." Other outside observers noted that EAL's labor and management were "working more like a team," while a lead consultant on the partnership argued, "There's more change and innovation at (Eastern) than anywhere else I know. . . . the mistrust is being eliminated" (all from Dubin, 1985, pp. 54–55).

The old quality-circle program, which had been tainted for bypassing the IAM, had been abolished in favor of a new initiative, "Employee Involvement" (EI). But the governing structure consisted of only top Eastern executives, except for a brief period in late 1985 when the three leaders of Eastern's unions were admitted to the council (Meek, 1988). Token participation and post facto invitations to join the process never go over well with organized labor, especially during times of stress.

On the bright side, the sweet appearance of success looked wonderful to most outside observers. But just beneath the surface was the ugly reality of seething hostility and crisis. Instead of the anticipated profits, EAL lost $67 million in the final quarter of 1985, leaving the company with only $6.3 million for the year. The sixty creditors exerted heavy pressure for immediate and drastic changes—mainly centered on reduced labor costs of $450 million. Borman obtained a no-strike clause from the flight attendants and then promptly laid off 1000 of them. He cut the pay of 23,000 other Eastern workers by 20 percent and hoped that these desperate tactics would keep his major creditors from forcing bankruptcy. The unions joined forces, wearing lapel buttons that read "We stand together" as their leaders began to re-open contract talks with management.

Within a month, however, the biggest shock to hit Eastern's unions occurred—Borman offered to sell the company to Frank Lorenzo, head of Texas Air/Continental. The chairman's decision stemmed from his analysis of the crisis: "It was either fix it, sell it, or merge it" (Rudolph, 1986, p. 63). Nearly a decade of failed attempts to fix things had not worked, so Borman basically just caved in. Four days later, TWA announced it was acquiring Ozark, only half a year after raider Carl Icahn had bought TWA itself. Those two mergers came on the heels of others, such as People Express buying Frontier and Northwest Airlines' acquisition of Republic. It was a frantic period of mergers, and Eastern got caught up in the frenzy.

To Borman and his colleagues, the merger was unfortunate but also an admission of failure. To industry experts, the deal was questionable, since it would make Lorenzo the head of the largest U.S. airline, dropping United to second place. Some 55 million passengers would be carried annually to over 300 destinations, and Lorenzo's ability to trigger fare wars and slice jobs would be greatly enhanced. To the government, antitrust implications raised many questions. To the workers, the proposal was a sellout, a $600 million betrayal with Borman in the role of Judas Iscariot.

A pivotal confrontation between Borman and the IAM's leader, Bryan, provided the final proof that the fragile partnership was unraveling. While Eastern's pilots and flight attendants agreed to 20-percent wage cuts, the machinists did not. Bryan agreed to wage concessions of 15 percent, but only if Borman would resign. He assumed that "the colonel" would rather quit and lose face than turn Eastern over to archrival Texas Air/Continental. Borman balked, assuming that Bryan would never agree to a takeover by Lorenzo, a despised union-buster. Both parties exchanged personal insults and attacks during the final Eastern board meeting, each blaming the other for the crisis. According to one of the combatants, it ended in a "shoot-out at the OK Corral" (Rudolph, 1986, p. 63).

After the board agreed to sell EAL, the remaining vestiges of labor-management cooperation melted like warm butter. Lorenzo appointed Phil Bakes as president of Eastern and removed labor leaders from the board of directors. He issued orders to cut labor costs by $490 million, some 30 percent. Together, Lorenzo and Bakes flooded employee mailboxes with a carefully orchestrated campaign to arouse fear, force early retirements, and pressure some workers to resign. Eastern pilots had enjoyed average annual salaries of $112,000, twice those of Texas Air. They knew that Lorenzo had reneged on his labor contracts after taking over Continental, firing all 12,000 workers and rehiring only those who were not militant and who would accept a 50-percent pay cut. With this awareness of Lorenzo's history, Eastern pilots were prepared to battle for their careers and paychecks.

At the outset, Lorenzo's rhetoric was conciliatory: "We're not union busters, we're airline builders" (Rudolph, 1986, p. 63). But soon after the deal was legalized, Bakes was ordered to start surgical operations on the "cancer" of labor costs. By the end of 1986, the IAM had filed 1353 grievances against the company, nearly triple the previous year. "This is all-out war," said the union's grievance administrator (Pauly, 1987, p. 49). Work that had been performed by labor-management teams once again began to be contracted outside Eastern, leading to layoffs and increasing tension.

"Going-by-the-book" tactics heightened the conflict, as supervisors were told to "get tough" and take control. EAL even began using form letters to notify employees of firings or fines, thus engulfing workers and unions with paperwork. Minor infractions, such as a twenty-second delay, would result in the loss of a full day's wages. Charlie Bryan began to grumble, "This isn't union-busting 101 . . . this is advanced union-busting" (Pauly, 1987, p. 49).

The conflicts escalated further in the months that followed. During a speech at Stanford Business School, in May 1988, some in the audience hurled catcalls of "Hitler" and "greedy" at Lorenzo as he entered the auditorium and then tossed eggs at him. In that speech, Lorenzo not only defended his management style, but he announced that Eastern had hired psychiatrists to study union newsletters and handouts and accused organized labor of "brainwashing" the membership. EAL's pilot union responded that "We're very sane people; we're very serious about what we're doing," and suggested that it was Lorenzo himself who needed therapy (Associated Press, 1988).

By that autumn, Eastern had cut service to twenty-one cities to save money and tried to lay off 4000 union workers, the largest layoff in Eastern's sixty-year history. The union sued to block the layoffs, so the company announced that $161 million in new wage concessions would be exacted from employees. As the battle escalated, Lorenzo began "upstreaming" millions of dollars from EAL to Texas Air—management fees, fuel-purchase commissions, airplane rents, airport gate fees. Continental's losses during this period ($315 million) were even greater than Eastern's, leading to "cannibalizing" of jet equipment from Eastern planes in order to keep the rest of Lorenzo's empire afloat. Some fifty planes were sold off, and EAL's high-tech reservation system, one of its crown jewels, was sold to Texas Air for under half its market value. Perhaps worse, Eastern's other greatest asset, the Northeast Shuttle, was sold to Donald Trump for $365 million, and its London route was also dumped on the market.

On March 4, 1989, the IAM struck against the company, and the pilots and flight attendants shocked Lorenzo by supporting the machinists. The entire AFL-CIO joined in the struggle. Millions of dollars of support came from unions across the country, providing strike benefits and interest-free loans. The company responded by filing for bankruptcy, hoping to use Chapter 11 to force changes as it had at Continental. With planes grounded and lenders angry, the situation became even more confusing.

The unions hoped that creditors would join in their demand that Lorenzo be thrown out. They argued in bankruptcy court that the judge should appoint an independent trustee to develop a reorganization plan. Political pressure led Congress to enact a bill directing President George Bush to create an emergency board and take control of EAL. Such action had been done thirty-three times in U.S. history, consistent with Railway Labor Act provisions. According to precedents in the transportation industry, this action would get Eastern planes flying again and impose prestrike conditions while a new settlement was being reached. The president, however, refused to act, in spite of urging from his own appointees at the National Mediation Board. Lorenzo's lobbyists had exerted significant influence throughout the Reagan years and Lorenzo expected that labor would continue to be the loser. He was correct.

Lorenzo pushed for pilot salary concessions of 19 percent, on top of a 32-percent reduction over recent years. When the pilots refused, he began contracting for strikebreakers to replace existing workers. Support for Eastern labor spread across the nation, perhaps typified by the sign a pilot waved at a rally in Atlanta: "United We Stand, Divided We're Continental" (Perlman, 1989, p. 11).

In the weeks that followed, various attempts were made to extricate Eastern from impending disaster. The government's antitrust division announced that it would block Lorenzo's attempt to sell EAL's Philadelphia airport gate to U.S. Air, but another eleven gate sales had been approved. The AFL-CIO put together a $50 million loan guarantee to encourage an outside investment group to purchase Eastern, rescuing it from Texas Air. Former baseball commissioner Peter Ueberroth also attempted to put together an investment group to save EAL, but Lorenzo blocked the deal by refusing to support the appointment of an independent trustee to run the firm while purchase negotiations were being finalized.

A *Washington Post* poll reported that 27 percent of the American public supported Eastern management versus 46 percent in favor of the strikers. *Fortune* magazine suggested that Lorenzo was so bad a boss that readers should count their blessings if they didn't work for him. Conservative columnist William Safire wrote that Eastern management sought "profit from dismemberment" and that Lorenzo "was out to plunder the company." He argued that Texas Air's holdings were "a collection of little leveraged buildings on a Monopoly board," predicting that "when loyalty dies . . . the company dies with it." One striker synthesized Lorenzo's role in the company's bankruptcy as "greed, total greed," while another reflected, "Lorenzo stepped on us for three years. He treated us like garbage" (all in *Solidarity,* 1989, pp. 8–9).

With virtually all its planes grounded, Eastern was hemorrhaging at a daily rate of $4 million. A stunned Lorenzo confessed, "I never believed we would be here today," while Bryan characterized the conflict as "the purist case of evil vs. good" (Castro, 1989, p. 52). Under revised bankruptcy laws, EAL might obtain breathing room for 120 days, but management lost considerable clout also since the court could take over the firm.

So Lorenzo turned to doing what he knew best—beginning to lay off 9500 non-union Eastern workers. The few flights that had still been operating were ticketed at only 15 percent of the original fare prices in order to entice travelers. But with understaffed counters, poor service, and the hassle of airport pickets, all flights soon ceased. Passengers were left with $250 million worth of prepaid tickets, and they too would have to get in line with other Eastern creditors. Meanwhile, Lorenzo continued to strip company assets, selling off all routes from the United States to Canada.

In the weeks that followed, a former Piedmont Airlines head attempted to purchase Eastern, but bankruptcy-court officers rejected the proposal. Eastern next proposed breaking up the firm and rebuilding as a small, profitable carrier, consisting of some 4000 non-union employees who would give fifty hours of work each week for forty hours of pay. All such efforts were futile.

Lorenzo and his lawyers fought to get relief from paying retiree health benefits. Pilots who tried to return to work during the strike sued EAL because it hired replacement pilots. The firm tried to defend itself, but lost in court and was told it would have to pay $25–$75 million in back wages. The chairman's attempt to sell additional assets was also blocked by various judges in the months that followed. When the IAM called off the strike in July 1991, only half of its 10,000 members remained, the rest having taken other jobs or moved away. The federal government launched new investigations into Lorenzo's extraction of half a billion dollars from the EAL employee pension fund. Eastern was also accused of unsafe airplane practices and the falsification of maintenance records that the firm had instituted, thereby endangering public safety. Juries in Miami indicted several managers on criminal charges.

Ultimately, a judge ruled that Lorenzo was incompetent to make decisions at Eastern and a court-appointed trustee was installed to manage the liquidation of what had once been America's leading airline. Northwest, United, American, and Delta each sought chunks of the Eastern empire when routes, gates, and planes were auctioned off to appease creditors. In the end, the much-touted labor-management partnership at Eastern turned into mothballs. A six-decades-old symbol of global transportation was reduced to the scrap heap of history.

Contrasts in Partnership Strategy

When we compare the attempts to create a partnership at Eastern Airlines on the one hand, and the transition at Fremont from GM to NUMMI on the other, we find a number of similarities. Both firms were involved in transportation-related industries and both were heavily unionized. They had both faced economic crises, and economic tensions and pain provided the impetus to try to cooperate. Labor in both instances was strong and had a militant reputation. Each operation suffered from years of financial losses, high labor costs, and extensive problems of absenteeism, grievances, and work stoppages. Neither firm had positive records with respect to customer service. Both operations were led by authoritarian managers who were strong on attempts to control employees. The consequences were alienation and low morale. Finally, the two companies were caught in a changing business environment, which included foreign competition, cheaper products and services, inhospitable policies toward unions (which flowed from the nation's White House and spread across the country) and declining national union membership. Table 8.3 summarizes a number of key elements that tended to interfere with the partnership process.

Clearly, the prospects for success in both cases were low. Yet for NUMMI, the outcome has been a resounding success, at least so far. In the case of Eastern, the result was organizational genocide.

In Chapter 1 we noted there are ample benefits to be gained from building partnerships of labor-management cooperation: greater productivity and financial profits for the firm, higher quality, lower labor costs, less absenteeism, and reduction

Table 8.3
Negative Factors in Attempting to Build a Labor-Management Partnership

Factors	Eastern Airlines	NUMMI
Labor-management history	High conflict during various periods of militant strikes	Poor labor relations, resulting in eventual shutdown of the factory
Readiness for change	Short-term crisis mentality; events forced change upon Eastern, but there was little inner commitment to make it work	Long-term development perspective; change was congruent with Toyota's corporate culture and objectives
Past collective-bargaining agreements	Rigid work rules; inter-union tensions at times between machinists, flight attendants, and pilots	Rigid work rules; intra-union conflicts between political factions within Local 2244 itself
Top-management philosophy and style	Military background created an authoritarian regime (Borman); aggressive union-busting actions which fueled conflict (Lorenzo)	Under GM, the Fremont factory was run by authoritarian principles; under two Japanese CEOs, the style was based on organizational consensus

Union leadership	IAM leader perceived as tough, distrusting, and cynical; pilots and flight attendant officials were viewed as substantive, rational, and more level-headed	UAW leaders were very critical of management under GM; under NUMMI they were invited in as partners and became converted to a new philosophy
State of equipment and technology	EAL shifted from older planes to 77 modern, fuel-efficient jets	Original plant and equipment was old but adequate; new technology and facilities were added since 1985
Finances	Strong revenues but low profits (or losses); huge debt ultimately totaled $2.5 billion	After years of GM losses, NUMMI sales started slowly and grew; initial investment was some $500 million, with profits increasing each year
Workforce	Older employees, high skills, many had spent their entire careers at Eastern	Older employees, skilled trades, long-term GM workers

(continued)

Table 8.3   *(continued)*

Factors	Eastern Airlines	NUMMI
Role of top international union officials	Leaders of pilots and transport workers were neutral until the strikes broke out; IAM was generally against union-management cooperation	UAW officers in Detroit were somewhat supportive of the NUMMI experiment; it fit with other labor-management joint efforts in the auto industry
Organizational climate	Top-down decision making; poor communication; high distrust; management spies; flood of grievances from management and labor; strict work rules and periods of tight enforcement; union and management tried to manipulate each other; wage concessions led to resentment and defensive tactics; this heightened supervisory threats and intimidation	Under GM, Fremont was the "battleship"; workers were alienated and hostile; lack of openness and trust; over 100 job classifications and numerous grievances; high degree of game playing; little worker commitment to quality or productivity; antagonism eventually culminated in GM shutting down the factory

| Wage and benefit package | EAL paid average rates for the airline industry until deregulation, when new, non-union competitors appeared; at that point management demanded concessions | Workers under GM were paid according to the pattern of the auto industry; under NUMMI the same standards prevailed in pay rates |

in scrap. For workers, the benefits are greater job satisfaction and improved working conditions. For unions, cooperation provides labor with new access to information, influence, and security. The research of Meyer and Cooke (1990) suggests that in firms where labor-management cooperation is practiced, return on sales had significant growth during a ten-year period, compared to firms that attempt union-avoidance strategies. Earlier data from Schuster (1983) and Voos (1987) report other performance outcomes for companies as well as unions.

Given all the potential for positive outcomes, we may find in the cases of Eastern and NUMMI reasons why the results varied so greatly. First of all, *Eastern and NUMMI engaged in different approaches to labor-management cooperation.* While a few of the specifics were similar in both cases, the overall pattern was radically different. Generally speaking, Eastern and its unions were engaged in an ongoing, reactive mode, while the parties at NUMMI exhibited a proactive process of interaction. Failures at Eastern led to greater distrust and resentment, while the early successes at NUMMI fueled satisfaction, confidence, and increasing commitment to work together. GM, the lenders, and the international UAW did not interfere or put undue pressure on the NUMMI experiment, while just the reverse was true at EAL.

There were other significant differences as well. *Eastern and its unions could not seem to balance the traditional, adversarial process of collective bargaining with a new attempt at collaboration.* They relied instead on the old-fashioned skills of pointing fingers and fighting, and they used the press to air all their dirty laundry. In contrast, NUMMI's effort was low key. Problems were worked through confidentially, and the resolution was shared after the fact. While GM and the UAW had a long history of confrontation, NUMMI's management emphasized its interest in consensus and the UAW responded.

Another difference was in social psychology: the personalities of the major players involved. At NUMMI, Toyota managers were reserved and extremely sensitive to the concerns of the UAW, and union leaders reciprocated. At Eastern, the flight attendants and pilot leaders were likewise somewhat reasonable in style and mode of interaction. Charles Bryan, however, got elected on a platform of "taking on" management, and he tried to be true to his mandate at every opportunity. This complicated everything he did. Sarcasm and personal accusations became the hallmarks of his approach, his meetings, his role on the board, and his inflammatory rhetoric with the media. Bryan's counterpart in management, Frank Borman, relied on his military past as the metaphor for leadership style. "The colonel" used authoritarianism to make decisions and, in essence, used the thrust of a court martial when the unions seemed to hold a different view. He invested in technology rather than in his "troops," pushing EAL over $2 billion in debt. Top management as a whole tended to exhibit certain negative assumptions about employees: that they were lazy, irresponsible, interested in working as little as possible, and requiring constant supervision. Workers responded in kind, and when Borman was eventually replaced by Frank Lorenzo, any hope of industrial peace completely evaporated. In the end, EAL was not a case of mere sibling rivalry. It was a repeat of the Cain and Abel story—fratricide.

An additional factor that differentiates the two cases is that *at NUMMI workers shared in the fruits of cooperation,* enjoyed increasing market success, and had 100-percent job security. Top management committed to a no-layoff policy at the outset. When the company was later faced with the usual twists and turns of the auto industry, jobs were not cut. Worker morale soared as a result. In contrast, Eastern's workers sacrificed hundreds of millions of dollars in wage concessions, only to be pressured to give up more. Insufficient job security and yearly demands for concessions led to a lack of good faith and demoralization.

Certainly another vital difference was that *in Eastern's case, neither the unions nor management ever learned how to juggle their habits of collective bargaining and adversarial relations with the polar opposite of labor-management collaboration.* This is evidenced in the failure of many other attempted partnerships. For example, UAW leaders at Hyatt Clark Industries, a GM factory bought by its workers, had real difficulty wearing the two hats of cooperation and conflict (Woodworth, 1986). Every time a crisis at the company arose, labor instinctively reverted to its militant behaviors. Management reacted similarly. Both were trapped by past decades of tension and mutual finger pointing. The same was true at Eastern, while at NUMMI the presence of a fresh, new partner, Toyota management, facilitated a change in UAW Local 2244's pattern of response. Each positive step encouraged reciprocal changes in the other party. This is the

essence of being a true partner, not management as the big partner and labor as second-class citizen.

A very complex aspect of achieving a new partnership has
to do with *the extent to which more-participatory leadership styles
and empowerment tactics are disseminated throughout all levels
of the organization.* At NUMMI, the process spread through the
entire organization, from the shop floor to the executive suite. At
Eastern, efforts to create a more democratic, cooperative system
tended to be concentrated at the top. According to a *Business
Week* article (Dubin, 1985), the head of the pilot's union, Larry
Schulte, was aware that "changes in attitude haven't filtered
down past top management." Eastern's senior vice president of
human resources, Jack Johnson, proposed that upper executives
spend a week going through a training program in employee involvement, claiming that "Investing that much time and money
says commitment" (p. 55). The sad fact is that spending only one
week signifies only a very weak interest in changing one's personal leadership style.

Related to the limited time and energy actually spent on
changing the inner self, one observer notes that four EAL vice
presidents quit their jobs because "they could not stomach participation." George Smith, a pilot union official, intimated that Borman in the past had been "notorious for barking out an order and
expecting results. Now he goes about things a little differently. . .
[because] he couldn't make the other way work." Even IAM official Bryan declared that Borman was sharing power more and
delegating decisions and that executives had developed a "total
commitment" to alter "the whole image of the labor/management
relationship" (all in Simmons, 1985, pp. 15–16).

On the whole, Borman's words intimated a new view. Re-
calling when he fired a top EAL executive for not considering
ideas from subordinates, the chairman at Eastern declared:
"Changing your style is one thing, but your basic tenets don't
change. You must be big enough to recognize the need to change"
(Dubin, 1985, p. 55). Yet union officials were skeptical whether
Borman would ever move beyond lip service. The pilots' head,
Schulte, said that Borman had told him: " 'Look, you have to understand, I'm not going to have the monkeys running the zoo.'
That told me more about his thinking than all his protestations
about how involved in E.I. (Employee Involvement) he is and
what's going on" (Simmons, 1985, pp. 17–18). EAL slogans like

"working together" were widely seen as mere frosting on a sour company cake. And, of course, when Borman was eventually replaced by Frank Lorenzo, the level of condescension and bitter animosity escalated into all-out war.

This inability to internalize a more cooperative and participative style was not only a weakness in Borman and top EAL executives. The unions, too, suffered from similar dilemmas. For instance, the pilots' head, Smith, was ultimately ousted from the union's executive council for not being sufficiently belligerent and Schulte became chief of the pilots' union. Generally, the pilots resented Bryan's success in softening corporate demands for wage concessions on the part of the machinists, so the pilots became even more militant, trying to outdo the IAM. Bryan, for his part, saw no need for learning activities like team building and sensitivity training. In fact, over time he grew increasingly autocratic with his own union, working alone and making his own policies. Said one observer, "He's as bad as Borman, if not worse, on wanting to control the situation" (Simmons, 1985, p. 24).

Thus, at EAL both sides tended to manage their people and interact with one another through the use of put-downs, backsliding, and occasional cooperative programs. Widespread and deep-seated change in the relationship between management and labor never really took hold.

The Process of Partnership Creation

The contrast between the EAL environment and NUMMI's substantive commitment to a new partnership with the UAW is dramatic. The keys to any partnership success may lie in the strategic steps by which change is designed and implemented. When NUMMI and Eastern are examined in detail, deep and important contrasts begin to appear. The results tend to correlate with eventual success or failure. Table 8.4 summarizes the critical strategies that should be carried out to achieve a genuine labor-management partnership. The table suggests that the absence of even a few conditions can lead to disaster and shows how recommendations from the previous chapters all fit together.

As the table suggests, Eastern and NUMMI developed and implemented very different approaches for organizational change. With ill-conceived, almost fatal flaws in the partnership at Eastern, the only outcome possible was self-destruction. In

Table 8.4
Key Steps in Building a Labor-Management Partnership: A Two-Case Analysis

Steps	Eastern Airlines	NUMMI
1. Start-up: Each party separately assesses problems in both their relationships and company performance; third-party consultants are selected and a new process begins.	There was a great deal of focus on industrywide crises, blaming of the other party, and inflated expectations that profits would soon turn things around. Management hired antiunion consultants to obtain concessions; the IAM sought antimanagement experts.	After Fremont closed, the UAW admitted it could have done more to counter the crisis; GM did likewise; Toyota's entry gave labor and management a new chance. Neutral consultants sought mutually beneficial strategies as the goal was a win-win outcome.
2. Determine readiness for change and joint sharing of concerns.	The primary motives for change were threat of competition, financial losses, lender pressures, and mutual accusations. Top management used warnings of Chapter 11 bankruptcy. IAM countered with threat of strikes. Neither side saw its own complicity in EAL's decline.	Deep-seated commitment to find a better way, a higher path for union-management relations. Both parties admitted their responsibility for past problems. NUMMI managers were interested in long-term culture change. UAW leaders were desperate to move from unemployment to a more secure future.

3. Agreement to proceed, research other models, and build a parallel system of cooperation alongside the structure of collective bargaining.	Agreements were often reached only as crises and events demanded a change; these were sometimes only temporary stop-gaps rather than deep commitments; little research on other cases of labor-management cooperation; primary model was a labor relations strategy: at times backed by a project-centered approach.	Open discussions prior to the agreement between GM, NUMMI, and Toyota; wide-ranging studies of other successful U.S. programs of cooperation were done as well as drawing upon Toyota's years of experience; 450 U.S. workers were sent to Japan for hands-on factory training; joint agreement on cooperative partnership model.
4. Creation of written charter: new structure, vision, mission, objectives, and ground rules.	Both parties created procedures and processes which they tried to "inflict" on the other. Often rebuffed, they engaged in intergroup fighting to try and manipulate the opposition. In the end, structures and systems were basically negotiated by each	Management and UAW parties together fashioned a clear explication of cooperative agreement through discussions and joint planning. They then spelled out their shared vision, common objectives, and norms and expectations. NUMMI viewed the UAW

(continued)

Table 8.4 *(continued)*

Steps	Eastern Airlines	NUMMI
	sides' lawyers. EAL tended to employ cooperation to weaken or manipulate the union and reduce wages; the IAM returned the favor.	as a legitimate partner, paid union wages, benefits, etc. Local 2244 reciprocated by committing to build a prosperous business.
5. Guarantee of no jobs lost due to cooperative improvements in efficiencies.	EAL disciplined and cut numerous workers. At times up to 1000 workers were laid off at once. There was a high degree of uncertainty and career insecurity.	Assurances of lifetime employment were adhered to, even when business dropped and there were hundreds of workers in excess of what was necessary. All were retained and paid to be trained and/or to do maintenance work.
6. Determine criteria for first pilot project(s) and launch the effort; ongoing monitoring and reciprocity.	Lack of diagnosis and clear criteria; rather, the test was to get as much from the other parts as possible. Benefits were usually one-sided; management would win while the IAM would lose; next time the tables would be reversed. Both	Careful study and diagnosis. The framework for success included identifying key issues to work on and then spelling out joint processes for their pursuit. Critique and evaluation were on-going. Local 2244 and NUMMI managers both

7. Ongoing evaluation of projects and use of anticipatory problem solving.

parties were loath to give any positive reinforcement to each other. Instead they conducted "disinformation campaigns," blaming the "enemy" for all EAL problems.

Eastern did assess projects but often the other party would be accused of not being accountable, honest, etc. The EAL process was primarily a reactive approach. When business crises occurred, EAL lacked a coherent set of ground rules for dealing with the unexpected. Company forecasts tended to be unrealistically high, exacerbating the shock and pain of further difficulties.

tended to share credit for small and/or large successes. Internally, extensive meetings, memos, and newsletters conveyed ongoing successes, joint problems, and future plans. Mutual respect was shown in most public communication, such as the press.

The NUMMI process was one of ongoing monitoring of events, and making adjustments when needed. At NUMMI, the process was more proactive. There were clear, well-established procedures for addressing unforeseen problems. The bargaining contract spelled out what constituted a violation and how parties were to respond.

(continued)

Table 8.4   *(continued)*

Steps	Eastern Airlines	NUMMI
8. Institutionalization so that organizational norms, values, and practices become embedded in corporate and union cultures.	The abrupt changes and frantic attempts to put out fires created such chaos that the EAL labor-management process never did become institutionalized. Rather than reward those involved in change, the result often was further concessions. EAL's efforts tended to be a series of individual "programs."	The labor-management partnership evolved gradually and was refined and adjusted as time passed. Quarterly feedback was given to all teams, and year-end bonuses were provided. Extensive training was coupled with core values and norms of consensus. As time passed, this all became not an experiment or project but a cultural pattern, "the way NUMMI does things."

contrast, the mutually beneficial strategies of NUMMI management and the UAW made all the difference in the world. That process defied all outside observers and doubters who predicted that the partnership would not be workable, and the result has been tremendous success. The lesson of Chapter 8 is that the various strategies and tools we discuss throughout this book must be integrated into a coherent whole in order to achieve a true labor-management partnership.

References

Agreement Between NUMMI and the UAW. Fremont, CA, July 1, 1985.

Agreement Between NUMMI and the UAW. Fremont, CA, July 1, 1991.

Arnold, Bob, and Dubin, Reggi Ann. "A Union Deal Pulls Eastern Back From Default." *Business Week,* February 25, 1985, pp. 32–33.

Associated Press. "Lorenzo Calls in Psychiatrists on Air Strike." *The Salt Lake Tribune,* May 18, 1988.

Barber, Randy. "Breaking New Ground: Pension Fund Bargaining at Eastern." *Labor Research Review,* Vol. 4, Winter 1984, pp. 75–92.

Bryan, Charles. Interview with Warner Woodworth, February 1982.

Castro, Janice. "Eastern Goes Bust." *Time,* March 20, 1989, pp. 52–53.

Chethik, Neil. "Old UAW Local Ain't What it Used to Be." *San Jose Mercury News,* February 9, 1987.

Cohn, Gary. "Eastern Airlines Angers Unions in Keeping Cuts." *The Wall Street Journal,* January 2, 1985.

Cohn, Gary. "Labor's Big New Role Inside Eastern Airlines Seems to Be Succeeding." *The Wall Street Journal,* October 31, 1984.

Dubin, Reggi Ann. "Why Frank Borman Finally Has Something to Smile About." *Business Week,* April 29, 1985, pp. 54–55.

Firing Line, "The Battle for Eastern Airlines," Public Television Documentary, 1989.

Fraser, Douglas. Personal interview with Warner Woodworth, January 1985.

Inside Track, Vol. 1, No. 2, November, 1986 (NUMMI team members' in-house publication).

Joedicke, Robert. *The Goose That Laid the Golden Egg.* Unpublished monograph by the firm of Lehman Brothers Kuhn Loeb, New York, 1981.

Krafcik, John. "Learning From NUMMI." Working Paper, International Motor Vehicle Program, MIT, September 15, 1986 (unpublished paper).

Kuttner, Robert. "Power Sharing at Eastern Airlines." Unpublished manuscript, dated 1985.

Locker, Mike, and Abrecht, Steve. "Searching for Eastern's Bottom Line." *Labor Research Review,* Vol. 4, Winter 1984, pp. 65–74.

Meek, Christopher B. *Labor-Management Cooperation, Employee Ownership and the Struggle for Control of Eastern Airlines; The International Association of Machinists and Aerospace Workers at Eastern Airlines.* Washington, DC: United States Department of Labor. Unpublished report, 1988.

Meyer, David G., and Cooke, William N. "Labor Relations in Transition: Strategy Implementation and Effects on Financial Performance." Unpublished working paper, 1990.

New United Motor Manufacturing, Inc. Fremont, CA: February 1992 (unpublished).

Pauly, David. "Lorenzo Starts His Attack." *Newsweek,* February 2, 1987, p. 49.

Perlman, David L. "Strike Solidarity Grounds Eastern, Lorenzo." *AFL-CIO News,* March 18, 1989, pp. 11–12.

Raine, George. "Building Cars Japan's Way." *Newsweek,* March 31, 1986, p. 43.

Rudolph, Barbara. "Musical Chairs in the Skies." *Time,* March 10, 1986, pp. 62–63.

Salpukas, Agis. "Eastern's Unions Agree to Pay Cut and Accept Stock." *The New York Times,* December 9, 1983.

Salpukas, Agis. "New Era for Eastern's Unions." *The New York Times,* April 20, 1984.

Schuster, Michael H. "The Impact of Union-Management Cooperation on Productivity and Employment." *Industrial and Labor Relations Review,* Vol. 36, No. 3, 1983, pp. 415–430.

Simmons, John. "Managing Participation: Frank Borman at Eastern Airlines." Unpublished manuscript, second draft, July 11, 1985.

Smith, Joel. Personal interview with Warner Woodworth, March 1986.

Smith, Joel, and Childs, William. "Imported From America: Cooperative Labor Relations at New United Motor Manufacturing, Inc." *Industrial Relations Law Journal,* Vol. 9, No. 1, 1987, pp. 70–76.

Solidarity, "Lorenzo Must Go." May 1989, pp. 8–9.

Staff Reporter. "Toyota, GM Venture Says It Will Go Ahead with Bumper Facility." *The Wall Street Journal,* July 15, 1993, p. A-5.

Stansbury, Jeff. "NUMMI: A New Kind of Workplace." *Solidarity,* August 1985, pp. 11–15.

Taylor, Frederick Winslow. *Scientific Management.* New York: Norton, 1911.

Urra, Marty. "Research, Experts and Building Solidarity." *Labor Research Review,* Vol. 4, Winter 1984, pp. 37–53.

Voos, Paula B. "Managerial Perceptions of the Economic Impact of Labor Relations Programs." *Industrial and Labor Relations Review,* Vol. 40, No. 2, 1987, pp. 195–208.

Walsh, Joan. "Cultural Exchange on the Production Line." *In These Times,* April 17–23, 1985, pp. 8–9.

Woodworth, Warner. "Blue Collar Boardroom." *New Management: Magazine of Innovative Management.* Los Angeles: University of Southern California, Vol. 3, No. 3, 1986, pp. 52–57.

9

The Future of Labor-Management Partnerships

This book began with the premise that business and labor must evolve from past traditions of adversarial relationships and move toward the design and implementation of cooperative strategies and new organizational configurations. We argued that the high costs of work stoppages, infighting, and finger pointing are not acceptable in today's new, fast-changing global competition.

For several decades, too many U.S. firms and unions have not coped effectively with these issues. In many cases, the problems and tensions were simply ignored as both parties hoped the conflicts would "just go away." Others engaged in flight behavior, installing new plants offshore as a means of escaping the stress and strain of poor labor relations, accusations of blame, strikes, and a state of war. In still other instances, management dealt with the problem by employing union-busting tactics, win-lose efforts that often led to lose-lose outcomes in the bitter end.

None of these approaches is likely to facilitate the creation of a stronger, healthier U.S. economic capability. Putting our collective heads in the sand, engaging in fight or flight, will produce only short-term relief; the fundamental causes of stress and strain will remain.

We argue that the most promising strategy for addressing these issues is to redesign the relationship between labor and management to create a genuine partnership of trust and openness. Throughout U.S. history progressive owners and managers of capital—as well as labor leaders—have experimented with collaboration. But these cases grew out of the personal values of the individuals involved or were reactions to specific short-run events, such as World War II. We argue that now is the time for a major overhaul, a restructuring of attitudes, power arrangements, and organizational interaction between American unions and companies.

The Range of Labor-Management Partnerships

In many instances, the primary effects of collaboration involve human resource issues, improved communication, and the implementation of new technologies. But in other cases, organizations are evolving into proactive models for coping with changing markets and increased interdependence among various stakeholders, including unions and firms. Joint decisions on the shop floor, as well as at the strategic level, when successfully structured and monitored, can evolve into genuine cultural change and institutionalization. The following brief sketches capture the magnitude of these new strategies.

General Motors Hydra-matic Willow Run Plant/UAW Local 735: Organizational changes began in 1981 with a loose team structure, but within two years the effort became more formalized with a plantwide steering committee to oversee cooperative efforts. Among the activities has been the creation of Comprehensive Process Planning Teams, which involved workers in new-equipment purchases before bids are sought. Others worked on restructuring shop-floor layout of the transmission line. In other areas autonomous work groups have been established, as well as Joint Customer Satisfaction Improvement Teams, Joint Ergonomics/Human Factor Teams, and other impressive structures as examples of cooperative problem solving.

Oil, Chemical and Atomic Workers Union (OCAW) Local 4-100/AMOCO Pipeline Company, Texas and Louisiana: Letters of agreement have been signed on joint decision making of both parties in the design and installation of a new system of Employee Involvement. They define their common mission, trust, and consensus process, and commit the parties to work together in creating a cooperative partnership between the two parties. They have recently expanded the process to include a gainsharing plan (1990–1992), and similar efforts have now begun in Wyoming.

Kellogg Company/American Federation of Grain Millers: Both signed an innovative 1991 charter for creating "Labor-Management Partnerships for New Work Systems." Corporate officers and international union leaders have established a Joint Steering Committee to support and facilitate the process of various plant efforts in restructuring the existing organization and push decision making downward. Team-based, multiskilled workers will operate in a new, collaborative mode and be paid according to knowledge and performance. Extensive management and shop-steward training has been carried out to develop more effective, democratic leadership styles. Ground rules of volunteerism, no job loss, and other appropriate guidelines are adhered to within the spirit of the overall charter.

United Steel Workers of America (USWA)/National Steel: The union and company reached a unique agreement that resulted in a policy of no layoffs and open sharing of all financial data with the union. "The Cooperative Partnership" began in 1986, transforming the company from Chapter 11 bankruptcy into a prosperous business. The annual report for stockholders now includes "A Letter From Labor," and National runs advertising in *The Wall Street Journal* headed "We're Partners With Labor Because We Can't Imagine a Future Without Them." The company is 100-percent unionized, including 140 office and technical workers at corporate headquarters in Indiana. Management credits labor with much of the 1991 cost reductions of over $100 million. The USWA has initiated similar agreements with some twenty other companies, including, most recently, Allegheny Ludlum. Says international president Lyman Williams, "We believe we should come together and establish a pattern for the future. This can only occur on the basis of partnership, in which workers are genuinely empowered" (Bryne, 1993, p. 10).

Scott Paper/United Paperworkers International Union: In 1989 the parties signed an "Enabling Agreement" which specifies guidelines for the creation of a "truly joint, cooperative change effort." A steering committee has been established and trained, and it has begun to implement various projects to increase productivity and quality, better train workers, provide for continuous improvement, and offer job security to all.

Communication Workers of America/AT&T: The parties finalized a "Workplace of the Future" agreement to establish labor-management teamwork at different levels—top management and union human resources board to address broad, strategic, global issues; business-unit or division councils to facilitate union participation in business decisions such as deployment of new technology; and workplace teams at the factory level where managers and labor representatives determine strategies for increasing effectiveness and better utilizing human capital.

This summary of recent initiatives toward labor-management cooperation lists but a few of many such innovations. There are numerous other examples as well: Boeing and the IAM, GM Lake Orion and the UAW, Cummins and the diesel workers, Budd and the UAW, Goodyear and the rubber workers, Boise-Cascade and the PWU, and Alcoa and the aluminum workers.

The new values, structures, and practices within U.S. industry today imply systemic changes and the creation of a new paradigm. Table 9.1 attempts to distill certain elements, drawing

Table 9.1
Emergence of a New Organizational Paradigm

Factor	Traditional System	New System
Decision making	Top down	Shared, democratic
Work rules	Specific, rigid	General, flexible
Career basis	Seniority	Performance
Organizational culture	Hierarchical	Egalitarian
Degree of change	Incremental	Revolutionary
Labor relations	Adversarial	Cooperative
Core organizational unit	Individual	Team
Structure	Bureaucratic	Decentralized
Planning frame	Short term	Long term
Power	Zero sum	Non zero sum
Business purpose	Productivity, profits	Quality, add value
Strategy	Attack mode	Alliance mode, partnership
Time-to-market speed	Slow	Fast
Meaning of work	Means to other ends	Source of personal fulfillment

upon our research, case experience, and OD interventions described throughout this book.

The Future of Cooperative Partnerships

Whether the surge in coordination between labor and management in recent years is a genuine shift that will last or a short-term blip on the screen before reverting back to the adversarial past is debatable.

On the dark side, there are those personalities who thrive on conflict. The ranks of labor still include many union leaders who grew up in the era of confrontation, programmed, so to speak, for attack. These are the ones whose personalities, values, and assumptions about corporate America have been cast in the heat of "the wars," as workers at Eastern Airlines describe it. Many managers in the corporate suites have the same kind of orientation. Power, not performance or profit, is the primal force driving their decisions.

In 1993 some 178,000 U.S. workers engaged in new strikes against employers. After the Foote & Davies Company shut its Georgia plant in response to the graphic communications union strike, some 500 unionists marched in protest, leading to seventeen worker arrests in Atlanta. A strike against Austin Cable Vision in Texas resulted in five worker arrests at a protest rally against the firm. And on May 27, 1993, AFL-CIO supporters of a group of sixty workers at Taylor Made Office Systems clashed with a police line in San Francisco, resulting in the jailing of twenty-two people. At PPG Industries California Glass Plant, the strike was over health benefits. Some 14,000 mine worker unionists engaged in selective strikes at certain targeted coal companies for months. At Alaska Air Group, flight attendants protested company schedules and work rules with a new weapon: a "Campaign for Chaos." The union would call for sudden work stoppages for an hour or even half a day. The company had to send between three and five managers on each flight in case of surprise attendant backlash. At Diamond Walnut, Teamsters have continued a strike since 1991 against the firm's actions to permanently replace the largely female, minority workforce. Similarly, the Las Vegas Frontier Hotel has been embroiled in a three-year battle with Hotel Employees Local 226, suffering huge losses and negative national publicity since

1991. Perhaps the most costly 1993 strike was the contract dispute between flight attendants and American Airlines, a conflict which only lasted five days but cost the corporation $190 million. And as of press time, 1994, some 70,000 teamsters are involved in a lengthy strike against major trucking companies across the nation.

On the other hand, new policies in the White House, after a decade of union bashing, are more favorable to labor and support greater cooperation. Bill Clinton's rhetoric during the presidential campaign, as well as the policy proposals and maneuvering that we have seen since the inauguration, suggest a leveling of the playing field. During his first year, President Clinton overturned President Ronald Reagan's federal ban on rehiring fired air-traffic controllers, paving the way for at least some of the 11,400 PATCO strikers to regain their old jobs. Labor Secretary Robert Reich argues forcefully for changes such as greater worker participation, worker training and empowerment, and the creation of higher-paying jobs, including rasing the minimum wage. The former professor at the Kennedy School of Harvard University told the Senate that firms ought to give workers more of a voice, and declared that the decline in union membership "isn't healthy." He has created a new agency, "The Office of the American Workplace," implying that he will be more supportive of workers than any cabinet official in recent history (Salwen and McGinley, 1993). Clinton, Reich, and others are working to ensure that the North American Free Trade Agreement (NAFTA) protects U.S. jobs. A more objective and reasoning NLRB is being fashioned with new, more objective appointees. Changes in right-to-work and the hiring of company scabs during a strike are legislative issues in the process of being considered.

Impressively, the Clinton administration organized a "Conference on the Future of the American Workplace," June 26, 1993, in Chicago, hosted by U.S. Commerce Secretary Ron Brown and Robert Reich, Secretary of Labor. Some 600 leaders from government, business, labor, and academia attended, as well as invited shop-floor workers. The first of its kind, the objective was to explore how to transform more firms into high-performance organizations and create better labor-management partnerships. Through case presentations and round-table discussions, one of which was led by President Clinton, strategies and potential new policies were identified to help reinvent the workplace. Further dialogue and research are occurring as follow-up to that event, and further collaboration in designing and implementing the work of this new coalition will continue (Brown and Reich, 1993).

Yet other legal and legislative matters still need to be addressed. For instance, in December 1992 the NLRB ruled that Electromation, Inc., an Indiana firm, had established a certain type of labor-management cooperation which violated the 1935 National Labor Relations Act. The federal law was designed to protect unions by prohibiting managers from dominating worker organizations. Electromation's defense was that it had, in recent years, established "action committees" as a tool to increase communication and enhance productivity. But the Teamsters sued, claiming this was an unfair practice, a tactic for preventing the union from successfully organizing non-union employees ("Labor-Management Cooperation," 1992). The NLRB's unanimous 4-0 vote affirmed labor's position and sent shock waves through many companies attempting worker participation. For us, the implications are clear: Only an honest and equal partnership between labor and management is acceptable and workable.

Unions are divided about the use of worker-manager teams to increase U.S. competitiveness in today's global markets. Personnel managers say they want such approaches to be free from the 1935 NLRB legislation so as to foster more effective organizations. Labor fears this will effectively lead to the creation of in-house, company-controlled unions, which will pre-empt AFL-CIO organizing campaigns. To complicate matters, the NLRA intended to protect labor by building a system of industrial relations based on antagonism. Today, if managers and unions seek greater efficiencies through joint decisions, how can they avoid the legal limitation on such efforts?

Of course, our book argues that the two approaches not be assimilated into one system, which could violate American labor law. Instead, we advocate the creation of parallel structures, one based on the adversarial system of collective bargaining, the other built on noncontractual issues of cooperation. Further, in Electromation's program, management designed the form of participation, selected specific workers for each team, prohibited them from being members of more than one team, and assigned a manager over each team. We argue, instead, for equal membership of labor and management representatives, voluntary participation, and joint design of the structure and process of cooperation.

In 1986 the U.S. Department of Labor initiated a study to determine whether current labor laws interfere with the degree of union-management cooperation necessary in today's competitive environment. Congress has also faced various proposals, such as the American Competitiveness Act, sponsored by thirty-three Republicans in 1991, to amend the NLRA so that nothing prohibits quality circles or joint production teams involving unions and managers. Likewise, the American Bar Association in recent meetings has debated the applicability of current, rigid labor laws new to corporate programs regarding participative management and worker empowerment. So far, after discussion and further analysis, the general agreement has been that the 1935 NLRA is not a barrier to collaboration between workers, unions, and companies, if done appropriately, and that further legislation is not necessary.

To further study these issues and to explore methods for enhancing productivity through labor-management cooperation, the Clinton administration launched a Commission on the Future of Worker-Management Relations, chaired by former Labor Secretary John T. Dunlop. A series of hearings, field trips to work sites, and other research efforts have been organized to document innovative efforts and formulate needed public policy on workplace participation (Clark, 1993, p. A-18).

Likewise, the AFL-CIO's Executive Council held its winter 1994 meetings in Bal Harbour, Florida, to review and adopt a new report, "The New American Workplace: A Labor Perspective." By unanimous vote, the report was officially approved as union policy, declaring, "The time has come for labor and management to surmount past enmities and to forge the kinds of partnerships which can generate more productive, humane, and democratic systems of work organization" (Hardesty, 1994, p. 1). Over the coming years, the AFL-CIO will work to design and implement specific strategies to empower workers in changing the traditional union-company relationship of conflict and move toward having an equal voice in organizational renewal.

In spite of past adversarial relationships, as well as legal and legislative concerns, our prediction is that strategies supporting labor-management cooperation will continue to grow. From a few, isolated experiments in the 1970s, the breadth and depth of these efforts is increasing exponentially in the 1990s. Whether at the subunit, plant, company, industry, or community level, a rich range of approaches to collaborative problem solving is developing. New labor relations systems are being retrofitted into company cultures. More effective use of human capital is leading to the design of a new organizational architecture. Partnerships between firms and customers, manufacturers and vendors, are also necessitating joint structures between labor and management.

Our view is that macro economic and social factors will foster further cooperation in the future—globalization, unified Europe, new workplace technologies, increased worker education, pressure to convert military production into peaceful uses, and so on. As employee ownership continues to grow, collective decision making between managers and worker stockholders will likewise increase. More labor leaders will gain seats on enterprise boards of directors, facilitating shared governance from the top down into the shop floor. Troubled firms will also be more likely to open their doors to unions as they seek relief from costly labor contracts, and this shared pain will give impetus to joint development of new innovations to cope with crisis. Heightened competition from foreign firms exporting products to the United States or building factories on U.S. soil will generate greater awareness of the advantages of a cooperative corporate culture with labor as partner—illustrated by German-, Korean-, and Japanese-owned organizations already established in our country.

Over the past year evidence has mounted that new worker-management ties are being forged. In the steel industry, for instance, recent collective-bargaining contracts have stipulated the appointment of union representatives on company boards of directors, including LTV Corporation, Inland Steel, and USX. The United Steelworkers continues to set up ESOPs and create new cooperative partnerships with firms rather than go on strike. Likewise, innovative systems of cooperation are increasing in the airline industry. TWA emerged from Chapter 11 bankruptcy through a labor agreement in which workers gave $600 million in wage concessions for 45 percent of the firm's equity. Union and management initiated a number of joint problem-solving committees and labor received four of fifteen board seats. Similarly, Northwest Airlines swapped $886 million in concessions for 37.5 percent of the company and five board positions. Labor has veto power over corporate investments, management changes, as well as any asset sell-offs or breakup of the company (Kelly and Bernstein, 1993). Finally, United Airlines and its unions agreed in March 1994 to a $4.5 billion radical restructuring scheme which will end up giving 53–63 percent of UAL stock to 77,000 workers, the largest employee-owned firm in the United States. A new twelve-member board will be created, two of whom are union appointed, four independent directors, and five directors elected by stockholders. Cost reductions and labor peace are the primary objectives for reinventing UAL, and a new partnership culture is seen as the means to achieving such goals (McCormick, 1994).

Certainly, some American executives will pursue other approaches, such as flight, out sourcing their products, or building plants in other countries, such as the *Maquiladoras* along the Mexican border. Others will seek to fight, remaining as management-dominated and authoritarian as possible. But increasingly, as we see it, progressive companies will choose the strategy of building labor-management partnerships. They will do so not "to make workers feel good," or to simply "cave in" to union power. At the same time, we envision more and more unions, at the local as well as the international level, seeking a more collaborative, problem-solving approach to dealing with corporate America. Labor's motives will not be to embrace management out of love, or as a tactic to gain access to the executive suite, like the Trojan horse.

No, our prediction is that both parties will jointly seek this new, common strategy not by default but by design. They will do so for one fundamental reason—it simply makes good business sense. Economics, rather than enlightened social philosophy, seems to drive this movement toward cooperation and a redistribution of power. Creating labor-management partnerships gives American industry a new organizational capability. It promises greater competitive advantage.

References

Brown, Ronald H., and Reich, Robert B. "Workplace of the Future." *A Report of the Conference on the Future of the American Workplace.* Washington, DC: U.S. Department of Commerce and U.S. Department of Labor, 1993.

Bryne, Michael. "Unions Show Partnerships Help Companies, Workers." *AFL-CIO News,* March 1, 1993, p. 10.

Clark, Lindley H. "Yet Another Clinton Commission—on Unions." *The Wall Street Journal,* April 6, 1993, p. 18.

Hardesty, Rex. "Unions Aim for Health Care, New Workplace." *AFL-CIO News,* March 7, 1994, pp. 1–13.

Kelly, Kevin, and Bernstein, Aaron. "Labor Deals That Offer a Break from 'Us vs. Them.'" *Business Week,* August 2, 1993, p. 30.

"Labor-Management Cooperation." *The Wall Street Journal,* December 8, 1992, p. 1.

McCormick, John. "Will Workers Stay on Course?" *Newsweek,* January 3, 1994, p. 62.

Salwen, Kevin G., and McGinley, Laurie. "Labor Designee Reich Urges More Input by Workers to Aid Job Quality, Safety." *The Wall Street Journal,* January 8, 1993.

Index